The Cameo Murders

©1999 Barry Shortall

Published by
The Bluecoat Press
Liverpool

Book design by
March Design
Liverpool

Printed by
Cromwell Press
Trowbridge

ISBN 1 872568 60 2

Front cover: George Kelly

The Cameo Murders

Barry Shortall

The Bluecoat Press

Acknowledgements

To produce a work that is as true and accurate as possible. bearing in mind the time which has elapsed since the case came to prominence, needs the help of many people. Of particular mention is Vincent Burke. LL.B. M.Phil., businessman, academic, criminal historian and friend whose encouragement kept me going through a maze of statements. myth and facts. My thanks go to Vincent for reading the manuscript and for his constructive comments and suggestions.

Journalist Malcolm Handley has helped immensely, both in gaining information and with constructive comments. I wish also to thank the Liverpool Daily Post and Echo for access to their cuttings and photographic library and to Les Rowlands, the librarian for his unstinting help and to Roger Phillips of Radio Merseyside who, by giving publicity to the case and renewing public interest, helped considerably in my research. The work and dedication of Lou Santangeli for his efforts to clear the name of Charles Connolly must also be recognised.

I would also like to thank the Merseyside Police Authority for allowing access to the archives of Liverpool City Police and to Tony Mossman, Publicity Officer of Merseyside Police Authority, for his kind assistance.

Thanks also to Lady Esther Livermore for reminiscing with me about the case and for access to the files of her late husband, Sir Harry Livermore. No mention of the Cameo case would be complete without an acknowledgment of the efforts on behalf of the accused and their families, throughout the years, of the Liverpool solicitor, Mr. Rex Makin. The unstinting efforts of Peter and Agnes Kelly and of Tommy Gill, over many years to have the case reopened, must also be recognised.

The research to produce this book has taken a number of years, the results only possible through innumerable questions and the help of people who, virtual strangers to me, shared their reminiscences and memories of the case. I acknowledge all this help

Foreword

Times change but memories remain and forever in Liverpool folklore there will be the memory of the terrible Cameo murders. It is now fifty years since the murders took place at the old Welsh Chapel which became the Cameo cinema. It has long been demolished and replaced by a block of flats. The area itself, once a part of the teeming life of Liverpool, has become somewhat derelict and run down.

The murders led to six hearings which lasted a total of twenty three days. The investigation resulted in 9500 houses visited, 75000 people interviewed, 1800 fingerprints taken, handwriting samples taken from 1840 woman and 1200 telephone calls received. Though Chief Inspector Herbert Balmer, who was in charge of the investigation, receives some criticism by the author for his methods, his dedication and commitment to this case cannot be doubted. If we are to judge not only his methods but those of the police force, it is important that we do so in the context of that time. There have, of course, been many changes since, not least of which is the Police and Criminal Evidence Act of 1984 and, in particular, the procedures which now have to be followed when suspects are questioned.

George Kelly's conviction and execution for the murders was one of the milestones which played a part in examining the possibility of miscarriages of justice and the ending of capital punishment. Although the case took place some time before the execution of Timothy Evans, James Hanratty and Derek Bentley, the concern about George Kelly's execution may well have accelerated public opinion towards favouring abolition. The Member of Parliament who actively campaigned for abolition was Sidney Silverman, a founder of the well known solicitors' practice in Liverpool. Harry Livermore, his partner, was the solicitor who so diligently represented George Kelly.

This well researched story of the Cameo murders is a refreshing change from previous accounts which have trivialised what can only be described as an awful tragedy. It is as accurate and definitive an account as possible of what took place although, of necessity, the full court proceedings have been compressed. The scenarios developed are based on numerous interviews with those who were prepared to talk about the case and about the short life and times of George Kelly. Mortality has taken its toll and the eroding effect of time on the memories of those involved must be taken into account.

While the writing of this book is entirely the work of the author, I am pleased to have been of assistance in discussing the case and generally encouraging him to embark on what was a gargantuan task. The question we should ask ourselves is, given present day methods of investigation, would George Kelly be found guilty of murder and would the threat of hanging compel Charles Connolly to make a false confession?

Vincent Burke, LL.B., M.Phil.

Saint Patrick's Day

In the March of 1949, Liverpool still showed its war wounds, the old seaport cratered with the reminders of war – great, toothless gaps in the once-proud Georgian and Victorian terraces. The city was grey with the pallor of a war which had not long finished, in the process of recovering from the blitz which had destroyed much of its heart.

Everywhere there was deprivation, rationing and scarcity, the drab sombreness of the greyness lightened only by the khaki, blue-grey and blue and white uniforms of the servicemen and seamen from numerous nations around the globe who paraded through the down-town streets, seeking amusement in a city which even then clung to its ability to amuse and be amused.

This particular day reflected an aspect of the polyglot nature of the city's teaming population and its ancestry from another country. St Patrick's Day was celebrated by the Catholic half of the city, those of Irish stock who wore the small green shamrock as a token of their Irishness.

It was damp and still and cold, without the relieving north west winds which would remove the sulphurous pall of smoke which tens of thousands of chimneys spewed over the city, shutting out the light under a khaki-coloured umbrella. The sounds of the Mersey bounced dolefully up the slopes of the hills which fringed the city; up Everton Brow, Islington and Low Hill. The mournful cry of the big ships, the liners and cargo carriers and the excitable blasts from ant-like tugs alternating in a muted cacophony with the shrill blasts from the ferry boats as they made their way through the fog which cloaked the river, dodging larger boats as they slowly emerged from the orange gloom.

As the evening approached, the fog began to thicken as the fires were stoked higher in an attempt to suppress the all-pervading damp and cold, the smoke spreading out covering the city in a sulphurous soup so dense that it was almost impossible to see houses across the street. In the hushed bustle and murmur, the main arteries into town were lit up by a multitude of instantaneous sunsets, splashes of white light from the overhead wires which gave the trams their life, sparking and spreading across the underside of the fog blanket, creating a sudden rosy brilliance over the streets below as the wires buckled and swayed under the changing pressures of countless poles.

Those sparks were reflected in the resilience and cheeriness of the people, a special vitality which refused to be dominated by the hard times, their sense of humour unequalled, warm smiles readily accessible to those who needed cheer. It was nowhere truer than in the close-knit, Irish Catholic communities represented in almost every street which fringed the inner city, marrying, bearing children and dying, sinning and praying together – the Murphys and Gallaghers, Byrnes, Kellys, Callaghans, Skellys and O'Malleys.

There was, of course, another side to the city, as there was to every city in the country at that time. Even in recovery and rebirth, it had its sinister side. The underworld, those who chose other ways to make a living than by the honest toil of the great majority, had other things on their mind, other ways of eating, living and dressing well. Ration cards were still a requirement, even for some of the necessities of life and the black market flourished. The hundreds of ships thronging the docks were a source of the unobtainable, with dockers'' allowance and contraband freely traded.

Other commodities emerged from the huge American Air Force base at Burtonwood, smuggled out secretly and freely bartered in the pubs and clubs of the city. Cigarettes and whisky, nylons, chewing gum and perfumes, carefully measured, drop by precious drop to be savoured by the ladies of Liverpool as they lay in their beds, dreaming that the man beside them was John Garfield, or perhaps George Raft or even, for those who aspired to higher things, Clark Gable.

Sarah Kelly's barrow, on the bombed site at the corner of Lime Street and Ranelagh Street, had been busy all day. The first delivery of shamrock had already sold out and now she waited for her sons to arrive with more boxes overflowing with the small green clover. Business had been good, the early daffodils had sold quickly, together with the small bundles of flowers she had carefully and painstakingly prepared herself that morning for her regular customers, the office workers who, on their way home in the evening or at lunch time, would stop by her stall. Some she kept back for other, more generous customers, the American servicemen who came into the city in the afternoon, buying flowers to impress the girls they were to meet.

All in all it was a good day and when it was time to pack up the stall and return to the small flat on the top balcony at Trowbridge Street, near the Bullring, a circular 1930's tenement block, two of her sons, Frankie and Joey were there to help her.

It was a rare occasions that so many from the family were together, rarer still that they ate together, some fortunate enough to find a place at the table, others spread out around the small room. Later, when they had finished their meal, the two younger men, together with their father, left for a drink at the nearby Bents pub in Great Newton Street, the women to follow later.

The pub was warm and full, those sitting near the door complaining every time it was opened it allowed tendrils of fog and damp cold air to be sucked in. Soon an impromptu party was in full swing, old songs repeated for the thousandth time, as they would be in many of the old pubs in the working-class districts of that city, until eventually the Irishness of the neighbourhood, a wistfulness for the perceived calm and tranquillity of the country which many of those present had never known, imposed its maudlin presence.

It was almost nine o'clock when a broad, stocky man shouldered his way through the crowded pub towards where the Kelly family were seated. George was the youngest of Mrs Kelly's sons, a twenty-six year old who lived on his wits, with no regular job, from day to day seeking the main chance. This time he was in the company of an occasional drinking partner, Jimmy Skelly.

George knew the market traders and barrow boys, the pubs and street corners which were the outlets for the stolen and smuggled goods which flooded daily into the city. Because of this, George was well known to the police and to those for whom he acted as sometime fence and informer. In some cases these overlapped, becoming inextricably intertwined as each used the other for individual gain.

An opportunist, his activities as a minor fence and police informer kept him, at times, in more funds than his hard-working brothers. One day he would have money to burn, the next without a penny to his name. Although a snappy dresser, closer inspection would show that the suit he had on, the one he usually wore, had a neat darn at the collar but it was clean and fitted well and helped George's appearance. He liked to think he was the well-dressed man about town, fancying himself as a

Hollywood look-alike. As he made his way towards the family group, the heads of some of the women in the pub turned towards him. George was attractive to women, his quick wit and rapid way of talking making him welcome company in any surroundings. But he was also a complex character, a man whose charm and generosity, still acclaimed by those who knew him was, according to others, negated by his treatment of women. Inevitably, women and drink were his weaknesses.

His criminal record included a conviction for beating up a prostitute in Manchester, the newspaper reports claiming she was pregnant, something Kelly denied, and in 1944 he had been bound over for twelve months for threatening to beat and assault his wife. Too many drinks and he became a bully, even his mother not immune to his oafish behaviour which, at times, had led to him pinning her menacingly against the wall when he was in the need of money.

George Kelly had married his childhood sweetheart soon after he joined the Navy but he was now separated. The marriage was a disaster which had left him with a young daughter, his Catholic background preventing him seeking a divorce.

As usual, George was welcomed by everyone he knew, his mother beckoning him over, a worried look on her face.

"That Mr Balmer was around again today, Georgie, asking after you." Kelly's face hardened, the frown quickly replaced by his usual smile.

"Don't worry, mam. Probably a bit of business. You know Bert Balmer."

George knew Chief Inspector Herbert Balmer. He knew him well because George was not only a useful informer on those minor criminals who crossed his path, or intruded upon his patch but was also a useful conduit in the movement of goods which Balmer and some of his men would not be loathe to buy from Kelly; desirable and barterable goods, suits, cigarettes, whisky, nylons, coffee. But it was an unholy alliance between the two.

Jimmy Skelly shouted across the crowded pub.

"Don't you worry, Mrs Kelly. George has Balmer where he wants him. He knows too much." Skelly grinned.

"I still laugh every time I think of it. You know, when Balmer went to arrest Georgie. When he left his ship." Skelly broke into a fit of laughter, unable to continue as his audience waited for the rest of the story, familiar as it was to his family. Frankie took up the story.

"Balmer came in through the front and George did a runner. Balmer sent the copper he was with round the back and went after George himself. The back door was loose on its hinges and George threw it at Balmer. It knocked him out." Frankie turned to George.

"Never forgiven you for that, has he, George? Bet that's the only time that's happened to Bert Balmer."

Kelly's father muttered quietly.

"You went to Durham for that, though, George."

"And the trousers, Georgie. Don't forget the trousers." There was ribald laughter as George tried to stop Frankie recounting the story, his embarrassment showing as he went to the bar for more drinks, Frankie carrying on unabashed as others who had not yet heard the story craned forward to listen.

"Georgie was at Doris O'Malleys. It was just after Christmas. Anyway, he was rotten drunk, so bad he'd soiled his trousers. Balmer called in and saw how bad he was and brought him home. Not as a favour like, he just has a thing about O'Malley, probably wanted Georgie out of the way. Anyway, when he came into the house, Balmer was carrying a brown paper bag with George's soiled pants in it. Georgie shouted to us all, "Hey folks, look at the great Inspector Balmer carrying Georgie Kelly's shitty trousers." Balmer was mad. "I'll have you one day for that,George," he said."

There was raucous laughter but George's father failed to join in.

"I don't know how you get away with it, George. Taking the mickey out of him all the time. You want to watch yourself." There was genuine concern in his father's voice.

"Don't worry about George, pop. Like Jimmy says, he's got too much on Balmer. He'll never touch him."

"I know, but... always standing up to him and laughing at him. He's a bad man to cross, George. Just you be careful. That quiet voice of his doesn't fool me."

Joey Kelly quickly changed the subject. "How's the job going, George?"

George grinned at his elder brother. "What job? Why? Need a sub, Joey?"

Joey Kelly smiled. George's last job, which had lasted for only ten months, was as doorman and sometimes minder to Jackie the Greek who ran the Primrose cafe in Cases Street in the centre of the city. It had paid well, the restaurateur trusted George, he liked his flamboyance, his quiet sometimes mocking sense of humour and his general manner which added a touch of style to his restaurant. But bad timekeeping and unreliability had made him an expensive luxury and for some time George Kelly's only regular work had been travelling to Ellesmere Port, on the opposite side of the River Mersey to work as a labourer at the huge oil refineries.

"Pity about that job, George, the Greek liked you. Told me he would trust you with his life." Kelly turned as one of his mother's friends passed, bending to kiss him on the cheek.

"You've got style, Georgie. You'll do alright."

George shrugged.

"Got too many other things on. You know what it's like." Another voice shouted out above the general hub of conversation.

"What's this about a girl friend up in Aigburth, George. Posh is she?" Kelly remained silent. The woman was married and now pregnant. But the affair was over.

Soon he was joining in the singing, with more vigour than harmony, the repertoire gradually becoming more maudlin. Rebel songs and love songs, maudlin songs and homesick songs and the songs of old Liverpool – 'The Mountains of Mourne' and the 'Leaving of Liverpool'. Few knew all the words but George Kelly had a good singing voice and soon he was hauled up to stand by the battered piano, customers in the old pub falling silent as his light tenor voice moved easily into the soft verses of 'Galway Bay' before voices from elsewhere in the pub called to him.

"Give us a Joe Locke song, Georgie." And he obliged, the pub joining in a foot-stamping, hand-clapping version of 'Goodbye' a popular song of the time.

It was 10.30 when George left, shouting a goodbye to his friends and family before jumping a tram on Brownlow Hill which would take him to where he lived in Cambridge Street with his current girl friend, Doris O'Malley.

It was almost mid-afternoon of the following day and the pubs had shut their doors by the time Kelly, again accompanied by Jimmy Skelly, arrived at the small terrace in

Cambridge Street, Kelly pausing, pursing his lips as he saw the black saloon parked outside number 67.

That it was a police car he had no doubt. That it was Chief Inspector Bert Balmer's he also had no doubt. The detective had become an unwelcome visitor to Doris O'Malley's home over the past months. It irritated George who had more than a suspicion that the visit was as much to see Doris as it was to seek information from himself.

Kelly let himself in, Skelly following. Balmer sat up stiffly from where he was sprawled on the leatherette settee in the front parlour. Doris was in the armchair opposite, her white Persian cat cradled in her lap. Balmer nodded to him,

"Hello, George. I've been looking for you everywhere. Just called to see if you had anything for me?"

"Not that, anyway, Mr. Balmer." Kelly nodded his head towards the glass of whisky in Balmer's hand. Then he grinned and burst out laughing, turning to Skelly.

"Never thought I'd see the great Inspector Balmer in his shirt sleeves and braces, did you, Jimmy?"

O'Malley's smile was strained. An attractive dyed blond, she was about thirty, several years older than George. She was also an occasional prostitute and, with the advent of Balmer's attentions, had become the talk of the neighbourhood.

Balmer climbed to his feet, a big man, towering over Kelly, as he pulled on his coat.

"You'll open your mouth once too often, George. Mark my words. You just watch your tongue."

"Jealous are we, Mr Balmer? Does your wife know you're here?" Kelly bridled, his temper always near the edge when he had been drinking.

"I know your style, Chief Inspector Balmer." He turned to O'Malley.

"Know what he does, Doris? Calls at people's houses when they're out, suspects, you know. Gives the kids sweets and then asks the woman if she's alright for money." He turned to Balmer.

"That it, Mr Balmer? And then, guess what, Doris? The next thing he's after is sex. Has he tried it on you yet, Doris?"

Balmer paled, holding himself in check. He shook a finger at Kelly.

"You've been warned before, George. Remember what happened with your missus." Kelly grinned insolently.

"Only probation, Mr Balmer. It was nothing." His expression hardly changed as he continued sarcastically: "No disrespect, Mr Balmer. Any way, I might have something for you in the week. Might see you in the Beehive."

Balmer grunted and walked to the door, murmuring a few words to O'Malley before leaving the house, the woman cowering back as the door slammed.

Skelly moving between Kelly and her.

"You be careful with him, girl." Skelly spoke to her as he pushed Kelly into an armchair. "He's real taken with you. Can't you see it. He's never away from you. It's not George he's coming to see. It'll only lead to trouble. You too, Georgie. Just back off a bit or he'll have you."

Kelly's reply was obscenely blunt.

Murder

Saturday, 19th March1949 was an unusually mild March day, the weather had changed, fresh westerly winds had cleared away the suffocating fog of the previous two days and occasional sunshine added to the early spring warmth although, by mid-afternoon, drizzle had started to enhance the greyness of the day.

Shoppers, mostly women, hurried along the pavements past the bombed sites which, even then, at almost 1.30 in the afternoon, were thronged with people who crowded around the barrows and stalls offering cheaper goods than the shops of the city.

For George Kelly it would be a typical Saturday afternoon, moving from pub to pub until the money ran out and he could scrounge more. He was wearing one of his favourite brown suits and a smart tie, as he chatted with friends and acquaintances in the bar of the Midland Hotel in Ranelagh Street. Soon Skelly arrived and they finished several pints before leaving and strolling the short distance to another of their haunts, Tracy's public house, the Empire in Hanover Street.

They stayed at Tracy's until closing time before retracing their steps and walking back to Sarah Kelly's flower stall where George helped out for half an hour or so, earning a few shillings until, soon after 3.30, they jumped a passing tram to Princes Road and the Ludo Club.

It was a useful club for George, its habitues a cross-section of Liverpool society, professional people and petty criminals and those who who lived on the edge of crime. Renee Brown, the owner, was a well known receiver of stolen goods. The club, even at that time on a Saturday, was a place where illicit deals were concocted, where prostitutes met their clients and where knowledge of jobs and opportunities, seldom honest, were passed from mouth to mouth and uneasy partnerships established.

It was to be a familiar story, the free-spending Kelly again running out of money and borrowing from one of his acquaintances, sharing it with Skelly and continuing their drinking spree. At a time when the mild beer they drank cost less than seven pence a pint, it soon began to have an effect.

It was shortage of money as much as anything else which forced them to leave at 5.30, catching another tram to Crown Street, at the back of the city's university and to the Royal William, another of their favourite haunts, a small pub frequented in the week by students but now a stopping place on their random way home. They stood outside for a while, talking to friends, hoping for an invitation for a drink, before going in. The small pub was busy; a large fire burning in the snug, the bar thronged, many of the customers having walked from the football match a few miles away across the city at Goodison Park. The conversation was about that day's result, the sad news for some that the home team had lost against Aston Villa, but of little interest to Kelly and his mate as they found themselves space at the end of the bar.

They were lucky, Yorkie Bob, his greasy flat cap on the back of his head, was standing at the bar talking to a seaman friend. They joined him, accepting an invitation for a drink and then another from the seafarer and it was about 7.30 before they moved on, crossing the road to the Liverpool Arms. By now, Skelly was much the worse for wear and they were asked to leave, only to continue their drinking at the next port of call, the Coach and Horses on Low Hill, less than ten minutes walk away.

After a few more pints, Skelly could hardly stand up, the licensee having already remonstrated with him for wanting to sing, and at about 8.30 George had had enough. He knew Skelly would manage. It was not unusual for his friends to take him home or pile him on to a tram with instructions to the conductor to pour him off at the stop nearest his home. It would happen again this night.

Kelly walked to where he could catch a tram which would take him along Picton Road and the nearest stop to the Leigh Arms, his local, and it was shortly after nine when he called in looking for Doris O'Malley, to be told that she had been in earlier looking for him. He ordered a pint and, and after finishing it, walked back to the Spofforth Arms, another pub they sometimes visited together.

Doris had not been seen and after yet another pint, George walked back to the small terrace in Cambridge Street which was Doris's home. There was a note in the usual place, the sugar basin on the sideboard – 'Gone to the Spofforth'. By now, Kelly was becoming irritated and, after a quick word with O'Malley's neighbour, Hilda Kelly, he left for the short walk back to the Leigh Arms.

This time he was in luck. Doris was sitting with Mrs McGuiness and her daughter; friends who lived nearby. Kelly nodded to the other women brusquely before beckoning Doris to him and grasping her by the arm. The strength of his grip made her wince.

"Where have you been Doris? I've been looking for you."

"You must have just missed me, Georgie. I was here before, looking for you." Kelly shrugged.

"Never mind. I'm skint. I need some money." She shook her head, unsure of which way his drunken mood would take him.

"I haven't any Georgie. Sorry."

"Then get some then, Doris. I need a drink."

"Where from? I can't George…" her protestations died away as she saw the look in Kelly's eye. She got up to leave, Kelly following her and grabbing her by the arm. She tried to twist from his grasp but he held her with one hand.

"Just get some, Doris. I'll pay you back. And get back here quickly."

He returned to the bar, ignoring the two women and joining another friend, Harry Harrison. Harrison was a bookmaker's runner, always in funds and able to offer Kelly a drink. They stood talking until, fifteen minutes later, O'Malley returned, handing Kelly a few notes.

"Thanks Doris. I'll see you back later." He nodded to the two other women as he left the bar with Harrison who refused his offer of a drink and made his way home.

Mrs McGuiness commiserated with Doris O'Malley.

"Why do you put up with it, Doris? Why do you let him treat you like that?" O'Malley shrugged.

"He's not that bad. It's just the drink."

"He's a bully. I'll never forget the other week when you came in the corner shop with two black eyes. We told you then…"

The woman shut up as tears flooded O'Malleys eyes. Every gesture and word showed that she idolised Kelly and what they said would not change her feelings for him.

"He's generous when he has money."

"I know." Mrs McGuiness's daughter spoke in defence of Kelly who she found attractive.

"And he's generous with the kids, always giving them money. And he always buys his round when he's in the money."

"Drinks all round, I know, that's all very well but it's still no excuse for the way he treats Doris" Mrs McGuiness sighed. "He does have his good points, I suppose."

Doris smiled at the women, wiping her eyes with a corner of her handkerchief before finishing her drink and leaving for Cambridge Street, a few minutes walk away.

The police car was parked outside the house, Bert Balmer's bulk behind the wheel. He climbed out when he saw Doris approaching.

"Christ, Doris! What's wrong? You look upset."

O'Malley shook her head.

"It's nothing, Bert. Really."

"It's Kelly, isn't it? George bloody Kelly. He's been having a go at you. I'm right, aren't I, Doris?" Again O'Malley's eyes filled with tears as she opened the door, Balmer following her inside.

George Kelly knew nothing of Balmer's visit that night. After waving a goodnight to Harrison, he went into the buffet bar where there were others he knew. He began celebrating his new found wealth by offering them a drink, as free with Doris's money as his own. By now, it was 9.45 and last orders would soon be called. He stayed until 10.15 when he returned to Cambridge Street only minutes after Chief Inspector Balmer had driven away.

In another Liverpool pub, on the edge of the city centre, another scenario was being enacted that night. At 9 o'clock, the Beehive public house, near the junction of Mount Pleasant and Brownlow Hill, was filling up. At one end of the passageway which ran along the side of the pub, and near the small snug at the rear, Jacqueline Dickson, a street-walking prostitute, sat with Jimmy Northam, one of her pimps. Also there was another young criminal, Donald Johnson and one more acquaintance, an occasional visitor to the Beehive, a man who also took a share of Dickson's earnings, unlike the others, only sipped at his drink.

Northam had been released from gaol only that morning, arriving back in Liverpool at midday, the train from Durham bringing him into Exchange Station. From there he had taken the electric railway under the river to his parent's home in Birkenhead, returning to Liverpool to meet Dickson in one of the city's small pubs before spending the afternoon at Dickson's flat in Parliament Street, just around the corner from the Boundary Hotel.

Northam needed money and Dickson, the dominant partner in their relationship, had found a way he could make some. He sat quietly as the plan was explained in detail.

"It's a picture house, Stutty. Just down the road. Must be about 500 quid there. They won't argue with the gun. It'll be a cinch." Johnson was a regular habitue of the cinema and sounded convincing.

Northam glanced quickly around before taking the large automatic from his pocket and passing it under the table to Johnson, who slipped it into his overcoat pocket glancing at the third man present.

"You keep watch. Let me know if anyone comes near the office." The man nodded as Johnson spoke again to Northam who had refused to have anything else to do with the robbery.

"See you back at Jackie's flat after, when I've done the job. Settle up then. That OK?" Northam nodded. He was nervous, his stutter more pronounced as he spoke.

"Jackie tells me it's an easy one. You sure of that, Johnno?"

"It's a cert. If Jackie lets me in there'll be no problem. Up the stairs by the door." The third man present spoke for the first time.

"We've already checked it out."

Johnson described the layout of the cinema, the small spiral staircase to what was once a chapel balcony, concealed behind a panel in the foyer wall near the fire exit.

They sat and finished their drinks before leaving, Northam returning to Dickson's flat, the others walking down Smithdown Road towards Webster Road and the Cameo Cinema.

Gangsters and crime were the themes of films showing in the city that weekend. 'Bond Street', a thriller in which there were two murders, was showing at the Cameo Cinema. 'Scarface', starring Paul Muni, was showing twice nightly at the Royal in Breck Road. 'Circumstantial Evidence' was on at the Princes in Granby Street and 'The Road to Alcatraz' was showing on the West Derby Picture House. In another world, at the Empire Theatre in Lime Street, The Covent Garden Opera Company were performing La Boheme.

The Cameo Cinema was about three miles from the city centre, a red brick building in a densely-populated district of narrow terraced streets, just off Smithdown Road, one of the main arteries into the city. The cinema was only sparsely-occupied, the second feature film, a thriller, during which the cashier took the night's takings from the cash desk, through the vestibule, near the side entrance to the cinema and climbed the short, narrow, spiral stairway which led to the manager's office

As she did this, Donald McDermaid, one of the patrons that night, was leaving the cinema. He had been there since about 7pm. The showing was continuous and, now that the big film was halfway through, he had sat through until it reached the part which was showing when he had arrived.

It was about 9.30 as he left the cinema, pulling his coat collar up against the slight drizzle. At the top of the short flight of steps which led up to the entrance to the cinema he was stopped by a young woman who peered past him towards the ticket office.

"Has the cashier gone up yet, luv?" She held the door as Donald glanced back inside. The small cash desk was in darkness. He nodded to the woman.

"Yes, she's gone."

"Thanks, son." The woman turned and walked down the steps and around the corner of the cinema into Bird Street as Donald continued on his way home.

The manager's office was in what was once the chapel gallery which had been partitioned off to make offices and staff rooms and could only be approached by an iron spiral staircase on one side and a steep iron staircase on the other. The bottom of the spiral staircase was near the side entrance on Bird Street and was reached through a small, narrow, wooden door which, to the casual observer, appeared to be part of the wooden partition.

The cashier let the spring close the door after her as she went up the stairs, waiting with the staff supervisor as the manager and assistant manager checked the takings. It took less than four minutes. Only then did the two women go through the fireproof door to the staffrooms on the same floor.

"What was that?" The supervisor turned to her colleague as she heard a series of sudden staccato bangs, as familiar as the many heard in the auditorium almost every night and coming from the direction of the office. A few seconds later, there were more. Together they ran along the passage, joined on the way by the cinema fireman. The door of the manager's office was rattling as someone pushed against it and there were more shots before the door burst open, the three standing in sudden bewilderment as a man ran out, a black scarf over his face, the brim of his hat pulled well down.

"Let me go, get out of the way or I'll blow your heads off." He shouted at the terrified group as, with his overcoat flapping loosely around him, he stumbled down the narrow spiral stairs, pushing past the projectionist who had just appeared and was gazing in disbelief at the weapon in the man's hand. After a few stunned moments the projectionist and the fireman followed, out of the fire exit into the narrow street which ran alongside the cinema, the gunman by now well ahead of them, disappearing from sight towards Garrick Street and busy Smithdown Road where he was soon lost in the crowds.

Quickly they made their way back inside the cinema, running upstairs to where the supervisor had forced open the door of the manager's office against the dead weight of a body lying behind it. She was in a state of near hysteria. The manager was lying on the floor, breathing heavily as she tried to help him, the assistant manager a few feet away on the floor.

Quickly the fireman retraced his steps, cursing in frustration when he realised the telephone had been disconnected. He turned and ran from the cinema; living nearby he knew which of the neighbouring houses had a phone.

Donald Johnson, for reasons he never could himself understand, had been waiting outside the Boundary Hotel to see what would happen as ambulances and police cars, sirens blaring, raced along Smithdown Road before turning into Webster Road, so engrossed in events that he failed to notice the police constable until he was standing in front of him, demanding to see his identity card. Johnson focussed on what the policeman was saying, breathing a sigh of relief as, satisfied, the policeman handed him back the card and boarded the tram which had just drawn up at the stop.

By this time all the Cameo patrons had left. No record was kept of their names and addresses, how long they had been there or whether they had seen anything out of the ordinary that night.

Kelly did this

It was the last day of a brief holiday, four days away from work which Chief Inspector Herbert Balmer had taken only at the insistence of his wife. Work was his life, work and the power which his position gave him; a position in which even judges and juries pandered to him. Power was his god.

Balmer was born in 1902 in Cairns Street, in the south end of the city, near the docks, his young days, as one of seven children, surrounded by a forest of masts and rigging. Seafaring was in the family, his father a carpenter and chantryman who had sailed on the great square riggers and who instilled in his son that the sea was the only career for a man.

His schooling was at St Silas's Church of England School in High Park Street which he attended until he was sixteen, when he began an apprenticeship in shipbuilding with H&C Grayson Ltd at their yard at Garston. At that time, it was a major company with five slipways and its own dry dock but, three years after the young Balmer joined them, the yard closed down, partly as a result of a strike and partly due to lack of orders. Balmer was eighteen months short of finishing his apprenticeship. It was the last shipbuilding yard in the city of Liverpool and its failure created in Balmer a resentment towards the strikers who had precipitated the failure. Even from those early days, he no longer felt an affinity with the working class into which he was born.

Balmer's only option then was to go to sea, subsequently seeking a career in the Liverpool City Police which he joined in May 1926. It was an inspired choice, his early police career outstanding and he was decorated twice by the Liverpool Shipwreck and Humane Society, receiving their silver medal for rescuing a woman from the Mersey. This accelerated his movement through the ranks and, by 1930, he had achieved his goal and was made a detective.

When war came, his affinity with the sea and the docks continued and he was involved closely in security work at the docks and was responsible for breaking up a black market racket operating from the PX stores at the American Air Force base at Burtonwood. For this he received a letter of thanks from Edgar Hoover, the Head of the FBI, which Balmer treasured almost as much as any of his other awards.

Bert Balmer was a Walter Mitty character, with all his characteristics and self-delusion. He lived in an environment of his own choosing, his crusade to rid Liverpool of its scum; the petty, minor criminals whom he felt were a threat to the city's recovery. He was, as he himself would claim, the Elliot Ness of Liverpool, an avid reader of books about the FBI and G men, even aping their appearance and manner.

He was also an excellent self-publicist, claiming that his was the first murder squad in the history of the Liverpool Police Force, the detectives, all good, reliable men, personally chosen by him, with many young detectives willing to give their right arm to join.

Much of this was true. Even his immediate superior in the CID, Chief Superintendent Bill Smith, was slightly in awe of Balmer and let him chose the men he wanted. These included Chief Inspector Jimmy Morris, who was a particular friend, Detective Sergeant Jack Farragher, a fingerprint expert and Scene of Crimes Officer, and Detective Sergeants Ernie Richardson and Jimmy Welsh.

A big, heavily-built man, those who remember him, and knew him well, attest to one particular attribute. Bert Balmer was a remarkable listener, attentive and capable of digesting a tremendous amount of information. He was also an excellent debater who gave people a compulsion to talk. An avid physical fitness enthusiast, he was a merchant navy boxing champion before he joined the police where he also helped form the Liverpool Police Rugby Club. He was also a rather morose man, his often sour countenance hiding a multitude of ambiguities of character. Even when being humorous, he seldom smiled.

A vain man, without the high social profile he craved, he was married,with two children, a boy and a girl. But attractive woman, no matter what their role in life, or their vocation, were a weakness with him.

Saturday morning, March 19, he was out later than usual for his early morning weekend walk. The morning was cold and damp and he shivered as he turned into the park near his home. He walked quickly, slowing only to inspect the early buds which were appearing on the trees. He was relaxed when, over an hour later, he returned home. He had walked the circumference of the park and had spoken to no-one. It was a peaceful, pleasant start to his day and to a weekend which usually bored him, except for the rugby that afternoon at the Police Sports Ground.

Today he would watch then enjoy a drink in the club after the game before returning home, sitting back in his favourite chair and opening the sports edition of the Liverpool Echo, his eyes only flickering over the main story on the front page before turning to the rugby news and then the boxing news on the inside pages.

It was almost 8 o'clock when he left the house again for the Liverpool Police Club, talking and playing snooker until about 10 o'clock when he made a short detour on his way home to call in to see Doris O'Malley, staying only 15 minutes. But it was time enough for his growing hatred of Kelly and his obsession with O'Malley to intensify. He left at ten past ten, only minutes before George Kelly returned to the house.

No doubt his mind was still preoccupied with Doris O'Malley as he drove into the short driveway beside his house, anger at the thought of Kelly living with and ill-treating the woman festering inside him.

His relationship with her was unlike any that he had had with the women he met in the course of his travels through the pubs and clubs of Liverpool's underworld. The prostitutes of that city were always a good source of information in return for taking a blind eye to their activities. But Doris O'Malley was different, a bit special, quite beautiful in an obvious, over made-up way. If he was to admit it, he was completely taken with her. But she was involved with Kelly.

And Kelly beat her. And used her. Balmer thought again of the tears in O'Malley's eyes when he had questioned her only minutes earlier.

In other ways also Kelly was beginning to cause problems and become more than just a nuisance, his role as an informer still useful but his activities escalating to a stage at which they could no longer be ignored. He knew too much and was becoming too cheeky, particularly in public and, although Balmer hated to admit it, Kelly always managed to upstage him with his personality.

The telephone was ringing as he turned his key in the front door, his wife coming into the hall to meet him.

"It's urgent, Bert. They've been after you for over an hour and the phone hasn't stopped ringing. A murder. At some picture house."

Balmer lifted the phone. For over an hour the calls had been almost continuous and he recognised the familiar voice of Detective Chief Superintendent Smith. His hatred of Kelly was suddenly forgotten as he waited impatiently for the squad car which was already on its way. This was the excitement he craved.

Within fifteen minutes, he was at the Cameo Cinema, one of the constables thronging the foyer pointing to the spiral staircase. Balmer made his way up the stairs, Smith crossing the room to meet him.

"Manager and assistant manager both shot. The manager's dead, the assistant manager's in Sefton General. In a bad way, I'm afraid."

Balmer glanced around the room, shaking his head.

"Christ. This is chaos."

It was almost 11.00pm and there were police everywhere, many of them tramping through the office upstairs, talking excitedly to the forensic team who were already powdering and photographing.

Balmer stood aside as the manager's body was taken out, again shaking his head. There was no indication of where the bodies had fallen but there was blood everywhere, a number of cartridge cases and bullets scattered around the room and the lock to the door of the manager's office lying on the floor.

He questioned the staff himself, but by now the women were in a state of hysteria, the men little better and it was with some difficulty that he was able to get a coherent account of what had happened. He continued his examination, getting the police presence together in the main auditorium where he gave them their orders, sending some to search the cinema, others outside to look for anything suspicious and, of course, the gun. After that, even though it was nearly midnight, they were ordered to conduct a house to house search.

Smith had already sent a message to the Railway Police, the Mersey Tunnel Police and those on duty at the Landing Stage at the Pier Head. With the help of the Lancashire Police, Liverpool was now, to all intents and purposes, cordoned off from the rest of the country. Then, as Balmer and Smith shared a police car back to the Central Police Station, Smith formally placed the Chief Inspector in charge of the investigation. When they reached Dale Street they were greeted by news from Sefton General Hospital. Bernard Catterall had died at 11.15pm. It was now a double murder.

Balmer arranged for an enquiry room to be set up near his office and arranged for a huge team of plain clothes detectives, together with every available uniformed policeman to conduct a house to house search in the area of the crime. The enquiries would continue through the night as a police net tightened around the city.

The description of the wanted man had already gone out to all forces:

'Between twenty and thirty, about 5' 4", medium to broad build and possibly with dark hair. Believed to be dressed in a brown, double-breasted overcoat with belt all round, black shoes and trilby.'

The biggest murder enquiry and man-hunt the country had ever known had been launched.

It was in the early hours of the morning before Balmer and Smith finally sat down to think rationally about the events of the night and to draw up a list of possible suspects, Balmer writing a list on a blackboard, the members of the murder squad clustered around. Finally, after eliminating a number of names, Balmer gazed around. He had already decided. There was one candidate for the crime. He seemed utterly convincing as he spoke to the team.

"George Kelly did this." There was no element of doubt in his voice.

He ordered Kelly's record sheet to be brought to the incident room, reading through it slowly, although much of it was familiar to him.

Born in 1922, Kelly's criminal activities had begun early. At eleven, he was sent to a special school for house breaking and larceny. When he was twelve, he was placed on probation for stealing 14 shillings and 7 pence which were found in his jacket pocket. When he was thirteen, he was again convicted, receiving probation for stealing four pence.

In 1938, Kelly enlisted in the Royal Artillery, falsifying his age. Fourteen weeks later he was discharged when his real age was discovered. It was something he remained bitter about for the rest of his life, his conscription into the Royal Navy no replacement for the Army, the discipline not to his liking and he deserted five times. He was discharged in 1945 and on the same day received a naval court martial and was sentenced to three year's penal servitude and twelve month's concurrent hard labour for prison-breaking and machine damage. He was released in April 1947.

In between these offences, when on the run from the navy in 1943, he was sentenced to nine months for assault on a young prostitute whom he was alleged to have hit in the face and kicked in the stomach when she was on the ground. He was discharged on the grounds of insufficient evidence but sentenced after a police bill of indictment against him. In January 1945, his record was brought up to date when he received another prison sentence for handling stolen goods.

Balmer looked up from the charge list. There was little in it to suggest a potential murderer. He pursed his lips as he remembered the time of Kelly's arrest for desertion.

"I'll go and see Kelly. Jimmy, you come with me."

It was 11.15am on the Sunday morning when Balmer and Detective Inspector Jimmy Morris called to see George Kelly in Cambridge Street. Kelly was already up and dressed. He looked cautiously at Balmer before the Chief Inspector spoke.

"Morning, George. We're making enquiries about the murder at the Cameo Cinema." There was no acknowledgement in his voice of his visit to see O'Malley the previous night.

"Yes, I heard about it. Doris, I told you. Didn't I tell you they would call?" He turned back to Balmer.

"Can we go to the back, Mr Balmer. She's got a visitor." Balmer followed Kelly into the back yard.

"What do you know, George?"

"Nothing, Mr Balmer. Only what's in the News of the World."

"Tell me about last night."

"Nothing to tell really. I was with Jimmy Skelly at the Coach and Horses. Jimmy got legless so I left him and came home. Must have been about nine. I was going to have a drink with Doris but she left a note saying she was out. I went to the Spofforth. She wasn't there, so I just had one drink and then went back to the Leigh."

"That's only about five minutes from the Cameo."

"I suppose so."

"Have you got a brown overcoat?"

"Brown. Never. Not for years. You know my style, Mr Balmer."

"Have you a gun in the house, George?"

George laughed at him. "I haven't got a gun."

"I'd like to search the house."

"No problem, Mr Balmer. I'll tell Doris and if you give me a lift, I'll take you to the chap I was with last night."

After Balmer and Morris had searched the house, they took Kelly in the police car. Kelly pointing out the Coach and Horses pub in Low Hill before they called in at Prescot Street Police Station for Skelly's address in Holborn Street. Balmer knew Skelly and that he also was no stranger to crime, with numerous convictions, including approved school, borstal and terms in prison for up to two years. Skelly was still feeling the effects of the night before as Balmer questioned him.

"Can you tell me where you where?"

"In the Coach and Horses. I was brought home rotten drunk at 10 o'clock."

There was little to be gained from Skelly and Balmer drove Kelly back to the corner of Cambridge Street. Kelly turning to the policeman as he climbed from the car.

"Are you satisfied now, Mr Balmer?" Balmer nodded.

"But I'll be checking your alibi, George."

Kelly looked stunned, Balmer's words ringing in his ears as he made his way to the Leigh Arms. He sat morosely by himself until the pub closed at 2 o'clock and then crossed the road to the telephone box at the corner of Cambridge Street, his call to Harry Livermore, a prominent Liverpool solicitor who had helped him in the past, answered almost immediately. The solicitor calmed him down, promising to help him confirm his alibi if Balmer decided to go any further with his suspicions.

The following day, Monday 21 March, the case made immediate headlines in the Daily Post.

The biggest man-hunt in the country for many years is being concentrated in the Lawrence Road district of Liverpool, following the murder of the manager of the Cameo Cinema, and his assistant on Saturday night.

One hundred plain-clothes detectives, together with every available uniformed policeman, directed by Chief Superintendent T A Smith, head of Liverpool CID, conducted a house to house search in the area for the assailant who is believed to be still armed. They hope to make an early arrest.

Mr Leonard Thomas, aged 39, the Cameo's manager, of Melwood Drive, West Derby, and his assistant, Mr J B Catterall, of Hampstead Road, Fairfield Liverpool, were shot in the manager's office at about 9.30pm, as they fought to protect the day's takings of £50.

Both the dead men had only been at the cinema for a short period; Mr Thomas, a married man with two children, Graham, aged nine, and Christine, aged five months was formerly employed in a Liverpool store. During the war, he served in the Forces until he was invalided out following a Bren-gun carrier accident. He became a special constable and joined the circuit owning the Cameo as an assistant manager of the Rialto Cinema, Liverpool.

Mr Catterall was demobbed from the Navy two months ago and came to Liverpool from Grimsby with his young bride.

Mr Thomas and Mr Catterall were seated at a table counting the takings. While one man grappled with the intruder, the other went to close the door. In the violent struggle which followed, during which papers and money were scattered all over the room, the assailant sent the manager to the floor with a fatal bullet wound in his chest. Mr Catterall, although wounded with a bullet through his right palm, fought on. Butt the intruder shot him in the right side of the chest and, as he fell, fired a third and what is believed to be fatal shot into his back. In his haste to escape, the gunman did not try the door but fired at the unlocked door.

The masked man left the money scattered on the floor, with Mr Thomas dead, a bullet through his chest and Mr Catterall dying with four bullet wounds. He died two hours later without regaining consciousness.

The Police are working on the theory that the man had carefully planned the hold-up. They believe that he must have visited the cinema on several previous occasions and made a survey of how the cash was taken nightly from the pay-box to the manager's office, which is up a spiral staircase.

The murderer was believed to have sat in the 1/6d stalls and watched the cashier come up the cinema aisle and cut through a passageway leading to the foot of the spiral staircase.

Minutes later, he left his seat and, in the narrow passageway, tied a black silk scarf over the lower part of his face and pulled the brim of his trilby hat over his eyes. At the foot of the stairs he cut the telephone wires. Mounting the iron staircase, he pushed open the door of the office.

The police have already interviewed several members of the audience who have told them of people leaving their seats about the time of the shooting.

The Cameo Cinema was formerly a Welsh Chapel, and the spire is still on the building. The shooting took place in what used to be the choir gallery.

A few days later, Balmer again saw George Kelly but his story was unwavering and later that day Balmer called at another house in Cambridge Street and interviewed a taxi driver, a neighbour of Doris O'Malley's named Currie. He was able to confirm a statement by the licensee of the Leigh Arms that Kelly came into his pub at about ten o'clock on the night of the murder.

Balmer next went to the Spofforth Arms public house in Spofforth Road, only three or four minutes walking time from the Cameo. Here again Kelly was identified by the licensee who confirmed that Kelly had been there.

Balmer was disappointed. Kelly would have been an ideal suspect and the one he wanted. But there was not a scrap of evidence to connect him with the murder and so far, his alibi was too strong for any jury to convict.

Jacqueline Dickson was a young, uneducated prostitute. Her real name was Morris and she was one of seven children, born into a poor family in the slums of Salford, her birth unregistered. In an attempt to escape her environment she had married a black seaman named Dickson but the marriage had failed, Dickson moving irregularly between Manchester and Liverpool, making a living from petty crime and prostitution. A thin, stooped woman, she suffered from chronic ill health and a weak chest which was to affect her for the rest of her life.

By April Fools' Day, she was panicking about her role in the affair, blaming Northam for supplying the gun, even though she had been one of the instigators of the robbery. The fact that the police had interview Johnson's mother had frightened her further. Worried that the others involved would turn Kings evidence to save their own necks, she was determined to protect herself at all costs.

On Monday 4 April, a letter arrived at Central Police Station, addressed to the Inspector, CID, Dale Street, Liverpool. As the officer in charge of the Cameo murders case, it was passed to Chief Inspector Bert Balmer.

Dear Sir,

This letter is not a crank's letter or sutchlike, nor am I turning informer for gain. You have been searching Wavertree and district for the person responsible for the deaths of the two men killed in the Cinema when the two persons responsible live no where near where the crime was commited it says in the papers that you are looking for one man, I know three and a girl, not including myself, who heard about his plan for the robbery. I would have nothing to do with it and I dont think the girl did. When I met her on Sunday she had not been with them and another man dropped out on account he wanted to unload the revolver before they went so only two went, the man he took with him lost his nerve and would not go in with him but said he would wait outside but did not, he has not been seen since nor has the girl he lives with been seen about the town, five days ago I seen the man who had done the job and we got talking. I said I wanted nothing to do with him and he said Im in it with him. What I want to know now is how I stand, I knew they were going to do the job but I did not go with them. I have proof I was in a pub not far from Dale St till 10pm and was talking till 11pm in Brownlow H. to two people. I want to know if I turn Kings Evedence or somthing like that will I be charged. I have a record you see, and he might say something to frame me with him, to prove I speak the truth the gun he used he threw it in the pond in the Park. The Park is on Edge Lane next to Littlewoods. He cut through the park for a 6a Car, I am scared of him he wants me to go away with him and I cant go down the town Im afraid of him finding where I stay. I dont know how you can get in touch with me. If I give my address you might charge me with being an accesory to the killing. If you put in the personal column of the Echo and give me your word that I wont be charged I will give you both their names also some of the bullets he left with me about 6 weeks ago. I can also tell you where he got the gun from he wants arresting for selling them. I can also tell you who ran that stolen motor lorry through the pub and killed a person some time back if you give me your word that I wont be charged. (sic)

The franking on the letter gave no indication of where it had been posted. There was a red stain in the envelope. Balmer replaced the letter in the envelope and sent both for forensic examination.

The letter appeared to rule out any link between Kelly and the murder. Kelly's home address was not Cambridge Street. He actually lived near Brownlow Hill which was further from the Cameo. Also, Kelly had definitely not caught a 6a tram.

But the letter was the first indication that more than one person was involved in the murder. Balmer drafted a reply and arranged for it to be put in the personal column of the Liverpool Echo that night, 'Anonymous letter received. Promise definitely given.'

After another week Balmer was baffled. The notice in the personal column had yielded no reply, neither had another one several days later and the search of the park lake had been carried out. It was a a stinking job, with a huge audience. After the Fire Brigade had pumped the lake dry, or as dry as possible, and even with over 100 detectives raking through the mud and debris for days, the search yielded only stolen bicycles, handbags and other property. There was a soft top layer of mud, the underlayer hard and there was no way the gun could have sunk into it. Yet no gun was found and eventually the search was abandoned.

But by now the forensic report on the letter was available. The red stain on the envelope was lipstick, which seemed to confirm the implication in the letter that the writer was a woman. Now the emphasis in the investigation changed.

Balmer instructed the murder squad.

"We're looking for a woman. She seems frightened. Perhaps she knows too much. I want you to interview every woman who has been arrested in Liverpool over the last ten years." Detective Sergeant Farragher shook his head.

"That will be impossible, Chief. What about prostitutes? They've got no fixed address, they move around. How can we find all them?"

"Maybe you won't but we have to try. Every one of them, whether here, or in any city they may have moved to. Get them to write the words that have been misspelled."

The search widened to the whole country; any woman known to have been convicted in Liverpool was interviewed, again without success.

A promise on the Holy Eucharist

The damp, grey days of March had gone. The year had moved on to a warm spring and Donald Johnson was a frightened man. On remand with his brother on a charge of robbery, uppermost in his mind was the seriousness of the crime in which he was involved. Within minutes of the murder he had been stopped by the police near the scene of the crime and they had also been to his home. Did they know more? Had the others talked? In his panic he showed too much interest in the Cameo case, so much so that the Wallasey police questioned him about it before reporting it to the Cameo murder squad.

Although only twenty three years old, Johnson's criminal record was worse than that of any of the other minor criminals who were the principals in the case. His career in crime had started when he was only eight years old, escalating through shop-breaking and larceny when he was twelve, eight cases of shop-breaking when he was sixteen, after which he moved on to house-breaking. In 1944 he was given 18 months for house-breaking and in 1946, when he threatened a woman doctor who discovered him in her house, he received a sentence of 12 months at the Liverpool quarter sessions.

It was then that the first symptoms of mental instability emerged when, during his imprisonment, he attempted suicide by hanging. On his release, however, his criminal activities continued and, in 1947, he was sentenced to three years penal servitude for house-breaking and larceny, after which, on release in April 1949, he was charged, along with his brother George, with robbery.

The message was on Balmer's desk when he arrived at his office at Dale Street Police Station at 9.30 on the morning of 2nd May. It was from the police in Wallasey. Johnson's behaviour was sufficiently incriminating that he should talk to him.

Detective Inspector Jimmy Morris and Detective Sergeant Jack Farragher were immediately sent to Wallasey, where they met Johnson minutes before he was due in court. In a small interview room, they introduced themselves before Farragher left the room, Morris sitting across the table from Johnson, laboriously taking out his notebook and a pencil, glancing up and staring hard at Johnson for long moments.

"First, tell me what you were doing on the night of March 19th. Can you do that?" Johnson was emphatic.

"I can, but I didn't shoot anybody." Morris leaned conspiratorially across the table.

"I know, Donald. I personally don't think you would do something like this. But I think you might know who did do it." He paused, sitting back in his chair before continuing. "You've already been interviewed about the murder?"

"No, but Inspector Gardiner came to our house and spoke to me mam when I was at work."

"And he seemed quite happy, did he?"

"Yeah, I suppose so. He never came back anyway." Johnson was relaxing.

"Are you sure you know nothing about the Cameo murders?"

"No."

Morris stood up. "I'll get you some cigarettes and a coffee. While I'm out, think it over. Okay?"

"I've got nothing to think over."

During this interview, Farragher had been interviewing Johnson's brother who claimed to have been drinking in the Dingle all that Saturday night, his alibi watertight, Farragher satisfied he had nothing to tell them.

Morris and Farragher returned to the interview room, throwing a packet of Woodbines at Johnson.

"There you are. Things aren't that bad. Have a ciggy and tell me what you know. Have you thought things over?"

Johnson avoided his eyes, nervy, moving restlessly in his seat, staring at the notebook in front of Morris before replying.

"Yes."

"Well?"

"I think I know who done the murder and I think I know where the gun is." Farragher remained impassive.

"Good lad. We'll get this charge against you quashed. It's only toffee. You won't be brought into the Cameo case. You won't even have to give evidence. Tell us about it."

Johnson began his statement, Farragher taking notes. (see Appendix 1)

It was a rambling story, Johnson laying the blame for the murder on a man called Charley Duggan who he had first met in prison. Duggan had asked him to go to the Cameo with him as he was going to do a job there but Johnson claimed he was scared and would not go.

As he gave the statement, Johnson became more and more agitated, his hands were clenched on the table in front of him and he was beginning to shake. He stopped for a while and when he continued, he appeared on the verge of breaking down and was almost incoherent, now claiming that Duggan was not the man's real name and, despite prompting, refusing to give another name, saying that he had promised Charley on the Holy Eucharist that he would not tell anyone.

Again Farragher tried to calm him down, asking him to draw a picture of a barrelled automatic pistol.

Now Farragher tried to persuade Johnson to take him to the gun, offering to wipe off any fingerprints. But Johnson shook his head, adamant in his refusal.

One hour later, Chief Superintendent Smith, who had arrived from Liverpool, interviewed Johnson alone. More persuasive than Farragher, he told Johnson that next time he was in trouble he was to go and see him, giving him a few pound notes, before placing a sheet of paper and a pencil on the table in front of Johnson. But still Johnson would not give any names. But Smith persisted.

"Are you courting, Donald?"

"Yes." Johnson looked wary. Smith's voice was friendly.

"I'll help set up a home for you and your girl."

Still Johnson remained silent and Smith left the room, returning half an hour later with a man dressed in priest's dark clothing, a clerical collar around his neck. But even that ploy was unsuccessful, Johnson shaking his head as he saw through the ruse.

"No, I can't. Not unless Charley Duggan lets me. It's no use."

"Come on Donald. Don't be stupid. Do yourself a favour." But still Johnson would not change his mind.

"I'm not going to say anything. I can find the man tomorrow if you'll let me go. I promised I'd give him a chance to give himself up. Once I'm free of the promise, I'll tell you who he is and about the gun. I know where it's planted."

Smith raised an eyebrow. There would be no opposition to bail on the robbery charge in the hope that Johnson would give them further leads. Farragher then put up the £20 bail.

Over the next few days, the police watch on Johnson was tight but he hardly moved from his brother's house where he stayed with Florrie, his sister-in-law. Several times over the next few days, on May 3rd, on May 4th, and twice on May 5th, he called Smith but without giving any further information. On May 6th, Smith was in his office when the next call was put through.

"Can you see me at half-past one outside the Gaumont?"

Smith was there with minutes to spare before Johnson arrived, pale and visibly trembling.

"I'm sorry, Mr Smith. I still haven't seen him. I can tell you I planted that gun, although I wasn't on the job but I can't tell you who the fellow is as I'm bound by my promise."

"You've had three days, Donald."

"I know that, Mr Smith, but until I see him I can't tell you."

By now, Smith's patience was exhausted.

"We'd better go up to Dale Street and you can tell me anything you want to say."

At the Central Police Station, Morris prepared to take down his statement. "You said you wouldn't go with him on the Saturday. But you saw him afterwards. You were outside the Boundary pub."

"You know that. A policeman stopped me."

"And then what happened? The whole story, Donald."

The door to the interview room burst open and Balmer strode into the room.

"Stand up, Donald John Johnson. I charge you with the wilful murder of Leonard Thomas. Have you anything to say?" Johnson's eyes were wide with fright.

"No."

"Do you want your mother to be told?"

"No."

Smith leaned over Johnson. "Then why won't you tell us? Here's a paper and pencil. Write down what happened."

"No. You can't charge me with murder. I will tell you the whole truth of what happened but I still won't tell you the man's name."

Morris sat down and started writing. (Appendix 2)

Johnson repeated much of what he had said in the statement taken on May 2nd, describing how he had been asked to go to the Cameo to look it over before doing a job there. He had arranged to meet the man at quarter to eleven outside the Boundary Hotel but was questioned by a policeman. When the policeman had gone, the man came over to ask what he had wanted and then gave him the gun, saying he had shot a couple of lights out. Johnson had then walked down Smithdown Road towards the Cameo and when he saw the police cars he got scared and climbed over the cemetery wall near the hospital and made his way home, planting the gun on the way.

The next day, he promised the man on the Holy Eucharist that he would not give him away and that he would give him the chance to give himself up.

Again Johnson refused to say who the man was because of his promise, adding that he had nothing to do with the job and the only way he had helped him was to get rid of the gun. Morris stopped him.

"Where is the gun, Donald?' Johnson shook his head.

"I can't tell you where the gun is because you would find his fingerprints on it and that would be as good as telling you who he is. If it wasn't for my promise, I would tell you."

He continued with his statement, saying it had been worrying him for weeks, he hadn't been able to work properly and even fell off the ladder at work because he was frightened. He then went on to say that the man had another gun and that he lived with one girl who was no good but was going about with another decent girl.

Johnson finished the statement by saying that every time he had seen the man since, he had given him a few bob and a few rums.

When Morris had finished writing, Smith read the statement back to Johnson, shaking his head in frustration, as again Johnson refused to sign it.

"No, I told you, I'm not going to sign anything but I have been talking to you for a long time and every word I have said is true." Smith stood up.

"Then I charge you that, knowing that a man known to you murdered Leonard Thomas, you did, on the same day and other days afterwards, receive, comfort, harbour, assist and maintain the said man."

The search of Wavertree cemetery took a week. It was old, overgrown in parts, graves and tombstones dating back to the early 19th century, soaring monuments and cupolas, carved stone filled with crevices offering many places to hide the weapon. But none was found. Evidence collected by Liverpool City Police confirmed Johnson's account of his movements late on that night. He was challenged at 10.15 outside the Boundary Hotel, by Constable Thompson and Constable George Milner reported that he had challenged a man coming from Princess Park into Park Road, the man claiming to have had a few drinks and to be walking it off. The man answered Johnson's description, the significance being that this would be on the route Johnson would take on his way home. Detective Sergeant Jack Farragher also confirmed that Johnson's verbal description of the wall he had clambered over in the cemetery had been strictly accurate.

Statements taken by the police and others who came into contact with Johnson at that time are revealing. They may suggest that his role may have been more than that of accessory. In a statement taken on May 6th, at Wallasey Police Station (Appendix 3) his brother, George, stated that after Donald had been interviewed about the Cameo, he had asked him what he knew and he had said, 'You'd be surprised.' George Johnson also said that his mother had told him that the police had been to see her to find out where Donald was on the night of the murder and she had said he was at home. George Johnson added that his own alibi was that, on the night of the murder he was in a Dingle public house. He went on to say that his brother had been looking very worried and when he asked him why he said it was about two girls, Clara Gallimore and Sarah Griffin.

Johnson's mother, Ellen Johnson, in another statement taken at the same time (Appendix 4) denied that Donald was not at home that night. She said he said he had gone to the Pavilion Theatre in Lodge Lane and came home shortly after 11 o'clock. She added that she did not know any of his friends. Clara Gallimore was interviewed.

(Appendix 5) She stated that she had not been with Donald on the night of March 19th and that he had told her he had fallen from a ladder at work.

This was supported by a statement taken on March 29th from the manager of the commercial cleaning company for which Johnson worked. He confirmed that he had remonstrated with Johnson about the condition of some windows he had cleaned, Johnson failing to offer any explanation for his unsatisfactory work.

When in prison, Johnson had written a series of long, rambling letters to Florrie, his brother's wife, as well as a number of letters to Catholic churches in Liverpool, asking if anyone had confessed to the murder. The letters could only have been a subterfuge, Johnson knowing full well the secrecy of the confessional.

His letters to Florrie are revealing. In one of them, (Appendix 6) he implicates himself in the crime and claims that he did it just for her and George, the children and Clara but would fight the case even though some people's names would appear in the papers. He continues by saying that if, 'I get a sentence and you know how large…' This could certainly be interpreted to suggest that Florrie knew the truth.

While on remand in Walton, Johnson also made a number of revealing statements which seen to suggest he was seeking an alibi. (Appendix 7) On the 13th May, Prison Officer Brennan stated that Johnson was visited by his brother's wife and that he had told her not to forget he was with Clara on the Cameo night. His sister-in-law asked if he meant March 19th and then agreed he was at her house and went with Sarah the following Saturday.

As the date of Johnson's appearance in the Magistrates Court approached, Jacqueline Dickson's nerve was going. On May 13th, she was in the Magistrates Court building in Dale Street on bail, waiting an appearance on a larceny case which could send her to gaol. Johnson was also due in court that day.

Her only way out, in case Johnson talked, appeared to be to strike a bargain beforehand. In the corridor outside the courtroom, where she was waiting to be called, she approached Sergeant Jack Farragher. She was well known to him and asked him if he wanted to know the writer of the letter which was sent to the police regarding the Cameo murders. Farragher took her to an interview room, sending for Balmer who was already in the building waiting to be called at the Johnson hearing.

"What do you know about the letter, Jackie? Who wrote it?"

"Not me. I never did anything but I'm up on a charge. I thought if I helped Mr Farragher, he could help me."

"You'll have to give me something before I see what I can do."

"I might need protection."

Balmer shrugged. "We'll see Jackie. What about the letter? Who wrote it?"

"I can prove it's from me. I put lipstick on it to fool you into thinking it was from a woman."

Balmer nodded. "It mentioned the lorry in Lime Street. Who drove that, Jackie?"

"He'll kill me if I tell. They'll all kill me."

"You tell us who he is and I promise I won't say anything."

"It was Jimmy Northam."

"And the Cameo?"

"That's all I'm saying, Mr Balmer."

"Who did it, Jackie?"

Dickson shook her head desperately as she tried to find a name.

"Go and see Charles Connolly. He knows about it. That's all I'm saying."

Balmer stared at her thoughtfully. "Good. You help me and I'll see what can be done about forgetting this charge."

The following day, Dickson was given bail but as soon as she left the Bridewell she returned to her flat, collected some of her belongings and left the city, failing to appear at her hearing on May 24th.

Accessory after the fact

Balmer leafed through Connolly's file. There was not a lot to see, except that he had been convicted of assault on a policeman. Connolly was a very minor member of the city's criminal fraternity. In 1938, he was placed on probation for larceny. Eighteen months later, he was fined ten shillings for disorderly behaviour and twenty shillings for assaulting a police constable. In 1941, he stole a postage stamp and was sentenced to one and a half days in prison but was immediately released. In 1946, he was arrested for being drunk and disorderly and was sentenced to one month's imprisonment but appealed and was fined £2 with £2 and 20 shillings costs. In 1947, he was fined £5 for grievous bodily harm in an assault on a policeman.

The convictions seemed trivial, particularly in comparison with those of others in the case. His Merchant Navy career was without apparent blemish and he left with a 'very good' character reference. He then worked as a labourer and as a railway porter, becoming unemployed for a period before starting work at Bibby's, a flour milling and refining company.

Early on the morning of May 14th, Balmer and Morris went to Connolly's home, and escorted him to Lawrence Road Police Station.

"Did you write a letter to the police regarding the Cameo murders?"

"No."

Balmer handed him a sheet of paper and a pencil, dictating what Connolly had to write. Connolly scribbled nervously before handing the paper back to Balmer."

"I know nothing about it, but who told you this? "

"A woman named Jacqueline Dickson, who said she knows you quite well."

" Aye, I know Jackie Dickson alright. I see her around Lime Street but she's telling lies when she says anything like this about me."

Balmer raised an eyebrow. "Where were you on the night of March 19th?"

"I was working in Bibby's then. I was on the afternoon shift and didn't get off until after ten."

Balmer showed him some photographs. "Do you know any of these women?"

Connolly nodded and pointed to one. "Yes. That's Jackie Dickson."

Connolly looked nervous, getting hesitantly to his feet when, after a few more questions, Balmer let him go. There was nothing to hold him on, he had denied all knowledge of the murder and his handwriting and spelling bore no similarity to that in the letter.

Balmer sent for Dickson to question her again but she had disappeared. Furious that his intended chief witness had fled, he started a much publicised search, her description and photograph circulated to police forces throughout the country. But Dickson was not to be found.

On May 26th, at Liverpool Magistrates Court, Kelly, together with Jimmy Skelly, were found guilty of stealing a pair of rubber boots and maliciously wounding a constable. The charge was dubious, Kelly proclaiming his innocence so much so that he had resisted arrest when the arresting constable approached him at the bottom of Brownlow Hill. Both defendants received a sentence of three months for the larceny, Kelly receiving an additional three months for the assault, Balmer making no objection when they successfully appealed against the sentence and were released on bail.

The following day, on May 27th, three weeks to the day after his arrest, Johnson, in the presence of his solicitor, Mr Leslie Black, made a further statement.
"I don't know anything about the Cameo murders. I don't know who did it."
The statement was witnessed by Balmer and Morris. The next morning Johnson appeared in Liverpool Magistrates Court, where he was committed for trial at the next Liverpool Assizes on a charge of being an accessory after the fact.

While on remand at Walton Prison, Johnson talked to a number of fellow prisoners. One of these was Bernard Joseph McBride, a 25 year old habitual minor criminal.
In a letter to the Governor, dated 30th May, Prison Officer J Le Poidevin claimed that Bernard Joseph McBride had some information about the Cameo murders. (Appendix 8). McBride claimed that Johnson had told him that his brother had done the murder and had given the gun to him which he had then got rid of. He had gone on to say that Johnson's wife knew all about it and that Johnson had told him he had taken the blame for his brother on a number of occasions because his brother was a family man.
As a result of this statement, Chief Inspector Jimmy Morris visited McBride in Walton Prison on June 7th. McBride was prepared to give a statement. (Appendix 9) He told Morris that Johnson had said that it was not he who had done the murder but his brother. He was in a woman's house that night and his brother came in and told him he had shot two men. He showed Johnson the gun and asked him if he would take it and that, while Johnson was out, his brother put the gun in his pocket and he didn't find it until he got home to his mother's house.
McBride continued to say that Johnson had had a visit from his solicitor who had told him that his girl friend was pregnant and that if he didn't tell the police all he knew, then she would. He said his girl friend was Clara Gallimore.
McBride finished by stating that Johnson did not say that Clara Gallimore knew anything about the gun but he got the impression that she knew something about it.

That the police had more in mind for Johnson than that of being an accessory to the murder is evident in the correspondence between the Chief Constable of Liverpool with the Airborne Forces Depot at Aldershot in which, in a letter dated May 26th, the Chief Constable asked for information on Johnson's proficiency with firearms. A reply was received, dated June 3rd, from the colonel commanding. It described Johnson's service in a Primary Training Centre and his subsequent desertion, apprehension and discharge on medical grounds, after a service period in the parachute regiment of only seven months.

'During his training at both the PTC and ITC he would have received instruction in the use of small arms. Such instruction would normally cover rifle, bren gun, sten, grenades and possibly PIAT 2 in mortar and pistol.

It cannot be said with any certainty exactly which weapons were taught during his abbreviated term of service. The first four weapons are almost certain to have been included in the PTC syllabus.'

On the 13th June, Johnson again spoke to a prison officer. In a letter to the Governor, Prison Officer Cork stated (Appendix 10) that Johnson had told him that the gun concerned in the case had been thrown into the Mersey. He questioned him as to how there were no fingerprints, considering the murderer did not wear gloves and Johnson replied, 'I never leave fin…' before correcting himself, saying, 'the bloke wouldn't be stupid enough to leave prints.'

During further conversation Johnson asked how Cork thought he would get on at Liverpool Assizes and when Cork reminded him of the gravity of the charge, Johnson replied that they could not 'top him' for it. He went on to say that if they found him guilty he would own up to it.

The trial of Donald Johnson for being an accessory after the fact opened on June 14th in the Crown Court. Mr Justice Lynskey was the presiding judge. The jury consisted of ten men and two woman. The defence counsel was Rose Heilbron, a young Liverpool barrister. For her, young and ambitious, the case was important and although the accused was not being charged with murder, a successful defence would enhance her steadily-growing reputation. She had decided, on reviewing the evidence presented to her by the defence solicitor, that a defence on technical grounds would have a strong chance of success.

Her case would rest on the fact that any statements made after the initial one on May 2nd were not admissible. This would have two strands, the legitimacy of the charge itself and the legitimacy of police evidence. This was emphasised in her opening statement.

"In my submission a man cannot be charged with being an accessory after the fact of murder alone. He can be charged with the murderer and after conviction of the murderer but he cannot be charged before the murderer."

She quoted numerous legal authorities from the volumes stacked on the benches in front of her, Mr Justice Lynskey listening intently.

"There are sound reasons of justice why an accessory after the fact in this particular case of murder should not be tried alone. If the man who was supposed to have assisted in this particular case should afterwards be tried and acquitted, you might have a situation where a man is convicted as an accessory to a man who is later acquitted and that is the anomalous position which might very well arise.

The killing in this particular case might be found to have been manslaughter and there is a position in the punishment section with regards to accessories. The punishment for accessory after the fact of murder is twenty years or penal servitude for life. The punishment for an accessory after other felonies is a maximum of two years."

The legal arguments continued until, ultimately, Judge Lynskey gave his judgment that the motion to quash the indictment must fail. It was his view that the accused could be tried as an accessory whether with the principal felon or after the felon or before the felon.

After a brief consultation with his counsel, Johnson then pleaded not guilty. It was an important development in the definition of English criminal law.

The prosecution was opened by Mr A Gerrard, KC who outlined the murder circumstances and was followed by the evidence of the policeman who had seen Johnson near the Boundary Hotel within about three quarters of an hour of the murder. Police Constable John Thompson described Johnson as 5' 6" to 5' 8 ", wearing a dark suit and, if he remember correctly, with a coat over his arm.

Gerrard then moved on to the next important date, the meeting between Johnson and Detective Chief Inspector Morris at Wallasey Police Station on May 2nd.

At this stage, Miss Heilbron objected to the admissibility of statements alleged to have been made by Johnson to the police, and the jury was asked to leave the court. Miss Heilbron then continued her case in camera, making allegations against the Liverpool CID chiefs, contending that they had offered to have another charge against Johnson and his brother quashed.

"A CID officer went surety for Johnson's £20 bail on the charge for which he was held at Wallasey and he was also told he would be kept out of the Cameo case. For this he was given sums of £1 and £2 by Chief Superintendent Smith, Head of the CID. He was later charged with the Cameo murders by Chief Inspector Balmer."

The police witnesses, in turn, denied this, except for confirming the issue of bail surety by Detective Sergeant Farragher.

"Why was this?" Miss Heilbron asked Chief Superintendent Smith.

"It was because we thought that Johnson was of more use to us in our investigations when free, than he would have been in custody."

"Mr Smith, it is a lie that you did not give Johnson a sheet of foolscap paper and an envelope to make a statement on the Cameo murders."

Smith answered with a veneer of politeness.

"I am surprised at you, Miss Heilbron, suggesting that it is a lie. It is not a lie."

Miss Heilbron then questioned Detective Chief Inspector Herbert Balmer.

"Did you approach the accused and say 'stand up Donald John Johnson. I charge you with the murder of Leonard Thomas'?"

"No. I did not."

"Mr Balmer, it is a lie that you did not charge Johnson with this murder."

There was no expression on Balmer's face as he replied, dismissively,

"That is definitely not true. He was never charged."

When the court resumed the following morning, the jury were again excluded as Johnson entered the witness box. Miss Heilbron asking him about the events of May 2nd when he was waiting to go into court on a charge.

"When you were in the Wallasey court before May 2nd, was bail strongly opposed by the Chief Constable?".

"Yes."

Defence counsel then took him step by step through the events of May 2nd at Wallasey Police Station.

"At about what time were you interviewed by officers from the Liverpool CID?"

"About 9.30 in the morning."

"Did Inspector Morris say anything to you?"

"Yes. He said he had come over to see me about the Cameo double murder. He said he was quite satisfied that I never had anything to do with it but he said, 'you know who did'."

"What did you say?"

"The only interest I had in the Cameo murders was like any other member of the public."

"What did he say to that?"

"He said, 'I can see you are worried. You won't be brought into anything. This charge here we'll have quashed.' He then asked me if I had been interviewed by the police as regards the Cameo and I said, 'Yes'. He asked 'Who by?' and I said Inspector Gardner had come down to the house, while I was at work, to see my mother and he asked what had been said and I told him. He said 'Are you quite satisfied you have nothing to do with it?' and I said 'Yes'. He said 'I will go and get you some cigarettes and leave you to think it over.'"

"Did you make any reply to that before he went out?"

"I said, 'I have nothing to think over.' He then left the room. He was out about a quarter of an hour."

"Did you believe him when he said he would get the case quashed?"

"Yes, I certainly believed him. When he came back he gave me ten cigarettes. He then called Sergeant Farragher in to give me a match. Farragher went out as soon as he had given me a light."

"When Farragher went out, did Morris say anything to you?"

"He asked me again about the Cameo business. He said 'Have you thought it over?' and I said, 'Yes' and he said, 'What have you got to say?' I said 'I think I know who done the Cameo murders and I think I know where the gun was,' and he said, 'Good lad, we'll get this charge quashed against you.' I asked, 'What charge?' and he said, 'The 30 shilling charge. It's only toffee. You won't be brought into the Cameo case or have to give evidence.' I never dictated a statement at all. I was never cautioned for a statement.

When Smith arrived Morris told him he had made a couple of notes and he gave them to him. He said, 'He's a good lad but he's a bit worried about this thirty bob charge but I have told him we will get it quashed for him.'

When the others had left the room Smith told me that if I ever got into trouble, to go and see him and he asked me if I was courting. I told him 'Yes' and he said he would build up a home for me and my girl."

"Did you say anything in reply to that?"

"I can't remember. Morris then came into the room and told Smith that I was wanted in court. Smith asked Morris to go and ask them to hold it back for a little bit longer. Smith then said he would get in touch with the Chief Constable and try and arrange bail. He told me it was only toffee I was up for. Farragher was there and he asked me where the gun was. I told him if I told him I would be breaking a promise.

Farragher said you won't be breaking a promise. We don't even want you to break a promise. If you will take us to where you have got the gun, we will wipe the fingerprints off. There won't be any fingerprints on the gun as it would have a rough surface. Then he showed me on a match-box and other things in the room."

"What was the promise?"

"I made a promise that I would not go to the police about this supposed Charley Duggan."

"When did you first mention Duggan?"

"When Morris came back with ten cigarettes."

The judge intervened."Did you tell him what your promise was?"

"I said I had promised on the Holy Eucharist that I would not divulge my knowledge to the police."

Miss Heilbron then continued. "What did you say that for?"

"A promise on the Holy Eucharist is a sacred thing and I knew it would be quite an order not to break a promise when made that way."

When Johnson had finished, Heilbron thanked him and made her submission.

"My Lord, I contend that these statements are inadmissible in that they were obtained by inducement. Pressure was exercised by the police, quite proper pressure. But if they apply pressure the penalty they suffer is that they cannot use it in any evidence. I submit there is no case to answer."

When she had finished, she remained standing, allowing herself a brief half-smile, confident that the Judge would have no choice but to allow her argument. He nodded to her and she sat down as he started to sum up the evidence which had been given in the absence of the jury.

"I am satisfied that at the time Johnson made his first statement, on May 2nd, there was no inducement offered to him and no threat used to him. I am equally satisfied that having obtained that statement, the police, particularly Chief Superintendent Smith, were extremely concerned and invoked the assistance of other officers to try to ascertain whether the story the prisoner had told were true. I am satisfied that in his duties to endeavour to discover the man who had committed the double murder, Superintendent Smith did his best to induce the prisoner to make a statement, both as to his own connection with the man and as to where the gun was, where the man was and who he was. For that purpose, I am satisfied, on Superintendent Smith's own evidence, that the police were not too strenuous in their opposition to bail at Wallasey, where Johnson and his brother were held on another charge. In these circumstances it seemed to me that this was sufficient inducement, from the legal point of view, to prevent the second statement made by Johnson being admissible as evidence. Therefore, all statements made after that on May 2nd should not be used in evidence."

The Judge nodded to the court usher.

"The jury may return."

Mr Gerrard stood up, waiting until the jury were settled in their seats before speaking. "I have given careful consideration to the Judge's ruling and in my view there is no other evidence I wish to offer on behalf of the prosecution."

The Judge thanked him before addressing the jury.

"In your absence we have listened to a great deal of evidence as to whether certain statements which the prisoner is alleged to have made and which he denied having made, were admissible in evidence as having been made freely and voluntarily and not because of some hope of favour.

The only possible evidence is the line in the statement, 'he spoke to me and showed me a gun and I know he did the murder. He asked me to go with him but I would not go.' Johnson's refusal to assist does not make him an accessory. I have to rule, having heard the evidence, that only one of the statements made by the prisoner is admissible in evidence, that the others were induced by him being offered the opportunity to bail and a police officer going surety for him.

The result of the ruling, although there is ample evidence before you and which you have heard, that a murder has been committed here, there is no evidence before you of the fact that this man, in the words of the old law did 'receive, comfort, harbour, assist or maintain' the man who is alleged to have done the murder. In other words, an 'accessory after the fact.'

The prosecution have come to the conclusion that the one statement which I have said is admissible in evidence does not give sufficient evidence on which they could ask you to convict this man. It is, therefore, my duty to direct you to return a verdict of not guilty."

Balmer remained impassive, only a slight twitching of facial muscles betraying his emotions as Johnson was taken from the dock to be escorted to prison, where he would begin the sentence of four years corrective training, passed on him the previous week for robbery. Chief Inspector Balmer had a case of inadmissible evidence against him and Johnson, who all through the investigation and subsequent trial did not mention George Kelly, could never again be tried.

Confession

The Cameo murder case had by now attracted countrywide attention and the pressure for a conviction was growing, even the Home Office questioning the lack of progress in an investigation which had resulted in an unprecedented use of police resources, 9500 houses visited, 75000 people interviewed, 1800 fingerprints taken, handwriting samples taken from 1840 women and 1200 telephone calls received. And Chief Inspector Herbert Balmer now had no strong candidate for the crime. Except for George Kelly.

Three months after the collapse of the case against Johnson, on 15 September 1949, Chief Inspector Bert Balmer's worst fears were realised. He received a call from DC Haynes of Preston police. Haynes had been contacted by a prisoner called Robert Graham, a 42 year old engineer from Preston, who was serving a sentence in Walton prison.

Graham was taken from Walton to Preston, where he was visited by Balmer.

"What do you know, Mr Graham?"

"Well, I was a cleaner at Walton Gaol when Johnson was in the hospital wing there."

"Donald John Johnson?"

"That's him. Just before the trial, his brief, Miss Heilbron, came to see him. When she left he was worried. It all depends on legal arguments, he said. If they failed, he would tell the truth but that could mean 20 years for complicity. Or the High Wing, the condemned cell."

"Johnson was acquitted."

"I know. And he was in great spirits. He said he could tell me that unless they found the gun, and they never would, they're finished."

"Did he tell you how he'd done it?"

"A bit."

"Go on. I'll just write it down. For the record." Balmer took the statement in his own hand, pausing and shaking his head several times. (Appendix 11)

Johnson said, 'I had the place lined up for some time. I often used to go there. Anyway, on this night I went up to the manager's office. I thought it was good for four or five hundred pounds. When I went in they were both sitting there. Both the manager and his assistant. When I asked them for the cash one of them went for me, so I let him have it right away. The other fellow then went for me, so I put a bullet into him too but it went into his neck and he dropped to his knees and turned over. The first was killed right away and I thought to myself, well, this bugger might recognise me so I shot him in the back to finish him off. I put three bullets into him before he went out, but the first chap went out when I put the first in him.

I got scared then and got nothing out of the bloody job. I took a powder then right away and, as I was going out, I bumped into the fireman by the top of the stairs.

How that fellow didn't recognise me, I don't know. He's the fellow I was scared of right through. I ran out and funny enough I didn't like to leave the district. I mooched round and then to finish it off, I was stopped by a copper. He asked me for my identity card and I thought he was going to search me but he didn't. If he had, I was finished, because I had the gun on me then. Anyway, I went and got rid of it right away.

I know I was bloody silly sticking round there but I couldn't leave. I think I must have been shocked because I didn't expect to have to do any shooting. I thought as soon as I showed the gun, they would be frightened. Anyway, they'll not get the gun and they can't get anyone to identify me when the fireman couldn't. In any case, they can't pinch me again for the job.'

He also said that when Miss Heilbron came to see him first, she told him that his only chance was the statement being thrown out on legal grounds. If she failed in this defence, she could only promise him life.

Last week he got three days punishment for insolence and he said to me, 'These buggers know I did the murders and they're going to make sure I do my full three years. I'll get this all the time I'm in.'"

Graham continued by saying that when he reported this conversation to Mr Brennan, one of the warders, Brennan told him that they all knew Johnson had done it but there was nothing they could do. Graham added that Johnson had also told a prisoner named McBride that he had done the murder.

Balmer finished writing and cursed. Graham would have nothing to gain from his statement, Johnson had been acquitted and could no longer be tried. He had suspected all along that Johnson was the murderer. He cursed again, loudly and long before sitting quietly, thinking. The murderer had gone free but there was still a potential suspect and Graham could be the vital link needed to establish that suspect's guilt. He leaned forward towards Graham.

"Forget about that, he was just kidding you, Robert. We know who did it. But you might be able help. There's something you could do for me."

"Anything, Mr Balmer."

"Right. If I need you I'll get in touch."

There was still a need for witnesses for the prosecution, witnesses who would support the story to be presented by Northam and Dickson. Norwegian Margie would be ideal.

She was young, dark, about 23 years of age, attractive and a frequent visitor to the Beehive, an essential rendezvous in the course of her business. Her nickname came from the fact that she had been married to a Norwegian sailor called Taanevig. From a decent home, her parents knew nothing of her activities. To them, she held a steady job in an office in town. She was also, as were many of the prostitutes in Liverpool, an informer for Balmer, not just by choice but in order to be able to continue her livelihood, Balmer not only able to take her living away but also in a position to formulate other charges which might put her inside for a long time.

Blackie the barmaid called to her, "He wants you, Margie. In the back room." Margie knew who 'he' was. Balmer told her what he wanted. But this time what he was asking was too much.

"But the fellow could be hung, Mr Balmer. I couldn't do that."

"Don't worry, Margie. We'll do a deal. He'll only get a few years. The other fellow will take the rap. This is what I want you to do. Remember it and we'll go over it again. All you have to say is that you saw George Kelly with a gun here in the Beehive on the night of the robbery and then the next day you were with him in a pub when the robbery was discussed and he admitted it. Got that?" Margie nodded dumbly.

"Don't take too long, Margie. You wouldn't want your mother and your father to know what you really do for a living, now would you? Margie shook her head, tears near the surface as she left the small back room.

That night, Blackie was on her way home when she saw Margie again, sitting on the steps of the tall terrace in Grove Street where she had a room. She was crying and Blackie spent some time trying to comfort her.

The conspiracy continued to unfold. Throughout the summer, and ever since he had been interviewed on the morning after the murder, Balmer made a point of talking to Kelly, usually in one of the pubs where he met his informants.

The Beehive public house at the bottom end of Mount Pleasant, a stone's throw from the Adelphi Hotel, was a small Victorian pub, inside the entrance, a narrow passageway led to a small bar, beyond that, at the back, a tiny snug. It was typical of the hundreds of small, cosy, dark and friendly pubs in the city, their back rooms a lunchtime meeting place for the brokers and solicitors, shop assistants and clerks of the town. In the evenings, a different clientele emerged as the pub became a forum for the petty underworld of the time, a meeting place to exchange ideas, plan the next robbery or the sale of the proceeds of their most recent crimes.

The back room of the Beehive was also a place where the police of the city would meet their informers. It was one of George Kelly's watering holes. He was a favourite with Blackie, a pretty, dark-haired girl who he would often present with left-over produce from the barrow. Blackie disliked Balmer almost as much as she liked George Kelly.

Balmer made a point of visiting the Beehive when Kelly was present, the Chief Inspector's high profile in the city having one of the effects he craved, the pub falling quiet for a few moments when his large, imposing bulk came in.

Kelly was invariably the first in the place to speak, chatting cheekily to Balmer.

"Hello, Mr Balmer. Who's getting it today?"

"Never you mind, George. Got anything for me?"

Kelly would often have information for Balmer, information occasionally about criminal activities in other parts of the city, or those who would intrude upon his own patch, and it was often information which would help bring convictions, Kelly being paid when the proceeds of the crime were recovered.

"Nothing yet, Mr Balmer. How's the murder investigation going? Any progress?"

"Not yet, George. Drawn a blank. Home Office are on my back now. But we're getting there. But don't you worry George. I know you're not involved."

"Any suspicions, just you let me know and I'll help you." Kelly nodded, his initial worries that Balmer would pin the murder on him had gradually evaporated, Balmer's constant visits to him for information had installed a false sense of security.

"If I hear anything, Mr Balmer, I'll let you know."

"I've got some stuff in the car, George. Want to bring it in for me?"

"No problem, Mr Balmer.' Kelly carried the box of Haig Dimple whisky from the car, putting it behind the bar.

There were other places their paths would cross. Balmer was a regular visitor, along with Ike Bradley, a long time friend from his seagoing days and now a stallholder in Birkenhead market, to the Cross Keys pub near the Liverpool Stadium which was the city's famous venue for boxing. George Kelly was another occasional visitor there, the same banter exchanged as the conspiracy closed around him.

During and after the Johnson trial and throughout the summer, Balmer had continued his well-publicised search for Dickson. Eventually an informer in Manchester told the police where Northam was working and through him they traced Dickson. On September 26th, a Saturday, Chief Inspector Tiffany of Manchester police called Balmer and he and Farragher brought her back to Liverpool. Together with Northam she was taken to Cheapside where they were placed in separate cells. Dickson was frightened.

"I just want to have a talk with you, Jackie."

"You know it wasn't me. I had nothing to do with it."

"You don't want to face that larceny charge do you, Jackie? Another stay in gaol wouldn't do you much good. You wouldn't last long, not with your bad health." Dickson made no reply and Balmer continued.

"Larceny and skipping bail. You didn't come forward. Obstructing justice is a very serious crime. I could make it real bad for you. You wouldn't want to die in a prison bed, would you, Jackie?" Dickson was trembling. She looked up tearfully.

"What do you want from me?"

"Just your help, Jackie."

"I won't tell."

"Who are you afraid of?" She shook her head.

"I'll tell you the whole truth but if anything happens to me, or this man, you'll be responsible."

"What about the anonymous letter?"

"Jimmy wrote that. I posted it."

"You said it was Charley Connolly. You said go and see Charley Connolly. I want the truth this time, Jackie." Dickson stared at him, wide-eyed. Balmer continued, showing her some photographs.

"You know Connolly. This is Kelly. Have you seen him before?" Dickson nodded.

"I know Charlie Connolly and I may have seen the other fellow around."

"Right, this is what really happened then, Jackie. Or do you and your boyfriend want... "

Dickson stared at him, wide-eyed and fearful, her silence her agreement, as Balmer outlined what he wanted. The conspiracy was underway, the rehearsals continuing the following day, Balmer prompting and testing both her and Northam.

The next stage was for a safe house to be found where Dickson and Northam could be kept as the tutoring continued, somewhere away from any other influences. There was such a place. Sergeant Jane Ashmore was a police college friend of Balmer. They had worked together on numerous occasions, often posing as a courting couple during surveillance work. Now Ashmore and her husband provided their flat, not only as a safe house where Northam and Dickson could be kept while their story was sharpened, but also for interviewing informants who did not want to go to the police station.

At Dale Street Police Station, on September 29th, the first two of a number of statements were written separately by Northam and Dickson. These, although in general agreement, also contain dramatic differences to those subsequently given as evidence at the forthcoming trials. They contain some interesting elements. (Appendix 12). After describing a meeting in the Beehive public house between herself, Northam, Kelly and Connolly, during which she alleged the murder was planned, Dickson then went on to say that, on the day following the murder, she and Northam stayed in Birkenhead.

The statement then continues with details about the meeting on the Monday after the murder and Kelly's alleged description of the murders, very much as she would present the evidence in court. But there were several important differences. She describes taking the bullets from Connolly and having tea with him at Littlewoods cafe in Clayton Square when Connolly told her what was alleged to have happened at the cinema.

She goes on to tell about meeting Kelly and having whiskies with him and thinking he was going to shoot her. Her statement finishes, 'When I saw Kelly in the Beehive public house on the 19th March, he was wearing a dark raincoat or overcoat with a belt around it.'

Northam's statement was also essentially the same as that of Dickson and the one they would both give later in court, but also with important differences. (Appendix 13)

Northam describes what had happened in the Beehive on the night of the murder and that Kelly said they would have to cut the wires there and when his coat or mac was open, Northam saw the two prongs of a pair of pliers sticking out. He continued by saying that the next day it was all in the papers about the murder and that Dickson and he stayed in Birkenhead all day.

Arrest

With the witnesses in place and the rehearsals complete, it was time to bring in the victims of the conspiracy. In the early hours of the morning, at about 2.30 on September 30th, Balmer went with Jack Farragher to Connolly's house. He cautioned Connolly that he had reason to believe he had murdered two men in the Cameo Cinema on March 19th that year. Connolly made no reply until he was told he would be arrested and taken to Dale Street Police Station, where he would be detained while further enquiries were made. When he did speak, it was only to say that he had never been in the Cameo Cinema in his life.

In the police car Connolly was quiet. When they arrived at the station, he asked,

"Tell me the strength of it, Mr Balmer, I have a right to know."

Balmer held nothing back. He spelt out all the details of the case, adding Kelly's name, and the names of the other persons who had been with him when the plans were discussed. Connolly shook his head. "I don't know any of them."

At about 9 o'clock on the same morning, Jack Farragher dropped a note through Doris O'Malley's letter box in Cambridge Street. Immediately Kelly read it, he left the house, going straight to his brother's house in Pleasant Street. He whistled up to the window to get Frankie Kelly's attention.

"Frankie, it's George. Balmer's put a note through the door, he has a ship for me."

"How come, George?"

"Well, he's let Jimmy Skelly off bail on the wellingtons charge to get a ship and get away from here for a bit. I thought I'd do the same. Have a change. You know Balmer can get anything he wants at the docks."

"Be careful, George. Don't trust that bastard."

"Don't worry. I'll see you later at Tracy's."

But it was an appointment George Kelly would not keep. Never again to be a free man. It was 10.45 am when he arrived at Dale Street Police Office. He stared at Balmer in disbelief and sudden fear when told the real reason for his summons there. Balmer left him in no doubt as to his position.

"George Kelly, I have reason to believe, that in company with a man called Connolly, you murdered two men at the Cameo Cinema on March 19th by shooting them with an automatic pistol." Kelly looked stunned, shaking his head in disbelief.

"Why me, Mr Balmer? I've never had a gun in my life. I don't know how to fire one. And I don't know any Connolly. Never seen him in my life and I've never seen the other people either."

At 3 o'clock that afternoon, an identity parade was organised in the main Bridewell in Cheapside, off Dale Street, where Kelly was identified by Jacqueline Dickson. He was then taken into the charge office where Connolly, surrounded by police officers, was held in the small pen used for prisoners. It would be apparent to anyone visiting that room at that time that Connolly was a prisoner. To Kelly, he was obviously the other man involved. He blurted out the first thing that came into his head.

"You've never seen me before, have you? You don't know me, do you?" Connolly stared blankly at him.

"No. I don't."

Now the case had to be strengthened, further exhaustive police searches documented for the jury. That same afternoon, a squad of detectives, under the supervision of Detective Sergeant Jack Farragher, arrived at the house of Kelly's parents in Trowbridge Street, pulling the place apart, even taking down the bricks in the chimney breast in a supposed search for the gun.

Soon after they had started, Joey Kelly arrived, remonstrating with Farragher, furious at their behaviour and concerned that his elderly father would suffer a heart attack. Leaving the house in a rage, he travelled immediately across town to the Central Police Station, demanding to see Balmer. Balmer met him in the corridor.

"Nothing I can do, Mr Kelly. You need a solicitor. Go and see Livermore. He'll help you." Balmer turned away, refusing to discuss the matter any further.

Harry Livermore was a prominent Liverpool solicitor, someone who believed passionately in the defence of the underdog. He had acted for George Kelly in the past.

Once George Kelly was held in Walton Prison awaiting committal proceedings, Balmer set out on his search for witnesses and the destruction of Kelly's alibi. One witness would be Fred Thomalla, the licensee of the Leigh Arms, an ex-policeman and acquaintance of Balmer. Balmer and Farragher sat chatting to him in the pub one evening in early October, Balmer making notes as Thomalla answered some informal questions.

"You're sure Kelly was here that evening?"

"Yes, I'm sure. I remember him clearly."

"What time was that?"

"Couldn't really say, Bert. The pub was full and I was busy. I couldn't put any time to it."

"He wasn't here all night, though?"

"Could have been. I remember talking to him."

Balmer finished his half pint, Thomalla accepting the offer of a lift to town for himself and his wife. In the car, Balmer turned in his seat, passing a sheet of paper to Thomalla.

"Here, Fred. Just sign this for me. Better do things properly. Save time later."

It was dark in the interior of the car and Thomalla had no reason to question what Balmer had written.

On the 2nd of October, Balmer received some unsolicited evidence. Hilda Kelly, a neighbour of Doris O'Malley, called at the Central Police Station asking to see the officer who was in charge of the case. She already knew Balmer from his frequent visits to her neighbour's house.

She gave a statement which she and her husband signed and which was witnessed by Balmer. (Appendix 14) The evidence was of startling importance. It would confirm George Kelly's alibi. She said that on the night of the murders, George Kelly had called at her house at 9.30 to her ask where Doris O'Malley was. He said that he had found a note in the sugar basin to say she was at the Spofforth, so he said he'd go there for her.

Balmer read the statement again after Hilda Kelly had left, before passing it to Farragher to file away. It could hardly be of use to him in his case against Kelly.

Several days later, on October 4th, Balmer received a note from Connolly asking him to go and see him as soon as possible. He sat across the desk from Connolly in the interview room in Walton Prison, waiting for Connolly to speak. The man was nervous, his statement rambling. (Appendix 15)

The essence of Connolly's statement was that a man called Skelly, of similar build to him, was a mate of Kelly's and that it might have been Skelly who was with Kelly that night and that Kelly was with Skelly up until 8 o'clock, when Kelly left. Connolly then went on to say that he knew Skelly but did not know Kelly at all.

When he had finished, Connolly refused to sign the statement but later on that month he claimed that his family had found an alibi for him, stating that he had been at a dance at St Mark's Church Hall when the murder had taken place.

COMMITTAL AND TRIAL

The witnesses are Liverpool witnesses

Harry Livermore had already defended Kelly in one of his minor brushes with the law and had recently obtained his release on bail on the charge of stealing wellingtons. Now he would act for him in the most serious of cases. Livermore was the people's lawyer, a valiant defender of the underdog, the compassionate Livermore contrasting markedly with Balmer whom he was known to describe as a 'big blunderer.'

Although he came from the North, his career in later years was always closely involved with his adopted city. He was knighted in July 1970 and, as an Alderman, became Chairman of the Library and Leisure Committee, the Merseyside Arts Association and the Everyman Theatre. One of his particular interests was the Liverpool Philharmonic Orchestra and it was at his instigation that it obtained the Royal accolade. He was elected Lord Mayor in 1958.

The committal proceedings took place over several separate hearings. They opened on October 1st, continued on October 10th, 17th and finally on October 19th when the final hearing took three days. It was held in No 2 Court, the largest in the building, before the examining magistrate, CG Gordon. The prosecutor was JR Bishop, who had also prosecuted Johnson.

The court was crowded with detectives, police officers, among them Chief Superintendent Smith, and members of the public. The press accommodation was full, with some reporters seated alongside the courtroom wall. It was 10.20 in the morning when the two defendants appeared in the dock, Connolly's age given as 26, his address as 110 Woolfall Heath Avenue, Huyton and Kelly's age as 27, his address as 39d Trowbridge Street. They were both dressed casually, Connolly, appearing relaxed but tired, was unshaven and wore a green pullover, khaki trousers and brown jacket. Kelly, also looking tired and unshaven, could be seen to be smaller and broader than Connolly. He wore a cream shirt and light brown jacket.

Harry Livermore, well aware of the publicity the case had attracted and also of the effect of reported proceedings on any subsequent trial, attempted to mitigate this by asking the magistrate that the press and public should be excluded but the magistrate rejected his plea, ruling that the case should proceed in open court.

Asked if they had anything to say, Kelly shook his head, Connolly standing up and leaning on the dock rail. "I apply for bail and legal aid."

The Stipendiary Magistrate refused the request for bail but granted legal aid. Still Connolly remained on his feet.

"Well I have a right to know who is supposed to have given evidence against me and implicated me in this." Connolly sat down dejectedly, his head between his hands as the magistrate shook his head.

"You can't go into that at this stage."

During the committal proceedings, Harry Livermore's line of questioning suggested that Johnson was still the main suspect in the case. He questioned Chief Superintendent Smith as to whether any evidence was being called by the prosecution to prove any association between Kelly and a man named Donald John Johnson. Smith agreed there was not.

During the proceedings, when Mr Livermore was examining Chief Inspector Balmer, George Kelly showed the first signs of the indignation which would hinder him throughout the hearings. When Balmer was asked how he came to arrest Kelly, he replied that he had cautioned Kelly and told him it was alleged that the hold-up had been planned at the Beehive Hotel, Mount Pleasant. At this point, Kelly stood up in the dock, shouting at Balmer that he had not told him that.

Balmer then went on to describe a visit to Kelly by Doris O'Malley. He said he was present at the interview and that O'Malley said, 'Oh, Georgie, isn't it terrible,' and Kelly had replied, 'Oh, you needn't worry about me. I'm alright. I was at the Coach and Horses with Skelly, and then I was with you.'

There was a commotion in the court, spectators craning forward to see what was happening, as again Kelly jumped to his feet in the dock, shouting at Balmer that he had not said that and that it was a confounded lie.

At the end of the three and a half days day's evidence, which Kelly then listened to in silence, both he and Connolly were bound over for trial.

On October 10th, immediately after Kelly and Connolly had been remanded for trial, Balmer further consolidated his case against Kelly, Northam and Dickson adding to their statement of September 29th. (Appendix 16) Northam's revised statement includes the fact that he was carrying his overcoat over his arm and he lent it to Kelly, who now did not wear a coat, going on to say that Kelly had a woman's small brown apron which he said would do for a mask. He put it in the overcoat pocket. Kelly then said that the gun was hidden in the soil of Wavertree Park and there was one bullet still in it. Later he said he had thrown it in the lake. Northam added, defensively, that when he lent Kelly the overcoat, it was before he and Connolly said they were going to do the Cameo.

At the same time, Dickson also gave a similar amended statement. (Appendix 17) in which she also introduces the loan of Northam's overcoat; that Kelly took a trilby hat from his pocket and that he showed them a woman's small brown apron. She adds, almost as an afterthought, that Northam lent Kelly the overcoat before Kelly and Connolly talked about going to the Cameo.

According to Balmer's report, it was was immediately after these statements that he went to the home of Northam's parents in Birkenhead where Northam gave him a brown overcoat which Balmer claimed to have sent to the Forensic Science Laboratory for examination.

On October 26th, Northam and Dickson made the final tuning to their original statement with additional details of a meeting in the Star public house on Sunday, the day after the murder, both retracting their original statement that they had stayed at home in Birkenhead on the Sunday.

The whole statement was signed by Balmer, Northam and Dickson.

By now, Harry Livermore had instructed a counsel he thought would be the most suitable for the case; the same counsel who had acted so well for Johnson.

Rose Heilbron was only 35 years of age, a strikingly beautiful woman, her pale skin and the bright red lipstick she favoured, contrasting vividly in court with the black of her gown. She was a native of Liverpool, the daughter of Max and Nellie Heilbron and had attended Belvedere, one of the city's prestigious girls' schools, after which she had graduated in Law with First Class Honours from the University of Liverpool. She was a Lord Chief Justice Halker scholar at Grays Inn in 1936 and was called to the bar in 1939. In 1945, she married Dr Nathaniel Burstein, ten years her senior. After the war, in which so many promising male colleagues had been called to arms, she took her chance, her rise was rapid and she became a KC in 1949. She was appointed Dame of the British Empire in 1974. Later in her career, she become Presiding Judge on the Northern Circuit from 1979 to 1982.

She and her husband had become good friends with Harry and Esther Livermore. The two couples lived near each other in a predominantly Jewish, professional class district of Liverpool. They frequently dined at each other's houses and Harry Livermore was responsible for giving her some of her early briefs. The Cameo case would be her first major murder trial.

On October 28th, Kelly and Connolly were both present when application was made by the prosecuting counsel, Mr William Gorman, the Recorder of Liverpool, at Liverpool Assizes, before Chief Justice Morris, that the opening of the Cameo murders trial should be fixed for November 7th. Basil Nield KC, the Conservative Member of Parliament for Chester, who was Connolly's counsel,and Harry Livermore, argued strongly that they would not have time for the preparation of an adequate defence if the case was heard at these Assizes. They requested that the trial be transferred to Manchester Assizes.

It was vital to the defence that they had time to prepare. They had only a handful of witnesses whereas the prosecution, with the police, had assembled a large cast to testify against Kelly. Despite this, the prosecution argued that the trial should go ahead.

"In my submission," requested Rose Heilbron, "the time suggested by Mr Gorman is inadequate to do justice to the defence in this case. Witnesses are still being interviewed. The prosecution have had to do an enormous amount of investigation and they have had rather longer time to do it in. My instructing solicitor does feel that unless he is given adequate time to prepare the defence he may not be able to do justice to it. It is a difficult matter to rush. Evidence may be overlooked if it is rushed. And vital evidence."

Mr Gorman argued against her.

"I should like to say two things. The first is, in my submission, that it is not right to send this case to Manchester. The whole circumstances are Liverpool circumstances. The whole of the witnesses are Liverpool witnesses. The solicitor appearing on behalf of Kelly made vigorous and public protests against any suggestion of delay. I am instructed on behalf of the Crown, quite definitely to oppose any suggestion of going to Manchester or taking the case away from the place where it should properly be tried."

Rose Heilbron shook her head."My instructing solicitor was anxious that these men be brought to trial. The whole proceedings were pushed forward so that the prisoner would know what evidence was to be put against him. That evidence, voluminous evidence, has now been given. Even though the trial were put off till next week or Wednesday week, it would not allow sufficient time for the case to be prepared."

"Could it not come to the next Liverpool Assizes?"

Again Miss Heilbron shook her head. "If that were the case it would mean that these men would be in custody for quite a long time with this charge hanging over their heads. In my submission they should be tried at the first available assizes subject to the defence being available."

The hearing was adjourned for the Judge to consider the arguments. When it resumed, the Judge accepted that the defence needed time but, despite the length of time the men would be held in custody, the trial would be held at the next Liverpool Assizes in January. He refused any further consideration of Heilbron's objections.

The trial date was set but the drama was still unfolding, an act again carried out in the back room of the Beehive. Blackie was passing drinks through the small hatch. Later she was to recount how she leaned towards the opening.

"Could I have a word in private, please, Mr Balmer?"

Balmer looked up, moving closer to the small serving hatch.

"What is it?"

"The trial, Mr Balmer, the Cameo murders. I was here. It wasn't Kelly had the gun. He wasn't here at all. But I saw the gun."

Balmer's face tensed, glancing quickly around before gesturing to her to move closer.

"Just what did you see then?"

"It was the girl, the blond one, Jackie Dickson. And the other fellow. They had the gun. I saw them from where I was standing. I didn't realise it was important until I read about the trial in the Echo. It definitely wasn't him, Mr Balmer."

"Who else was here, Blackie?" It was the first time he had addressed her by her nickname and a sudden presentiment flooded through her.

"Just the other one, her pimp. He gave her the gun."

"How do you know it was a gun?"

"It was a gun. I know it was a gun."

Balmer's hand shook as he pointed a finger at Blackie, his voice frightening in its intensity.

"You saw nothing. The case is cut and dried. Don't you be telling stories. I don't want to hear any more about this. Do I make myself clear?"

Blackie was scared. "But…"

"No buts. It will be the worse for you if you go spreading stories. Do you understand?"

"I don't know." Blackie was shocked and frightened.

"Just shut it. You saw no gun." Blackie nodded dumbly, Balmer staring at her for a few moments before returning to his seat.

Half an hour later, as he left the pub, his intense stare sent a shiver down Blackie's spine.

Later still that night, when Blackie arrived home, three of Balmer's detectives were waiting for her. One of them took her and her father into the small front parlour, the others standing in the hall. Farragher leaned conspiratorially towards her.

"You have to keep your mouth shut, Blackie. You saw no gun." He turned to her father.

"It might be better all round if she leaves town for a while. Is there anywhere she can go?"

"She could go to her sister's in Nottingham perhaps." Her father's face showed his concern.

"Good idea. Stay there, Blackie, until the trial is over." The detective turned to her father.

"We'll see you're alright for money." Farragher stood up to leave.

"Remember, Jackie. You saw nothing." Blackie sat quiet, numb with fear as her father showed the three detectives out.

Suicide

There were yet more bizarre twists to the case. Harry Livermore, as convinced as ever of his client's innocence, was constantly seeking information which would lead to the real murderer. At the committal proceedings, he had been far from impressed with the main prosecution witnesses, Northam and Dickson; their stories too glib, their knowledge too exact. He initiated his own investigation of Northam. On October 29th, it appeared to have paid off when he received information which confirmed his belief that Northam had been involved in the crime and that he had supplied the gun.

On the morning of Saturday, October 29th, when he was supposed to be attending the wedding of another Liverpool solicitor in Newcastle, Livermore took his wife to the station and saw her onto the Newcastle train. She recounts that she arrived at Newcastle with only her return ticket, without money, her friends there looking after her for the weekend and seeing her onto the Liverpool train on the Monday morning. In the meantime, her husband had been busy. After dropping his wife at Lime Street Station, Harry Livermore called for Rose Heilbron at her home in Menlove Gardens and together they embarked on what would be, looking back now, a venture doomed to failure. They drove to Smithdown Road Cemetery where they walked the paths for several hours, the solicitor even clambering to the top of several of the tall tombstones but even they, for all their determination, must soon have known it was a hopeless task. If the gun was there, it would never be found, and the police, in numbers, had already searched.

There was one more possibility. Harry Livermore had the address of a police informer, Sidney Smith, who had claimed to have information about the gun which he would reveal at a price. After dropping off Rose Heilbron, he drove to the man's address. A request for payment was refused until the information proved genuine but Harry Livermore managed to get the address at which the gun used in the murder was allegedly hidden. At this moment, Harry Livermore must have felt he was near success and that Northam was involved in the crime more than he had admitted. The address was that of Northam's parents in Birkenhead.

On arrival at Wood Street, just off Cleveland Street, the door was answered by the boyfriend of Northam's sister, Beatrice. Harry Livermore, saying only that he was connected with the Cameo case, asked if he could search the house for the gun which was supposed to have been used. It was a gallant effort on behalf of his client but he was not allowed in. Dispirited, he returned to Liverpool, his only recourse now, was to ask for police help in searching the house. His distrust of Balmer was implicit in his request that it would have to be in his presence,. At 4.45pm on Saturday, October 29th, Harry Livermore called at Dale Street Police Station and asked to see the Chief Constable in connection with the Cameo murders.

By this time, Sidney Smith, annoyed that Mr Livermore had got the information without paying a price, and in an attempt to curry police favour, had gone to Birkenhead Police with his information and, at 5.10pm that evening, Chief Inspector Balmer received a call from Birkenhead CID that a man named Smith had called with information concerning the Cameo murders. The man was a known informant and was therefore invited to Liverpool, where he was taken to Rose Hill Police Station. His information concerned Northam. He told Balmer that Harry Livermore had told him not to go near the police whatever happened, going on to claim that a mate of his, Peter Rowlands, had told him early in September that Northam had a gun. He had seen Northam at his house in Wood Street. Northam owed him some money and said he could not pay it back but offered him a revolver. He showed Rowlands the gun which had a magazine in the butt end. When Rowlands said he did not want it, Northam said he would hide it where no one would find it, on the shelf up the chimney stack.

While Balmer was interviewing Smith, the Assistant Chief Constable arrived at Dale Street to see Harry Livermore, the solicitor explaining what Smith had told him and demanding that the house be searched straight away, adding that he wanted to be present when the search was carried out. But he refused to give the address, unless he was allowed to go with the police to make the search and interview the two people involved after they have been questioned.

Mr J R Bishop, the prosecuting solicitor for the city, then spoke by telephone to Harry Livermore, pointing out the seriousness of withholding information from the police in the case of murder. Still the solicitor refused to tell, Bishop responding by telling him that he could not let him dictate the terms under which he would give information on such a serious matter.

At 8.30pm that night, Balmer and Farragher saw Rowlands, who confirmed that Smith had called him earlier that night, at about 7pm, asking if he could get the gun, Rowlands confirming that he remembered a fellow named Northam who said about the beginning of the year that he had a gun or could get a gun. It was the only time Northam ever mentioned a gun to him.

At 10.30 the following morning, October 30th, Balmer and Farragher together with Chief Superintendent Smith, went to Wood Street and searched for a gun. It was claimed that none was found and that there were no indications in the bedroom chimney that a gun or any other object had ever been secreted there. The soot on the chimney shelf was level and undisturbed.

An hour later, Sidney Smith telephoned to tell Balmer that Livermore had visited him the previous evening in order to find Rowlands and to try to get the gun. Smith alleged that Mr Livermore told him that he had first called at Walton Gaol to see Kelly and asked him to swear that none of his fingerprints would be on the gun if he found it and that Kelly was adamant that if he was to hang that minute, his fingerprints would not be found on that gun.

On Monday 31st October, Harry Livermore wrote to the Chief Constable to tell him that he had had an opportunity of discussing the position with Miss Heilbron KC, as a result of which he was now prepared to give the information which came into his hands on Saturday afternoon and upon which he had seen Mr Nichols at 5.30pm on Saturday.

The letter then gave information as to where the gun was believed to be hidden 'in a top bedroom in the chimney. We understand that there is a ledge inside the chimney and a recess at the rear of the ledge and the gun was hidden in this place.'

On November 1st, on the advice of Bishop, Solicitors Silverman and Livermore received a letter.

'The address which you supplied has already been the subject of a thorough examination by police officers engaged in investigating this crime and every part of the house, including the chimney you indicate, has been searched. The house has, in fact, been searched more than once, the last occasion being on Sunday last, the 30th. No gun or weapon was found on the premises and the police are satisfied that none was there.'

It was late at night, about 11.30 on November 10th, when Miriam Kronitz was chatting to one of the tenants of her tall terrace house in Grove Street. The young woman and the man she passed off as her husband, had taken a furnished room a year earlier but, only a month ago, the young woman had told Mrs Kronitz that the man was not her husband and that, after rowing, she had turned him out.

Mrs Kronitz asked her how her job in town was going and after talking for about 15 minutes, the woman, who had been drinking, left the house, returning five minutes later and going straight upstairs to her room. It was soon afterwards, just gone midnight, when Mrs Kronitz was called upstairs by her two daughters. There was a smell of gas coming from her tenant's room and no answer when they knocked on the door. Sudden apprehension shot through MrsKronitz as she ran downstairs for the spare keys to the room, her fears deepening as they had difficulty pushing open the door against the two coats and the roll of newspaper which had been wedged behind it.

Margaret Taanevig was already dead, lying fully-clothed facing the window. In her mouth was a rubber tube, the other end connected to a gas bracket above the bed.

Mrs Kronitz turned off the gas and opened the window, letting in the woman's cat which was crouched on the window sill outside. On the dressing table beside the bed, was a note, written on the fly-leaf torn from a cheap novel. It was a pathetic last testimony by a sad and frightened young woman.

"Please don't class this a disturbance of mind. I'm just fed up,
Terry knows why she has tried everything and Pinkie agrees
God help Tony. Look after…"
The note ran out at the end of the page.

The post-mortem was held on November 11th, the inquest a few days later. The coroner's report gave the cause of death as, 'carbon monoxide poisoning sustained on the 10th November when she killed herself by inhaling coal gas and that Margaret Taanevig did kill herself whilst the balance of her mind was disturbed.'

Margaret Taanevig was reported as being the former wife of Kjeld Taanevig, a sailor and Petty Officer in the Norwegian navy, from whom she had obtained a divorce. Miriam Kronitz gave evidence at the inquest and said of Margaret Taanevig that, 'she seemed to be a happy person, often under the influence of drink. I cannot identify her writing.'

Margaret's sister Francis, who travelled from Manchester and who identified the body, said, 'I have seen the note produced and the writing does not look like my sister's but I have been informed that she was under the influence of alcohol before the occurrence and this may account for my not knowing the writing.'

For 28 year old Margie, the role required of her was too much. And the shame, if she refused the role. But at her death, Margie's conscience was clear. Unlike those who had led her to that final, desperate act.

Chief Inspector Balmer had lost his corroborating witness and, just over a week after Norwegian Margie's death, on November 19th, he again visited Graham, handing him a typewritten statement. He explained what Graham would have to say.

"Got that?"

"It's a lot to remember, Mr Balmer."

"Don't worry. We'll go through it and refresh your memory and we'll get it right."

"I'll do my best. I like to help the police if I can. Do myself a bit of good."

"That's the ticket, Bob. I'll look after you. Read it carefully and sign it. When you worked on the hospital wing at Walton you passed messages between Kelly and Connolly. Say they had no other means of contact. Make sure you remember everything in there."

You don't know me at all

Public interest was at its peak, the occasion had rapidly become a 'cause celebre'. At that time, the use of guns was unusual in any crime and hundreds had waited outside for several hours to be sure of a place, St George's Hall having been built for just such an occasion. Even when, as on the morning of January 12th 1949, it was packed with people, they were secondary to the awesome solemnity of the courtroom – stained oak and mahogany seeming to take up more than their share of available space – as those who were in that room, by right or through patience, slotted into the spaces the furnishings allowed. Benches, tables and the witness box, the latter uncomfortably close to the jury's seats but facing away, so that they could not see the face of the prisoner, all coated in a veneer of Victorian efficiency, long disused inkwells spaced regularly along bench tops, dark holes in the oak as mellow, mahogany panelling reflected the artificial light from three small candelabra in every polished grain of wood.

The dock was the only place with room to spare, placed between the general public's standing area and the well of the court. Facing it was the platform, redolent of the full majesty of English law, from where the judge could gaze down at the wretched prisoner in the dock and hand down judgment. Between these two places of importance, in the well of the court, were the curving rows of advocates and solicitors' benches, behind them the few rows of seats reserved for special guests and prisoners' families.

It was a setting where, not only the unfortunate in the dock would tremble in awe but one in which even learned counsel would be unnerved by the solemnity of their surroundings, as they made their case under the gaze of one of the stern judges of that time, gazing down from under the great seal of the Crown.

In that setting, on January 12th 1949, there was an air of excitement. It reflected the feeling in the city at that time, the daily reports of progress in the case, like a film script unfolding, the majority verdict of the populace being that Kelly was guilty, that the gangs had got out of control and the police, ever diligent in looking after the welfare of their fellow citizens, had got their man. After the committal, very few people in the city remained ignorant of what had happened, the innocence of the accused was not presumed. And the prosecution was to play to this bias.

Outside the hall, the reporters and press photographers were kept busy, as officials and senior police officers arrived and, at the far end of St George's Hall, where a huge iron door gave entrance into the very bowels of the building, a small crowd was waiting as the police car bringing Kelly from Walton Prison arrived. There were shouts of 'good luck' and 'you'll be alright, Georgie.'

The presiding judge was Mr Justice Oliver. He was well known in Liverpool from his earlier days when, in 1931, he had successfully defended William Herbert Wallace, in what was still the most talked about murder trial in Liverpool's history. The case had helped to make his name, winning in the Court of Appeal, regarded by many as a most remarkable feat.

The Judge's entrance was announced by three bangs of the Clerk of Court's gavel and Judge Oliver came slowly through the massive oak doors behind his chair, one hand holding up his ermine-trimmed gown, a resplendent symbol of the majesty of the Crown, a bundle of papers in the other. A tall man, his close-cropped, ginger hair obscured by his wig, as he lowered himself onto his huge, elevated throne. He was the symbol of power, of legality – possibly of justice.

An awesome figure in court, Junior Counsel and even Senior Counsel would be intimidated by his stern and unsmiling visage. He had one glass eye and the popular assertion among the judiciary at the time, was that Judge Oliver's glass eye was his kindly eye.

There can be little doubt that Rose Heilbron felt the severity of that austere gaze. A young barrister, defending her first major murder case, it would be difficult for her to try and impose her own arguments or argue her case under Oliver's imposing demeanour. Yet she did both these things with skill and determination.

"Bring up Charles Connolly and George Kelly."

The Clerk of the Court's announcement echoed through the suddenly hushed courtroom, as the two defendants entered the dock between three warders. Their appearance was in marked contrast to that at the committal hearings, Connolly wearing a brown double-breasted suit with a blue tie, Kelly, stocky and square-chinned, wearing a well-cut, grey suit with a blue tie.

When they were seated in the dock, the Clerk of the Court empanelled the jury who were seated, five men and one woman to each row, the woman central, as if ordered. They were respectable and responsible, middle-aged representatives of the house-owning British public. Each read the oath, some easily, some stumbling over words, ill at ease under the attention of the court and the solemnity of the occasion. When they had finished, the clerk then asked the two defendants how they pleaded. Both answered 'Not guilty.'

Mr William Gorman KC, Counsel for the Crown, was now on his feet. He took the jury in careful steps through what had happened, each step unfolding to a jury who were supposedly new to proceedings they should never have heard before. But they had. They remembered previous evidence, it was catalogued in their minds, ready to compare with that to be given, this time for them alone. And some among them remembered that the evidence, as presented by the prosecution at the committal hearings, was amazingly inadequate.

Mr Gorman handed the jury various exhibits including plans of the Cameo Cinema, the surrounding district and photographs of interior and exterior views of public houses, before launching into his opening statement. Judge Oliver listened attentively, his large florid face peering intently at the prosecuting counsel.

William Gorman was precise, his statements detailed as he attempted initially to clearly define the exact time at which the shooting took place. After that there was an excited buzz in the court room, bringing a frown of disapproval from Judge Oliver, as Mr Gorman announced the introduction of a new witness.

"My Lord, members of the jury, you will hear prosecution evidence from two witnesses, Dickson and Northam, of how this crime was planned. And you will hear from a third witness who has come forward since the committal proceedings, a Robert Graham who, while on remand in Walton gaol, exercised with Kelly and Connolly and acted as their intermediary and to whom they talked freely of their part in this. It is the submission of the prosecution that Kelly shot and murdered and that Connolly took part in this nefarious and deadly scheme, to give such help as necessary."

The prosecution case was based on time and corroboration. Early in his opening remarks, after reviewing the evidence of the witnesses in the cinema, William Gorman defined the time at which the shots were fired.

"I stress that because there you have the time which the prosecution stresses is beyond doubt. The time of this shooting was, on the submission of the prosecution, about 9.35."

He followed this with a detailed account of what the police had found when they arrived at the cinema, before outlining the evidence which would be presented by the witnesses for the prosecution, of whom there were only ten, witnesses whose testimony related to times at which Kelly had been seen and his alleged knowledge of Connolly. This included the evidence to be given by Northam and Dickson about the planning of the robbery in the Beehive and, most crucial of all, the new corroborating evidence by Robert Graham.

Mr Gorman finished the case for the prosecution just before the court adjourned for lunch.

"It is the submission of the prosecution that the statements of Graham, Northam and Dickson are true. It is the submission of the prosecution that Connolly with Kelly set out on a common purpose to rob with violence and, that in carrying out this purpose, Kelly shot and killed the manager and that Connolly was there with Kelly to warn him, to give assistance, to prevent surprise and to help him if necessary."

After lunch, the prosecution called their first witnesses. The time of the shooting would be critical to Kelly's defence and, on the basis of the evidence in the magistrates court, this was not before 9.40. The first witness was Mrs Jackman, the cinema cashier. When she had presented her evidence, Rose Heilbron cross-examined her.

"How long would it take to check the money in the manager's office?"

"Only takes three or four minutes. I don't it think it would be as late as 9.45 when I heard the bang." Miss Heilbron reminded her.

"You said in the Magistrates Court, that it was 9. 45."

"I think it was between 9.40 and 9.45."

Phyllis Stevens, an usherette at the cinema, was called next. She said she saw a man come down the staircase and go to the exit door leading into Bird Street. She had a good opportunity of noticing him because the door stuck when he tried to push it open. He kept his left hand in his pocket. She thought it would be about 9.45 or 9.50 when she heard the bangs.

Mona Watkins, supervisor at the time of the murder, said she went into the operating room and the clock showed 9.35pm.

"Are you sure of the time the shots were fired?" Rose Heilbron was persistent. In the Magistrates Court, Mrs Watkins had said she heard the shots about 9.40pm.

"Definite. The first shots had been fired by 9.35."

Griffin, the cinema fireman, was next into the witness box. He had run after the man as far as Garrick Street and had then returned to the office to telephone the police, only to find that the telephone wire at the bottom of the spiral staircase had been cut off. Miss Heilbron reminded him that at the committal proceedings he had said that he had heard the bangs between about a quarter to ten and ten to ten.

The next witness, Mrs Simpson, who also lived in Garrick Street behind the cinema, told the court, that just a little after 9.30 by their clock, she and her husband heard a noise. The back of her house was very near the part of the cinema where the manager's office was situated.

John Alfred Owen, a night telephonist at Sefton Park Exchange, then told the court of receiving a 999 call at 9.45pm on March 19th.

The next prosecution witness was Police Sergeant George Armstrong, who gave evidence about pacing out the distances concerned between the Cameo and the Leigh Arms, Rose Heilbron getting to her feet and objecting to this line of evidence.

Judge Oliver looked up from the policeman's deposition in front of him.

"I do not think the times it took one to walk certain distances matters very much, or benefits the jury in any way. They have the distances on the plans and will have some idea themselves how long it took to walk the distances."

The next to be questioned was Barbara Bore, a barmaid in the Leigh Arms. She stated that a woman who was sometimes with Kelly came into the public house at about 8.45 and had a drink and left. She saw Kelly having a drink in the bar about 9.45 but could not say whether or not he was in the bar before 9.45.

"Did you get the impression he had been drinking a lot?"

"He seemed to be a bit merry."

Judge Oliver questioned her.

"You don't know the exact time he came in?"

"No. But he did seem to have had a few drinks."

She was followed into the box by James Sangster, a store supervisor at Lewis's, who said he knew Kelly and Connolly well and that he had seen them together in the street four or five times since last March, at the corner of Lime Street near the Adelphi, or the blitz sites opposite Lewis's and at the corner of Elliot Street.

The first expert witness to be called was Albert Allen, of the North-Western

Forensic Laboratory who said that six cartridge cases he examined appeared to have been fired from a 9mm self-loading pistol. The lock from the office door at the Cameo had three holes consistent with having been made by 9mm bullets. The ammunition referred to was of German origin, with the exception of a bullet recovered from a sewer, which was the same size and type as the others, but of American origin. The weapon used was a P38, a standard issue to the German Army during the war.

The pathologist, Dr Grace, then presented his report. He said that there was one bullet hole in the case of Mr Thomas. The bullet mark was underneath his left arm and the bullet, after going in through the arm, went into the chest and caused death. The post-mortem on the other man showed that there was a shot in the region of the right breast, one through the left hand and another shot in the back. The shot in the back was fired either when Bernard Catterall was kneeling, lying, or bending down.

Inspector George Reade of the Police Photography and Fingerprint Department, in cross-examination by Miss Heilbron, said that one of the wires was broken on the top of the telephone. He couldn't say whether it had been torn or cut. In further questioning, he confirmed that there were several areas of blood on the floor of the manager's office.

Patrick Dowling, a member of the Corps of Commissionaires, then gave evidence that he had seen Kelly come out of the Globe Hotel, Cases Street, next door to the Primrose Cafe, between 7.30am and 8pm on March 19th and that he turned to the left towards Renshaw Street. He said that he had not told Kelly he had seen him, because he thought that if Kelly was in Cases Street, he could not have been at Wavertree.

Next into the box was Edward Ellis, at the time of the murder the licensee of the Spofforth Hotel, who said that George Kelly came in there at 9.20pm on March 19th. He had a pint of beer and was there for about four minutes. He was wearing a brown suit but had no hat or coat.

Ellis was followed by James Currie, a taxi driver, who said Kelly arrived at the Leigh Arms at about 9.50pm. Kelly offered him a drink, and seemed excited and fidgety. Miss Heilbron cross-examined him.

"Did he appear to have had a lot to drink?"

"Yes. He patted me on the back and said I could have the best in the house. I looked at him and said 'Have you been in the sun?' he said, 'No, I've been having a go. You can't take liberties with Kelly.' A woman, Mrs Butterworth, who was with me, asked what Kelly meant by 'having a go' and I said, 'Oh, it means he has been having a fight.' But his hair was not ruffled and he did not look as if he had been in a fight."

"Are you sure he didn't say, 'Don't take any notice of me. I have been having a go on the bevvy'?"

"Quite sure. Kelly persisted in me and the woman having a drink and Kelly ordered drinks for himself and drinks for two other women in the buffet and ordered drinks for the manager and his wife and daughter. He insisted on them having the drinks. I went out about 10.00pm and Kelly was still in the buffet bar with some drink in front of him. He seemed to have had a lot to drink."

Detective Sergeant Ernest Richardson then gave evidence that he had known both defendants for about three years and said he had seen Connolly and Kelly together about eight or nine times before March 19th. He had seen the two more often separately than together. The last time he had seen them together was about three weeks after March 19th.

It was now the turn of Chief Inspector Herbert Balmer to give evidence. There was a perceptible buzz in the court as he entered the witness box.

He was composed. Having served as police prosecutor in the Liverpool Magistrates Court, he was both confident and effective as a witness. His voice, as usual, was quiet but firm as he started to give an account of his first interview with George Kelly on March 20th.

As he began to speak, Miss Heilbron stood up, objecting that he was reading from his notebook which he was not entitled to do. The Judge shook his head reprovingly.

"The officer is entitled to refresh his memory from his notes. Carry on."

"I visited the accused at 67 Cambridge Street, Wavertree, at 11.15 am on Sunday, March 20th, and saw Kelly in the presence of a woman named Doris O'Malley. I said to Kelly. 'I am making inquiries into the murder at the Cameo Cinema last night. Kelly said, 'Yes, I have heard about it,' and turning to the woman O'Malley he said, 'There you are, didn't I tell you they would call?'

I then asked if he would account for his movements on the previous night and he said, 'I can easily do that. I was with James Skelly at the Coach and Horses public-house just after opening time. He was on the booze, so I left him and arranged to see him down town. He did not turn up, so I went back at 9 o'clock and saw he was drunk, so I jumped a tram to the public house opposite our street in Picton Road and stayed there until 10 o'clock. When I came home I found a note from Doris in the sugar basin saying she was at Bramley's and we had a row over it.'"

Kelly frowned from the dock; there was an almost imperceptible tightening of the lips as he shook his head slowly to and fro. His expression showed anger and disagreement, frustration and exasperation all at once. Balmer did not even glance at him.

"I then asked Kelly if he had a brown overcoat, and he replied, 'Not for years.' When asked if he had any firearms, Kelly said 'I haven't got a gun.' I searched the house but found neither overcoat nor firearms. I took Kelly in the police car to the Coach and Horses public-house in Low Hill, which Kelly pointed out to me, and then we went to 46 Falcon Street where we saw James Skelly.

I told Skelly that I was making inquiries into the murder at the Cameo Cinema the previous night and asked Skelly where he had been. Skelly said 'I was in the Coach and Horses until I was brought home rotten drunk at 10 o'clock.' When I asked if Kelly was with him, Skelly replied, 'I suppose he was one of the fellows who took me home but I was too drunk to know.'

About two months after the murder, I went with another officer to Huyton and saw Connolly, who was asked to account for his whereabouts on March 19th. He told us he was at work at Bibby's, Great Howard Street, on the afternoon shift and did not get off until after ten.

Some days later, I told Connolly that I had information from Messrs Bibby that he was not at work on Saturday March 19th and Connolly replied, 'Well, I say I was at work. You say I wasn't. If I wasn't, then I don't know where I was. That is all there is to it.'

On September 30th, I saw Connolly at his home. I said to him that Kelly had gone into the cinema and had murdered the manager and assistant by shooting and that Connolly had remained outside. Connolly said 'I have never been to the Cameo Cinema in my life.'

When he was taken to Dale Street, Connolly said, 'Tell me the strength. I have a right to know.' I said that it was alleged that on the night of Saturday March 19th, he was at the Beehive public-house along with a man called George Kelly, another man named James Northam and a woman named Jacqueline Dickson and another woman who was dressed in black and who was heavily made up.

He was also told that Kelly planned the hold-up at the Cameo, that he and Kelly had gone to the cinema, that the woman Dickson accompanied them and then went back with Northam to the public-house, that the manager was shot by Kelly and that Connolly was the outside man.

Connolly replied, 'I don't know anything.' As I was leaving, Connolly said, 'Yes, I know Jacqueline Dickson, but I have never been in the Beehive or any other public-house in Mount Pleasant.'

Kelly was seen at the Dale Street Police Station and I told him we had reason to believe, that in company with Charles Connolly, he had murdered two men at the Cameo Cinema on March 19th and that the murder had been committed by him shooting with an automatic pistol. Kelly said, 'I have never had a gun in my life. I have never seen the other people in my life before.' He was then told he would be detained.

On October 1st there was an identification parade and then, at Kelly's request, arrangements were made for him to be seen by a woman named Doris O'Malley. She said, 'Oh, Georgie, isn't it terrible.' and Kelly said, 'You needn't worry about me, I'm alright, I was in the Coach and Horses with Skelly, and then I was with you.' The woman replied, 'Oh no, Georgie. Don't you remember, I left a note for you in the sugar basin where I had gone and you carried on because you didn't find me.'

I came into the charge room with Kelly immediately behind me. Connolly was sitting in the dock, a small pen and, as they came in, Kelly called out to Connolly in a loud voice, 'You have never seen me in your life before, have you? You don't know me at all.' Connolly replied, 'No. I don't.'

On October 4th, I received a note from Connolly asking me to go and see him as soon as possible and I went to Walton Prison and took a statement which Connolly would not sign.

On October 10th, I was present at an identification parade at which Connolly and Kelly were identified by a witness named Sangster. When Kelly was identified, his solicitor was present. As Sangster identified him, Kelly shouted across to me, 'If it is the last thing I do, I will get you for this, Balmer.'

On the same day I went to Birkenhead and took possession of a brown overcoat from James Northam."

William Gorman prompted him.

"You interviewed the licensee of the Leigh Arms and obtained a signed statement?"

"That is correct."

"The statement said that Mr Thomalla, the licensee, did not see Kelly in the pub before 9.50?"

"That is correct. He said I am quite satisfied George Kelly was not in my house at 9.30 but he was in the buffet at ten to ten."

Still finding fresh evidence

After a weekend's break, the cross-examination of Balmer for the defence was painstaking. Basil Nield KC MP, the defence counsel for Connolly, was a prominent Liverpool barrister and member of Parliament for Chester. A member of a legal family, his father had been President of the Liverpool Law Society. He was first to cross-examine Balmer.

"During your evidence, you have referred frequently to your notebook. Would you tell the judge and the jury how that notebook was made up?"

"At various times."

"Would it be right to say that it was made up sometimes a little time afterwards. On one occasion three-quarters of an hour and on other occasions very long intervals?" Balmer's voice was level, smooth, as he answered counsel's questions.

"I agree."

"Is the reason why you must look at your book this, that you cannot possibly remember everything that was said in the course of this case?

"That is so."

"Would you care to tell us how many persons you yourself have interviewed in connection with this inquiry?" Balmer replied almost conversationally.

"In the region of about two thousand, I should say."

The judge intervened, speaking to Balmer and the court's attention, which by now had started to lapse, was suddenly riveted again.

"So far as the people connected with the cinema were concerned, I wanted to know when they first made their statements." His voice was quiet, the members of the Press Box straining to hear him.

Balmer turned over pages in his notebook.

"I first saw Northam in the early hours of May 14th. It would be after I had seen Connolly."

"When did you first see Jacqueline Dickson?"

"At 11.00 on the night of May 13th. I took her statement on September 29th. I saw Graham on November l9th and I left the statement over until November 21st."

The judge nodded his thanks and Basil Nield continued his examination. "In the course of any criminal inquiry you would be interested to see whether a case rested only upon evidence of accomplices, or whether there is outside evidence to support them."

"That is so."

"Now Inspector, in the whole of your inquiries, and with the knowledge you have in this case, will you tell me, is there one word of evidence that Connolly ever went into that cinema?"

"I agree. There is not one word, to my knowledge, that Connolly ever went into the cinema."

"Or one word of evidence that he fired any shot?"

"1 agree again, there is not one word of evidence that he fired any shot."

"I want to follow those two wide questions by this. Is there any direct evidence of this man Connolly planning any active part in the plan, apart from Northam, Dickson and Graham?"

"That takes a lot of thinking out."

Judge Oliver intervened, addressing Nield.

"Mr Nield, I am not too sure that the question was not just a little vague. You know there is evidence to be given this week and I don't think you have a right to ask this witness such a question. These are really matters for comment which you can make in a speech, but I don't think you can ask this question."

Nield nodded, turning back to Balmer.

"Then I want to ask you this question, Inspector. Northam, Dickson and Graham are the only witnesses who speak of any direct part played in this plan by Connolly. You have made inquiries about them?"

"I have."

"Are they, all three of them, convicts?"

"They have all three got convictions."

Neil paused before resuming his questioning.

"Appreciating as you do that it is then, when a man's vitality is at its lowest, I want to know why you and three other police officers visited Connolly at 1.50 in the morning?" Balmer was not in the least perturbed by the question. He gave a slight shrug.

"It is invariably my practice, if I want to see a man rather badly, I go at the times when I am confident I shall find him in."

"You showed about half a dozen photographs of women?"

"I showed no photographs whatsoever to Connolly."

"And you asked him to pick out Jackie Dickson?"

"That is not so." Balmer's voice was almost scornful of the suggestion.

"Had you a photograph of Jackie Dickson?"

"Yes, we have."

"And he picked it out and showed you who it was?"

"That is not so."

"Are you saying that nothing was said about his finding Jackie Dickson?" There was mild derision in Basil Nield's voice.

"Nothing, at any time."

"Did you ever have it in mind and did you ever consider that Connolly might give evidence and not be a prisoner?"

"I did have that in mind."

"You referred to an incident in some part of the police office where Kelly was brought at the time that Connolly was there. Suppose a witness said this at the time, Connolly was the only other prisoner in the charge room, it would be obvious to anyone coming into the room that Connolly was a prisoner. Would you agree?"

"It would be obvious to Kelly that Connolly was a prisoner."

"By the time the committal proceedings had been completed, Northam and Dickson were your two main witnesses?"

"That is correct."

"Did you think that they were at any rate involved themselves?"

"They were present at the Beehive when the plan was discussed but did not take part."

The judge intervened when Nield repeated the question.

"You are asking this officer to decide whether they are accomplices or not. That is the question for the jury under my direction. Your point is that he was entirely desirous of getting corroborative evidence. Put it that way." Mr Nield nodded, turning back to Balmer.

"It was when you were was looking for fresh evidence that Graham was found?"

"I have looked for fresh evidence since March 19th and I am still finding it."

"When did you see Graham?"

"Graham was in prison at the same time as Connolly. I saw Graham on November 19th." The lie came easily.

"Did you know before November 19th that he was in Walton Gaol?"

There was no trace of nervousness or any indication that he was lying as Balmer replied.

"I knew at 6.40pm on November 18th that he was in the gaol. I received a message from a detective of Preston Borough Police. Graham sent for the Preston police and, because of that, they in turn sent for me and I went to the prison."

"Did Graham sign a statement?"

"Yes."

"Without persuasion?"

"There was no persuasion whatsoever to get him to do that."

"Have you ever used persuasion?"

"I suppose I have used persuasion on many occasions in my life but not in this particular case. I think that in some cases I would not object to persuading a witness to sign a statement. I see no harm in it."

"Did you get a signature from Dowling by persuasion?"

"I got his signature from him by assuring him of protection by the police."

"You conducted an investigation into the case of a man named Johnson who was charged with harbouring those responsible for the Cameo. The charges were being an accessory."

" The accused was acquitted."

"And you, in the course of that case, interviewed a man named McBride."

"It was the Chief Superintendent. The man named McBride did make a statement."

"Was he a prisoner?"

"He was."

"Was the position that Johnson was supposed to have said something to McBride, which McBride could give in evidence?"

"That is what the evidence would be. McBride was not called." Balmer's reply was quite off-hand. Judge Oliver intervened.

"McBride never gave evidence, so I don't see how it can be evidence against anybody."

"I am seeking to draw an analogy between the calling of Graham to say something spoken to another person, and the use of the man McBride, my Lord."

"If the man McBride had been called, I could follow but otherwise I cannot follow the analogy."

Mr Nield turned again to Balmer. "Tell me about the anonymous letter."

"I saw an anonymous letter, which was received by Chief Superintendent Smith. It was written by Northam, assisted by Dickson. The letter was in printed characters."

Mr Nield asked for the letter to be handed in as an exhibit and copies were handed to the judge and the jury. Nield then read the letter in full. When he had finished, Judge Oliver questioned Balmer.

"When Smith showed you the letter, had you any idea who had written it?"

"No, my Lord."

Mr Nield nodded to the bench and sat down, his cross-examination over.

A smasher

This would be Rose Heilbron's first major criminal trial since taking silk and she was determined to succeed. She stood up, Portia at the bar, a strikingly beautiful woman, to begin her cross-examination of Detective Chief Inspector Balmer. She questioned him at some length.

"When did you first interview Kelly?"

"On March 20th last year."

"Would you give us any idea roughly how many interviews you had with Kelly since March 20th in connection with this case?"

"I saw him specifically in connection with the case, when I asked him something regarding it, once only between the time I saw him on March 20th and the date on which I arrested him. Kelly did call to ask me about the case, how the case was progressing, on many occasions. I did not ask him to get information for me. The information he gave that was not in connection with the Cameo was a great help, that about the Cameo had proved to be wrong."

"Were your enquiries again directed towards the time the murder was committed?"

"Yes, but my attention was likewise directed to the hours preceding and following."

"What happened when you saw Kelly on May 20th?"

"I went to the house at which Kelly was living, accompanied by Chief Detective Inspector James Morris and there were, in the house, Doris O'Malley and a youth of nineteen who was in the army. While I was interviewing Kelly, I did have a notebook with me, but did not make any notes at the time. I could quite easily have done so, but did not make any notes until after I had interviewed Skelly, and that would be about 45 minutes later. The search of Kelly's house took about twenty minutes."

"No coat was found. No gun, no bullets and no mask?" Her voice sounded incredulous.

"That is so."

Miss Heilbron then commented dryly on the identification parade in which Northam and Dickson were separately asked to identify Kelly, pointing out that it may have been more desirable to have had it before a charge was made in open court. She then reviewed the evidence of the charge room incident, which was argued in detail during the committal proceedings.

"I suggest that what Kelly shouted to Connolly when he saw him in the main Bridewell was: 'I have never seen you in my life. I don't know you, do I?'"

Balmer replied, unshaken and unhurriedly.

"What Kelly did say was, 'You have not seen me in your life.'"

Rose Heilbron next questioned Detective Chief inspector James Morris, and there was a sudden gasp in the court when, her voice again full of incredulity, she commented on Morris's admission that he had refreshed his memory from Balmer's notes.

"Hardly what you would call independent recollection. I suggest to you that your recollection cannot possibly be accurate as to an interview as long ago as last March." Morris was unabashed.

"Without anything to refresh me, I would say that is right."

Constable James Nugent, of Liverpool City Police, was next in the witness box to say that he had seen Kelly and Connolly with a woman outside a billiard hall in Lime Street at 5.35pm on Monday September 26th. He was quite certain that it was Kelly and he had known Kelly and Connolly for about three years.

It was now time for Jimmy Northam,the chief prosecution witnesses to enter the box.

"Tell the court what happened on the night of March 19th."

Northam then gave a detailed account of what had happened. Even to the untrained observers in the court, his evidence came as a practised and smooth delivery. (Appendix 18)

"I was in the Beehive public-house with Jacqueline Dickson. Connolly joined us about 7.40 and Kelly came in 15 minutes later, at about 7.55. He bought some drinks and we all stood together talking. A short time afterwards, a girl came out of one of the back rooms. She was very dark and had plenty of powder on and lipstick. Kelly went over and spoke to her but I did not hear what was said. I was carrying a brown coat over my arm."

Mr Gorman held up an overcoat.

"Is this the one?"

"Yes, but the belt and two buttons are now missing. In the public-house Kelly said he was cold and he asked for the loan of the coat, which I gave to him. Kelly put it on and said it fitted alright. While Kelly, Connolly, Dickson and me were chatting together, the well-made-up woman stood in the background."

"What were you talking about?"

"It was about a job."

Judge Oliver spoke to Northam.

"Does that mean work?"

"No. It was breaking into a place. A particular job was mentioned in Islington but the idea was abandoned because it had burglar alarms."

"Another job at New Brighton was then mentioned by Kelly and Connolly, and they also mentioned a taxi-driver who was a 'stool pigeon' for the police. Then Connolly mentioned the Cameo Cinema and said it was a smasher."

Connolly, listening intently from the dock, shook his head in denial.

"What does a 'smasher' mean? Does it mean something that is worth smashing?" The judge looked genuinely perplexed.

"It means it is something worth doing. Connolly said that the cinema would have to be a stick-up job and that a gun would be needed. When he said this, Kelly pulled a gun out of his hip pocket."

"What kind of gun?"

"It looked like a flat automatic. There was no ammunition in the magazine. Dickson said 'Put it away, because you might be seen.' Kelly said 'I don't care who sees me, my name is Kelly' and then he put a shell in the breech. Then he put six more shells in the magazine and others that were left in his hand he put back in his pocket. Kelly then asked me if I was coming. I said no."

"Was there anyone else in the passage?"

"Just us and the well-made-up girl."

Northam continued, almost without interruption, to relate what had happened that night and the following day. He described how the well made-up girl had supplied Kelly with a brown apron and then told the court of a meeting they all had the next day at the Star public house on Brownlow Hill. He said Connolly appeared to be frightened and there was talk about him leaving the country, Kelly calling him a yellow bastard. Kelly then saying that he had a good alibi, telling Connolly that if Balmer came to him he was to say he didn't know Kelly and Kelly didn't don't know him. Then Kelly told Connolly to find himself an alibi and Connolly said he would fix one up with his wife.

Northam went on to describe a meeting in Liverpool on the Monday following the murder when Kelly returned the overcoat and described all that had happened in the manager's office and that when he dashed out he could not see Connolly. Northam went on to say that Kelly then told him that he had a cast-iron alibi which the police would not break in a thousand years, especially Balmer.

Northam finished his evidence by describing how, a few days later, Dickson gave him twenty-three shells in a handkerchief. He took six and told Dickson to take the rest back to Connolly.

Basil Nield cross-examined Northam for Connolly, questioning him about the anonymous letter and readily exposing discrepancies in Northam's evidence.

"I wrote the letter and I got some ideas that Jacqueline Dickson might be involved because she went to the car stop. She helped me with the spelling and the wording."

"Look at that letter. Did you write, 'If I give you my address, you might charge me with being an accessory to the killing.'?"

"Yes, but Jacqueline thought she might be charged with being an accessory to the murder."

"But it is your letter?"

"It is the letter of both of us."

"You were frightened of being charged, weren't you?"

"No. I was frightened of Kelly and not the police."

"Look at the letter. Immediately after the words I have referred to, did you say, 'If you put it in the personal column of the Echo and give me your word that I won't be charged,' do you still say you were not afraid of being charged?"

"It was only Dickson who was afraid of being charged, I was not afraid of being charged."

"Do you know what was meant by the phrase in a letter about turning King's evidence, or something like that?"

"When I wrote it, I thought the best thing to do was to tell the police. I wanted to tell the police so that I could have protection and give evidence."

Basil Nield then made a telling comment about the remarkable similarity of Northam's evidence with that which he had given at the magistrates' hearing.

"Is this the position? That you gave your evidence in chief exactly as it was given, almost word for word, in the police court without a single note?"

"Yes."

"Did you know the dark-haired girl you met in the Beehive and who joined you?"

"She was a stranger to me. I met her again the next day, but did not know who she was."

"'I know three and a girl, not including myself, who heard about this plan.' Who is the third man?"

"I meant myself. I meant there were five of us altogether. I meant myself, Connolly, Kelly, Dickson and the other girl."

"You have said 'You are looking for one man.'"

"What I meant was the one man who did the shooting."

"Did you, in that letter, refer to the part taken by Dickson in quite a different way a fortnight after? Didn't you say; 'I would have nothing to do with it, and I don't think the girl did. When I met her on Sunday she had not been with them.'"

"I did not want the police to know I was living with her."

"You go on, 'And another man dropped out on account he wanted to unload the revolver.' Who is that?"

"I meant Connolly."

"On account that he wanted to unload the revolver before they went?"

"What I meant was that Connolly would not go inside."

"You were saying about April 3rd, that Connolly had dropped out of this venture?"

"Dickson said it was not Connolly's fault."

"I suggest that you were telling the police Connolly had dropped out."

"I was saying that in the letter and meant that when they got to the cinema Connolly would not go in. Kelly and Connolly asked me to go to the cinema, but I said no, as I did not like guns, or the people who used them."

"Is it not correct that you said not one word before the Magistrates Court about Connolly fixing an alibi with his wife?"

"Perhaps not."

"On March 21st, you had said you and Dickson came to Liverpool and that you separated. Does that mean at the station?"

"At the corner of Lewis's, before I saw Kelly."

"Did you, in the Magistrates Court, say, 'Dickson and I again came to Liverpool. We saw the accused Kelly in Lime Street'?"

"I think that is so."

"Assuming you said, 'We saw Kelly', that would be incorrect?"

"I saw Kelly. I don't know why I said 'we'."

Northam was then taken through a list of previous convictions. He admitted that when he was only eighteen, he was put on probation for stealing. He was now twenty-three years of age. In 1942, he was convicted of shop breaking and larceny and, at that time, had 27 other offences taken into account. In 1945, he was charged with house-breaking and shop-breaking and was sent to Borstal. In 1946, he was convicted of house-breaking at Birkenhead Quarter Sessions and sent to prison for 28 days. In August 1947, he received a month's imprisonment for stealing a car and on January 17th 1949, he was convicted of receiving at Brampton and sentenced to three month's imprisonment."

"Who was the thief from whom you received on that occasion?"

"Some man."

"Was the woman Dickson convicted on that date with you, at the same place?"

"Yes."

"Did you have a gun?"

"No, I never had a gun."

Once again, Basil Nield showed his conviction that Northam's involvement was more than he had admitted.

"I suggest that you are saying that which is untrue. Do you take this view, that if someone else is convicted for this, you are alright?"

"Not necessarily."

Judge Oliver sat forward. "Are you suggesting he is a murderer?"

"I cannot do that, how can I?"

"I thought you were asking about saving himself from the charge?"

"From being charged as an accessory, as he himself has indicated."

"You say you are not making the suggestion. I say no more." Mr Nield paused for a few moments, seemingly seeking to control his own feelings, before resuming his questioning.

"Have you ever claimed to have been paid money by Mr Livermore?"

"Yes."

A buzz went around the courtroom, causing the judge to frown and glance around disapprovingly. Then there was an almost stunned silence as Northam continued by accusing Harry Livermore of trying to get him to change his evidence.

"Are you suggesting that you have been asked to change your evidence?"

"Yes."

"By whom?"

"By Mr Livermore."

"What are you saying about him?"

"That he offered me £150."

"When?"

"I am not sure."

"Would you give an approximate date?"

"I cannot give an approximate date."

"Did you keep the money?"

"I told the police straight away."

"What day of the week was it?"

"Tuesday."

"Can you remember the month?"

"I can't."

"Did he say he wanted you to change your evidence?"

"Yes."

"Did you, when reporting it, take the view that if it were believed, it would indeed be damaging, not only to Mr Livermore, but to the prisoner Kelly?"

"No."

"Can you think of anything more damaging?"

"No."

"I suggest from first to last it is wholly untrue?"

"It is not untrue."

Northam's cross-examination ended at this stage, the judge adjourning the hearing until the next day and asking the jury to leave the court, the press and the public allowed to remain for a brief legal discussion, during which the judge was told that when Nield had asked the question concerning Livermore, he knew what the answer would be.

Judge Oliver shook his head, pointing out that here was enough to be got through on the present case and he was not going to permit this point to be pursued any further, neither would he allow Mr Livermore to enter the witness box to deny the statement made by Northam as the matter was not an issue before the court.

The legal vixen

It was the fourth day of the trial, when Rose Heilbron stood up to cross-examine Northam. She was a forceful interrogator, her questions relentless but with no sense of bullying, Judge Oliver's presence looming as she attempted to destroy Northam's credibility.

"Do you remember an identification parade in October? Tell the court what took place."

"What I did was to walk up and down. I saw Kelly but didn't want to pick him out. I then said to Mr Balmer and Mr Livermore he had a hat and coat on that night."

There was a surprised murmur from some in court, those who had been listening intently shaking their heads in disbelief, remembering that Northam had said he had supplied Kelly with the coat. The judge interjected.

"In the end did you pick him out?"

"Yes." Miss Heilbron continued.

"What did you do on the afternoon of March 19th?"

"I arrived in Liverpool from Durham about 2pm and then went home to Birkenhead and I think, but am not sure, afterwards me and Dickson went to the pictures in Birkenhead and then went back home for tea."

"Not sure?"

"Dickson called for me at my house at Birkenhead and we travelled to Liverpool together. We didn't go to the Beehive straight away but walked along Lime Street and back again. I had been carrying my overcoat all day and thought it might be cold going back to Birkenhead at night."

Northam continued, his replies unhesitating as defence counsel questioned him vigorously, stating that there was no one else who was drinking in the passage at the Beehive on that Saturday evening but people were walking in and out into the room.

"Did it occur to you that your overcoat might be rather easily identified?"

"I forgot, after I handed it to Kelly."

"It was not going to be a good thing for you if a man went with your overcoat on."

"No."

"But it slipped your memory?"

"Yes."

"Although you saw him walk out with it on and with a gun?"

"Yes."

"Were you shocked when the robbery was discussed?"

"It was a general discussion between the four people. I was not shocked by the conversation. We were all standing together, myself, Dickson, Kelly and Connolly and the other girl."

"Why did you not go away with Dickson when the gun was produced?"

"I didn't like to."

"It didn't slip your memory that an armed robbery was being planned?"

"No."

"Would the barman have been able to have seen the gun?"

"It might have been possible."

"Did you suggest that Kelly was drunk in your statement to the police."

"Yes."

"Did you attempt to stop Dickson going?"

"No."

Judge Oliver looked up from the deposition open before him.

"If Dickson did go to lend a hand, one could make some sense out of this passage in your letter when you say, 'When I met her on Sunday she had not been with them.' Where should she go on that night, except go home with you?"

Northam blinked in some confusion, unable to answer.

"Do you mean that she went home with you that night?"

"Yes."

"If Dickson had merely gone with the others and not seen you until next day, you had very good reason to believe that she might be prosecuted?"

"I put that in the letter because the police might find out that she was with Connolly and Kelly."

"Was her part to be to help to get rid of the gun once they had finished shooting? Was that to be her part?"

"It might have been."

"And possibly to get rid of the disguise and the overcoat and the mask?"

"It might have been."

"You have heard of what people call in America 'gangster's molls'? Was that to be her part, to get rid of the gun and possibly the disguise and the overcoat?"

"It might have been."

Rose Heilbron had been waiting patiently while the judge questioned Northam. Now she continued to pile on the questions.

"Was the arrangement to meet next day made just as you were leaving the Beehive?"

"Yes."

"On the Sunday morning, you went to meet at least two people whom you knew had been involved in something very desperate. Nevertheless you went?"

"Yes."

"When did you first tell the police about the coat?"

"In September. I told the police about the overcoat but I did not tell them that I had had it back from Kelly. The police found the overcoat when they searched my house but I had told them about it before they found it."

"Why did you write the anonymous letter?"

"Because I wanted nothing to do with the matter."

"Didn't it occur to you that you could have put Kelly's name in that letter and nobody would have known?" Rose Heilbron's voice was as smooth a silk.

"Yes."

Counsel drove her point home.

"You see, there was no need for you to put your name but you could have put Kelly's name and you could have mentioned the Beehive and the overcoat?"

Northam responded weakly. "Yes."

"When you saw the advertisement in the press, you took that as an assurance you would get police protection. Were you worried about your part in the affair?"

"Yes."

"You accepted the promise the police had given you and the offer of police protection. In view of that, you did not, of course, go to the police?"

"No."

"And when you saw the police on May 13th, you did not say anything?"

"That is so."

Now, Rose Heilbron showed her velvet claws.

"Don't you remember saying in the police court, 'I should say it was about four weeks after the murder that the police interviewed me.'?" Northam made no reply, counsel waiting patiently before continuing.

"I will read on and perhaps it will jog your memory, 'they saw me then in connection with the Cameo murders.'"

"It might have been. They might have mentioned it."

Rose Heilbron continued to read from the Magistrates Court deposition,

"'I did not tell them what I am now telling the court.'?"

" Yes. It did occur to me that it might be my duty to say something but I did not."

"You did give this evidence, didn't you? You don't deny it was given? I will read this again, 'They saw me then in relation to the Cameo murders.'" Northam again was silent. He looked for help to the prosecution bench.

Miss Heilbron changed the line of questioning.

"Did you know at the beginning of May that a man named Johnson had been arrested?"

"Yes. I was not very much interested."

"But according to your own statements, you knew who had done the murder. You knew the man was arrested at the beginning of May, before you saw the police on May 13th, for his part in this self same murder. Are you telling the jury that you were not sufficiently interested to even read about it?"

"I didn't take much notice of it. I knew the man Johnson was alleged to have received the gun within an hour of the murder."

"But, according to you, the gun was in the lake in Botanic Park."

"Yes."

Rose Heilbron slowly shook her head, in mock disbelief, before directing her questions towards the matter of the overcoat.

"Where has the overcoat been all this time until you remembered about it in October and gave it to the police?"

"At my father's house."

"But the police searched your father's house in Birkenhead in May."

"I think he must have been wearing it at the time."

Miss Heilbron raised her eyebrows in an expression of feigned amazement before continuing.

"Were you asked at the Magistrates Court, when you received the shells in the handkerchief had you seen those shells before?"

"The bullets I had seen in the Beehive. I could not see the names on the back but I examined the twenty-three bullets out of curiosity and kept six for the police."

"And at the Magistrates Court, you said you kept six out of curiosity and now you tell us that you kept them for the police?"

"Yes."

Now defence counsel attacked Northam relentlessly.

"Do you still say that the other man, who dropped out because he wanted to unload the revolver, was Connolly?"

"Yes."

"You said the man had not been seen since but you told me yesterday you knew Dickson had seen Connolly on two occasions after?"

"There are two people's minds in this letter."

"You pledge the accuracy of this letter? It is absolutely true?"

"Yes."

"It is as true as your evidence?"

"Yes."

"You say, 'five days ago I seen the man who had done the job.'?"

"That is not true on my part, but it might be true about Dickson."

"It could not be. She was with you on the Sunday?"

"Yes."

"Why did you write that if it was not true?"

"I meant Connolly."

"It says 'the man who had done the job', I thought that was Kelly?"

"Connolly done the job as well."

"Well you say, 'Five days ago I seen the man who done the job' and that is also Connolly.'?"

"It must be."

"How can the two be Connolly?"

"You will have to wait until Dickson gives evidence."

"You say, 'I have proof I was in a pub not far from Dale Street.'?"

"I meant I was in a pub in Birkenhead but I did not want to say Birkenhead, so I said Dale Street."

Miss Heilbron glanced slowly along the line of jurors, as again, Northam was exposed as a liar. She spoke to the judge.

"I have no further questions."

William Gorman re-examined Northam for the prosecution.

"Are you saying what you have said, to protect yourself?"

"Yes." Northam stopped, checking himself before continuing.

"Oh no, sir."

"You were asked yesterday afternoon whether you had been asked to change your evidence. I want you to go into that carefully. The answer you gave was, 'I have been asked to change my evidence by Mr Livermore.'?"

"Yes."

"Will you tell the jury how the contact was made between you and Mr Livermore?"

The judge looked up from his notes and shook his head.

"I don't think there is any purpose in merely getting repetition."

"Will you tell us in what way you were asked to change your evidence?"

"He said that I had to say that I met Kelly and Connolly in the pub on the Sunday and that I had not seen them the day before in the Beehive, that Kelly was drunk and that he made a boast that he had done it and that later he had said he was only joking."

"What had you to say about that?"

"I was to say that it was only a toy gun. I was to say that I didn't take much notice and that when I first saw the police, I told them Kelly had made a boast."

Again the judge interrupted.

"I want to suggest to you that you don't want to go too far into this. If we are starting to try half a dozen cases I don't think we shall ever finish."

Northam continued.

"The statement I had given to Balmer was mentioned. I was told to say, after I had told the police that Kelly had only made a boast on the Sunday, I was to say that they turned round and said that it must have been on the Saturday."

Judge Oliver's one good eye glared reprovingly at William Gorman. His voice was cold and final.

"I am afraid I must intervene to point out once more that this is not the case the jury are trying. I have permitted you to re-examine. I shall tell the jury, apart from the effect it has on this man's credit, it has nothing to do with the case."

And Jacqueline Dickson...

It was the turn of Jacqueline Dickson to enter the witness box. There was a murmur of anticipation as she came into view, the clerk of the court announcing her as Mrs Jacqueline Eva Margaret Dickson. She wore a light grey suit and a powder blue hat with a feather in the side, her appearance so dramatically changed since the magistrates' hearing that Rose Heilbron, at one stage in the proceedings, was to ask who had bought her clothes for her.

Along with Northam and unlike other witnesses, she had waited in one of the police rooms before being called. Now she was allowed to be seated as Mr Gorman began his examination, concentrating on what she had claimed to have seen in the Beehive on the night of the murders. He led her through her statement, prompting and questioning. Her evidence was lengthy and detailed and almost identical to that of Northam. (Appendix 19)

She described what had happened in the Beehive and how Kelly joined her, Northam, Connolly and a heavily made-up girl in dark clothes. She said she had, at first, intended going with Kelly and Connolly to the Cameo but had then changed her mind.

She described how, after Connolly mentioned the job at the Cameo, Kelly had taken out a gun and she told him to put it way, someone might see him and he replied, 'I don't care. My name is Kelly.' She went on to tell how Connolly, Kelly and she left the

Beehive and went across the road to the tram stop but when the tram came, she ran back to the Beehive to join Northam."

At this stage, the judge leaned forward.

"Are you quite sure you did not go with them?"

"No, I did not, my Lord."

Dickson resumed her evidence to describe what she alleged took place in the Star Hotel the next day, her story, again, almost identical to that of Northam's.

She described how Connolly looked frightened and Kelly then came in with the dark girl and called him a yellow bastard. Kelly then told them that Balmer had been to see him that morning and, if he had had a gun, Balmer would not have been so cocksure of himself.

Kelly said he had got an alibi but Connolly would have to find one for himself and that Connolly said he was trying to get one with his wife.

Dickson then described how she met Connolly the next day and he gave her a handkerchief with some hard objects in, telling her to give them to Kelly the next time she saw him. Northam kept six before handing the remainder back, telling her to go and tell Connolly to do his own dirty work. On a Saturday, a fortnight afterwards, she claimed she again met Connolly and went to a cafe. Connolly then asked her to go to the Smoke with him but she refused and then he told her what had happened at the Cameo, saying he had waited outside and when he heard the first shot he ran away. Connolly also told her Kelly had thrown the gun in the lake.

That night, she helped Northam write the letter and, after finding six bullet in Northam's pockets, she took them and threw them down different drains behind the Adelphi.

Dickson then went on to tell how she had met Kelly in town and had a whisky with him in the Caledonian. He bought more drinks and she had said he must have plenty of money and Kelly said he would have had more if he had got what he went for at the Cameo.

Finally, as they were leaving, Kelly warned her not to say a word or he, or somebody else, would knife her.

"Did Connolly tell you that he ran away because he didn't know there was to be any shooting?"

"Yes."

"Do you also agree that in the Magistrates Court, you said that you didn't think the gun was going to be used, except to frighten."

"Yes. It was to frighten and not to shoot."

"Does some of the letter refer to you and some of it to Northam?"

"Yes."

"Everything in it was true?" There was a touch of incredulity in Basil Nield's voice.

"Yes. A good many of the things. All the things I said were true but Northam was putting things in the letter himself and these were things I didn't know."

Judge Oliver questioned her.

"But you put them all in under the title, I?"

"Yes."

Mr Nield continued.

"Will you look at the letter, the part where it stated, 'I know three and a girl, not including myself, who heard about his plan for the robbery, I would have nothing to do with it, and I don't think the girl did. When I met her Sunday she had not been with them.' Is that right?"

"Yes."

"If it were true, there was no question of waiting till Sunday to find out whether you had been with them?"

"It was not me. It was the other girl. The dark girl."

Mr Nield quoted the anonymous letter,

"'I have proof I was in a pub not far from Dale Street till 10pm.' What do you say about that?"

"We were not in a pub. If we had said we were in Birkenhead we could have easily been traced."

Basil Nield's voice was icy.

"You say you now explain two false statements in that letter. Do you remember me asking you if all you knew there was true and that you said, 'yes'?"

"I did not say 'yes'. I said some of it was true."

The judge reminded her.

"You said some of the things in the letter were true and that, so far as things were known to you, they were true."

Counsel continued.

"In that letter, there are facts spoken to you within your knowledge which are wholly untrue?"

"You know why we put those things in."

"I put it to you, that what you had said, so far as Connolly is concerned about the meeting in the public-house the next day and the days thereafter, was wholly untrue."

"They are not untrue; it is the truth."

"Why did you leave Liverpool in May?"

"Because I had been threatened. I was charged with an offence in Liverpool on May 13th and brought before the court and remanded on bail on May 14th, and it was while I was on bail that I went to Manchester."

"Do you say that under those circumstances with the police, in fact, very much at hand, you left because you were frightened?"

"I was told if I went near the court I would have my face split open."

"Were you re-arrested?" Dickson made no comment, until Judge Oliver asked.

"Were you brought back to Liverpool in custody?"

"Yes. I was."

Nield continued,

"In fact, you have been in trouble with the police?"

"Yes."

"In 1947, you were convicted of receiving stolen goods, weren't you, at Cumberland Assizes?"

"I was charged and was sent to a convent for six months, on probation."

"Did you plead guilty?"

"Yes."

"And as a matter of fact, there was an earlier conviction in 1946 for offensive behaviour in Liverpool." Dickson again made no reply until the judge spoke.

"Is that right?"

"I don't remember it."

Basil Nield continued,

"And in January 1949, were you charged before the Brampton Magistrates with receiving stolen property?"

"Yes. We pleaded not guilty."

"When you say 'we', who is 'we'?"

"James Northam and I."

"Did you go into the witness-box and take the oath and say you did not commit the offence?"

"Well, we had not. But we were found guilty."

"Did Northam also take the oath and give evidence?"

"Yes, but he had not done it."

"And was he convicted?"

"We were both convicted."

"After swearing that he was not guilty?"

"Well, we were not guilty."

"Were you then living with Northam?"

"I was."

Basil Nield nodded, satisfied that he had exposed Dickson as a liar. He

"I suggest your evidence before the Brampton Magistrates on oath was untrue."

"It was not untrue, I know it was the truth, although we were convicted and found guilty."

"Finally, that which you have said here today is untrue?"

"It is true, as far as I am concerned."

Basil Nield sat down and Rose Heilbron stood to cross-examine on behalf of Kelly. She could see that Dickson was weakening. Her voice was faltering and her answers less assured. Miss Heilbron stared intently at Dickson before questioning her, slowly and deliberately.

"Are Kelly and Connolly, who according to your story were involved in the murder, the sort of people whose company you would seek?"

" I don't seek anyone's company at all."

"But you had a drink of whisky with Kelly. Did you think a murderer was the right sort of person to give you protection?"

"I did not think of that at all. I went so that I would have someone with me."

"Were you afraid of Kelly?"

"I never was afraid of Kelly, only when he said what he would do to me. I was frightened of his people, his brothers."

"Are you afraid of Connolly?"

"I was never was afraid of Connolly. I met him on two occasions after the murder and on one occasion had tea with him."

"With this man you say were involved in the murder?"

"Yes."

"You were prepared to act as messenger between the two of them?"

"It was a good turn."

"For a man involved in a brutal murder?"

"I would do a good turn for anyone, even a dog."

"You must have known what was in the handkerchief."

"I didn't. I just put it in my bag. It was not mine and I had no right to look in it."

"You knew there were hard objects in the handkerchief given to you by a man you say was involved in murder and in whose company you had seen a couple of bullets?"

"Yes."

"I suggest the whole story is quite untrue."

"I know it is true."

"Why did Northam keep six bullets?"

"I suppose out of curiosity. I put them away because I was sick of looking at them. I went into Northam's pockets quite a number of times for other things. I didn't want them in the house at all. I had no idea why I put them down the drains."

"Were you asked if you had written the letter?"

"I don't think so."

"Chief Inspector Balmer has given evidence that you were asked about the letter."

"I mentioned the letter."

"But you denied writing it."

"I don't think I denied it at all."

"When did you first admit that you told the police that you had written that letter?"

"I can't tell you. I think it was in September, when I was brought to Liverpool."

"Was there any reason why you should not have told the police that you had written the letter?"

"After I had gone so far, I was scared to go any further and that is all there is to it."

"But in September you went the whole way?"

"Yes."

"You remember the sentence, 'five days ago I seen the man who done the job and I asked who was the I.'?" Counsel waited for a reply, Dickson was now very pale and merely stared at her questioner. The judge leaned forward.

"Are you feeling unwell? Don't go on giving evidence if you don't feel well. Would you like to have a rest?"

Dickson nodded, her voice distressed and shallow.

"Yes sir."

"I understand. She has been very ill."

Rose Heilbron looked stunned, she started to protest and then changed her mind, as the judge ruled that Dickson could continue being cross-examined on the following day.

On the following day, Jan 19th, Jacqueline Dickson again took her place in the witness box. Miss Heilbron rose immediately.

"I hope you are feeling better. I am sorry, I have to put a few more questions to you but I have a duty to perform. Take as much time as you like to answer." She paused for a few moments before posing her first question.

"I am suggesting to you that you did not know George Kelly."

"Oh yes, I did know George Kelly and I knew Connolly lived somewhere near Old Swan and that he was living with his wife and another girl as well." Rose Heilbron made no comment on this, although there were surprised murmurs from the rear of the court.

"Where was the letter to the police written?"

"At Northam's house in Birkenhead"

"Are you quite sure that you and Northam wrote it."

"I am positive of that. We wrote it just as it came into our minds and it just set out

72

what we knew. "

Behind the wide sleeve of his gown, the judge suppressed a yawn before addressing Dickson. "What you put undoubtedly was true?"

"It was true."

"The letter says; 'Five days ago I seen the man who had done the job.' Who was that I?"

"That was James Northam."

"And the man who had done the job was Kelly?"

"Yes."

"Why did the letter say that you were in a pub near Dale Street when you were in Birkenhead?"

"We did not want the police to know where we were living."

Rose Heilbron turned unhurriedly back to the witness.

"Why did you mention Brownlow Hill in the letter?"

"That did not really matter. It was not me who put that in. You will have to ask Northam about that."

"But you knew he was putting it in?"

"Yes."

"You knew it was false?" Dickson remained silent.

"You speak about two people. Who were the two people there?"

"I cannot answer that."

"But there were no two people?"

"No."

"You say in the letter, 'I'm scared of him. He wants me to go away with him and I cannot go down the town.' Is the 'I' there you?"

"Yes."

"Because you say Connolly wanted to go away with you?"

"Yes."

"But you said yesterday you were not really scared of Connolly?"

"That's right. I was scared that he would make me go away with him. That is why."

"What did you mean about the passage in the letter, 'about six weeks ago'?" Miss Heilbron's voice was almost cajoling.

"I don't think I wrote that. I dictated some of it. You must realise this letter is an awful long time back and I don't quite remember everything."

"But there could be no mistake about a few days or six weeks? Having seen that letter do you still say it is true?"

"Yes."

Counsel had no more questions, Judge Oliver indicating that Dickson could leave the court.

"You can go home. I hope you won't be asked for again."

The go-between

There was a renewed murmur of conversation as the court waited for the new witness it had been promised and Robert Graham took the oath. He was a tall, thin-faced man who had been brought to court from Walton Gaol.

William Gorman asked him to tell the court how he came to meet the defendants and Graham launched into a detailed account. (Appendix 20)

He described how he had exercised with Kelly and Connolly and Connolly had told him that, apart from being with Kelly that day, he had nothing to do with the killing and when the gun went off he ran away. Connolly then described being with Northam and Dickson in the Beehive, what had taken place there and that they had arranged to meet the next day in the Star. He went on to say that he had sent for the police officer in charge of the case to tell him everything but then changed his mind.

Graham continued, telling the court that the following day he had exercised with Kelly who told him all about the murder and that his life hung on five minutes. He said that before he went to the cinema he had been with Jacky Dickson, Northam and Connolly. Graham then went on to describe how he had passed messages between Connolly and Kelly and that Kelly told him that he had threatened Dickson in a pub.

When Graham had finished, prosecuting counsel questioned him, asking him if he had known that some of the things had already been given in evidence in another court? Graham shook his head emphatically.

That concluded the case for the prosecution.

Basil Nield cross-examined Graham, asking him to tell the court why he was in prison. Graham unfalteringly gave a record of his previous convictions, saying he was at present on a charge of receiving and that he had last been convicted of a criminal offence on January 11th 1949, for taking money by false pretences. For this he got twelve months imprisonment.

"When did you come out from that sentence?"

"In September, 1949. I arrived at Walton on November 14th after having been five days in custody at Preston. I was on remand at the prison and was lodged in one of the reception cells in the hospital as a prisoner awaiting trial and both Kelly and Connolly were also in hospital."

"Were they not in adjoining cells?"

"No. They were about twelve yards away."

Judge Oliver then spoke. "Are their cells in hospital?"

"Yes."

"Were you on the same floor?"

"Yes. The sections of the hospital were called lower, middle and bottom C. There were three cells set aside for people under close observation, I think, but I could not swear to that."

Mr Nield continued.

"Were these two men in the same section?"

"No. The hospital is a long corridor. Kelly was in the end cell in one section and Connolly was in the first cell by what is called the hospital centre."

"When you were in hospital on former occasions did you know a man called McBride?"

"Yes, I worked with McBride."

"When McBride was in the hospital was there also a man called Johnson?"

"There was."

"Charged with being an accessory to this murder?"

"There was."

"Did you not tell Connolly that McBride had been there and that Johnson had said things to you and that McBride was going to be a witness?"

"No. I didn't think anyone knew either."

"Did you say to Connolly, 'Why don't you turn King's Evidence.'?"

"No. Connolly told me the part he played and that he did not know there was going to be a murder committed. I told him that he should tell the truth about it and cover himself."

"During exercises, are prisoners sometimes visited by the police?"

"That I cannot tell you. I have never been visited by the police during exercise. I don't know whether anyone else has or not."

"I must put it to you that you left for about fifteen minutes and when you came back you told Connolly that you had a police visit."

"No."

"What I am putting is that Connolly at no time told you that he was concerned in this affair at all."

"He was quite insistent that he never thought murder was going to be committed at all. I told him he was a foolish fellow for not telling the police all about it."

"What you suggested was that he should give evidence?"

"I did, sir. I told him he should give all the evidence he could to the police."

It was Rose Heilbron's turn to cross-examine Graham.

"What did Kelly tell you?"

"He told him what he had done in the cinema office and he told me about borrowing a coat from Stutty Northam. Kelly told me he had shot both men and that the door had locked behind him. He said he had fired at the lock and then discovered that the door was not locked but that it opened inwards instead of outwards."

"Have you any doubt in your mind that Kelly confessed to you?"

"He repeated it throughout."

Rose Heilbron paused, frowning slightly as she stared up at Graham

"Were you not very shocked and troubled at this very rare confession?"

"I felt it was too great a responsibility for me to keep such a secret and that was why I reported it."

"When the confession was made to you, it was such a great responsibility, that you immediately told the Governor?"

"I asked the Governor if he would have a police officer to come to see me at the prison."

"Who took your statement?"

"I saw Chief Inspector Balmer at Walton Prison on Saturday, November 19th and saw him again at Preston Borough Police Station two days later."

"Did you ask Kelly what was the evidence against him?"

"No, I had no need to ask Kelly anything. He was telling me everything about it so that I could pass the information."

Counsel glanced down the line of jurors before asking, almost conversationally.

"Is it not a fact that it is quite possible for Kelly and Connolly to talk to each other through the bars of their cells?"

Graham shook his head emphatically.

"Absolutely impossible. Where they are situated it is impossible."

There was a murmur in the court, people straining to see as, at this point Kelly stood up in the dock, staring hard at Graham before leaning through the railings to speak to Mr Livermore. He took a sheet of paper and a pencil and returned to his seat, doing a quick sketch of the relative position of the cells. He passed it back to Miss Heilbron.

After this brief interruption, Rose Heilbron continued.

"I suggest to you that not only is it possible but at night they are able to talk across the corridor one with another?"

"No. If I could describe the position of the cells I could show you how it is impossible."

"Did he say I am not worried because I am innocent?"

"He said I am not worried because I have a lot of brothers and if they find Jackie Dickson she will never give evidence against me."

"What you are saying is that this confession was made to you quite voluntarily and in great detail?"

"When you speak to a man for five hours about a thing you get to know quite a lot of things."

"He told you all the details which the prosecution had, apart from the fact that he confessed to you about the murder and it was planned beforehand and what happened afterwards?"

"Yes."

Miss Heilbron had one final question.

"Is it true, Mr Graham, that earlier this year you spent some time in a mental hospital?"

Graham hesitated, glancing quickly at William Gorman before replying.

"Yes. From March to May."

The Saturday night dance

Connolly's involvement on March 19th if proven, would lead to his conviction for murder. For him to be guilty, George Kelly would have had to be proven guilty. Basil Nield emphasised this when he opened the proceedings for the defence of Connolly in which he would concentrate on Connolly's alibi which would be mainly by members of Connolly's family. He bowed, gathered himself and addressed the jury.

"There is a sharp and marked distinction between these two persons. In the six days hearing, not one word that Connolly ever entered that theatre has been heard, not one word that he ever fired any shot. Even if the whole of the Crown's case was correct, the jury have the fact that the witness, Northam, has told you that Connolly dropped out of the wicked adventure because he would not permit a loaded weapon to be there. Dickson informed you she was satisfied that Connolly would take no part in the expedition.

According to the Crown evidence, five persons were gathered in the Beehive Hotel in the planning. One had not been seen, another young woman dropped out. The four were Northam, the two accused, and Dickson. If everything reported was correct, Dickson heard all that had passed, all that was to be done, started out, reached the tram stop and then retreated. According to her, Connolly boarded a tram, went to the cinema took no other part and, according to Northam, he would not watch. He retreated from the adventure.

I will remind you that the vast majority of the witnesses for the prosecution never mentioned Charles Connolly. If you look fairly and squarely at the situation, I submit that you are driven to the view that there are but three witnesses who can give any direct evidence against Connolly.

The three witnesses cannot be regarded as reputable people. The first two were themselves of the party of five which was engaged in hatching the plot which had been spoken of in the Beehive Hotel.

I would submit, subject to the legal direction which you will have, that it is correct in law and in common sense, that you may not act on the evidence of accomplices unless there is outside evidence corroborating what they say and, I would submit again, that in a murder, to accept the evidence of accomplices would be quite unthinkable.

Connolly is twenty-six years of age, a married man with one small child and another expected. I want, at this early stage, to say to you that I am not presenting him to you as a faultless member of society. He has been in some trouble but, whatever he has done, I submit that it does not amount to very much. I will present Connolly as an otherwise decent person and a good husband. He had, in fact, served his country. He joined the Royal Navy at the age of eighteen and, at one stage of the war, he was in the Indian Ocean with what was called 'The Wolf Pack', chasing enemy submarines. He was actively engaged on D Day on the extremely hazardous task of acting as decoy for German batteries on the French coast and was released from the navy in 1946.

The first Connolly knew about the crime, or rather about his being in any way involved, was on May 14th when four police officers arrived at his house and he was taken to the Central Police Office and asked to account for his movements on the day of the crime. His statement on that occasion was that he was at work on the afternoon shift and that he was employed at Bibbys. The important point was that every one of these statements was true except that he was speaking of any other day than the Saturday.

Connolly's alibi is simple; that he was at a dance with his wife and members of his family at the time the murder was committed. The dances were in St Mark's Church Hall in Edge Lane and Connolly attended dances there on the Saturdays of March 5th, 12th and 19th. At the dance on the week before the murder, three things of vital moment happened. There was a crooning competition, in which Mrs Connolly was successful. There was a spot waltz competition in which Charles Connolly was successful and Connolly and his wife had a photograph taken by photographers who visit such dances. A deposit was paid by Connolly on Saturday March 12th and the arrangement was that he would collect the photographs the following week, Saturday March 19th.

At the dance on March 19th, three things of immense importance happened. Connolly arrived at the dance at 8.30 and entered a rumba competition at 9.30 but was not successful. One of the prizes was 20 cigarettes and when the winner handed the packet round, Connolly was one of those who accepted a cigarette. Shortly after the dance ended the photographer came with the photographs from the previous week."

Basil Nield nodded his head several times at the jury. His case was watertight. Now they could listen to the accused man himself. He called Connolly to the stand.

"Were you ever at the Beehive Hotel that night?"

"No."

"Or at the Cameo Cinema, outside?"

"No. I don't know where the Cameo Cinema is."

"What happened the next day?"

"I was in bed until twelve or one o'clock and then stayed at home."

"Did you see Jacqueline Dickson on March 21st?"

"No."

"Were you shown photographs by the police?"

"Yes. In the early hours of May 14th I was shown six photographs of men and women and asked if I knew any of them. I looked at them and said I knew one."

"Who was that?"

"Jacqueline Dickson. The photographs were full face and side face, and there was a number under each. I had known Dickson about six months before then but she was only a casual acquaintance. I used to see her walking up and down Lime Street and had spoken to her once or twice."

The judge interrupted.

"Do you mean that she used to walk the street in Lime Street?"

"Yes."

Mr Nield continued.

"When you left Messrs Bibby, had you any trouble at home with your wife?"

"Yes, but not important."

"Did you offer to help the police find Jacqueline Dickson?"

"I offered to help them to get in touch with Jacqueline Dickson and told them that she lived with Bobbie Woolerton. I told the police that I would locate Woolerton if I could and when I did see Woolerton and told him Inspector Balmer wanted to interview him, Woolerton said, if Inspector Balmer wants to see me he can come and get me."

"Where were you on the night of March 19th?"

"I went to a dance at St Mark's Church Hall. My sister got a black eye at the dance on March 5th. In view of that, I decided to go with her the following week on March 12th to give her protection. My sisters, Irene and Doris, were there and I went with them and my wife. There was a crooning competition and my wife won a bangle. We were both photographed there."

Judge Oliver looked up from his notes and spoke.

"Did you decide to go to protect your sisters?"

"Yes."

Connolly continued.

"Early on the evening of Saturday March 19th, after having tea with my wife and child, we went to buy a coat for the child. At five o'clock, I was in Littlewoods Cafe having tea with my wife and baby. She wanted to get the baby a coat and we went to Lewis's. We were there until just on closing time at 6pm. Then we went on the tram to my mother's home at Old Swan. I had an arrangement with my wife to go to a dance that evening and had tickets but when we arrived at my mother's house, I found my mother had toothache but she said I might as well go to the dance. I went alone and left my wife to get ready. It would be about 8.20 when I arrived at the dance and I used the half-price ticket which I had won the week before. My wife arrived at the dance about twenty minutes later and we entered for a rumba competition at about 9.30. It was won by a girl, I don't know her name. The prizes they won were a bangle and a packet of cigarettes. I asked for a cigarette and the girl handed round the packet which was finished in a couple of minutes.

Shortly before the dance ended, at 11 o'clock, the photographers who had taken my photo at the dance on March 12th arrived and I got two copies of the photo of my wife and myself. I gave the photographer the receipt I got when I paid a deposit of two shillings the previous week."

Basil Nield stood up and asked that the jury be handed a photograph showing Connolly with his wife. In it, Connolly was wearing a hat.

Connolly continued. "I went back to my mother's house at Old Swan with my wife and two sisters and then returned to my own home with my wife and child."

Mr Neild then questioned him about prosecution witnesses who claimed to have seen him with Kelly.

"Do you know a witness named Sangster who was a supervisor at Lewis's?"

"Yes. My wife worked for a time at Lewis's before the Cameo murders."

"So far as you can say, were you ever with Kelly when Mr Sangster was there?"

"No, not to the best of my belief."

"Do you know a police constable called Nugent?"

"Yes. He used to be on duty near the Seamen's Employment Exchange." Connolly turned towards the Judge, speaking emphatically, almost indignantly.

"He couldn't have seen me talking to Kelly in Lime Street on September 26th. I wasn't there, I was with my wife and child in a picture house, either the Futurist or the Scala. It was 'The Last Of the Redskins' and we came out about six o'clock."

"Constable Nugent's evidence is wrong?"

"Yes."

"Have you, in fact, ever known anything about Kelly, ever seen him, or met him or spoken to him before the crime?"

"No, sir."

"Do you drink?"

"No. Not unless I'm practically forced to. I do have a drink from time to time."

"When you were in Walton Gaol on November 14th, 15th, and 16th and were alleged to have spoken to Graham, did you ever tell him that you had been outside the cinema or took any part in this affair."

"No, sir. Graham asked me about my part in the Cameo crime and I told Graham that I did not wish to discuss it".

"Did Inspector Balmer ask you to turn King's evidence?"

"Yes, but I told him I don't tell lies. Never at any time had I been involved in that crime."

Basil Nield's examination of Connolly for the defence was finished. When cross-examining, William Gorman concentrated initially on the letter Connolly had written in prison. He asked him about it.

"It's one I sent to Inspector Balmer. I wanted to tell the police what Dennis Barker had told me. I knew nothing at that time about Kelly. I did know about James Skelly. I did say to Balmer – I want you to find who Nobby Clarke of Bootle is and where he is, also to tell him that a man named Skelly is a mate of Kelly's."

"Why did you say a moment ago that you knew nothing about Kelly?"

"Well I don't anything about Kelly. That is what I was told by Dennis Barker. I was just conveying a message. I heard Skelly say something to Dennis Barker. I told Balmer that Kelly and Skelly were together until 7.30 or 8 o'clock."

"Did you gather that Kelly had something to do with the murder?"

"No."

"Did you not send for Balmer to tell him the part you had taken in the Cameo murder?"

"No, I took no part in it."

"Is what you are saying this; that Kelly and Skelly were together at the murder and all these things that happened afterwards are funny?"

"Yes, a lot of things were going on."

"Did you say, 'can't you see that Kelly had his alibi fixed up right away. I have got to find one now.'?"

"Kelly had got his alibi all fixed up. I didn't know what it was."

"Did your people say something like this to you; look here, don't you be a fool, you send for the police and tell them what you know about it?"

"Yes sir."

"And it was because of that that you sent for Mr Balmer?"

"No, it was not that. It was because Barker told me to."

"You sent for Mr Balmer, but you changed your mind before he came?"

"No."

After an overnight adjournment, Mr Gorman continued his cross-examination. Connolly looked pale, the prolonged questioning taking its toll.

"Can you suggest how Graham got the information that you had talked to Balmer?"

"No, I just cannot explain. I didn't tell him anything."

"There is only one explanation, is there not? Graham is telling the truth?"

"No, he is telling lies. He used to be a cleaner in Walton. He knows the routine. He knows where to get information from. I have never been there before."

"Did you exercise with Graham?"

"Yes."

"Were you frightened at the time?"

"Well I would not say that I was exactly frightened. Just a bit nervous, that's all."

"Were you frightened of Kelly at that time?"

"Frightened of Kelly? No, why should I be?"

"Kelly had already called you yellow."

"That's according to Dickson's evidence. He didn't say that to me."

"Why did you tell Inspector Balmer, when he asked you, that you were working until after 10 o'clock on the night of the murder, if you did not know when it was, to within a week or a fortnight?"

"I did not say I was working at Bibbys on the night of the Cameo murders to Inspector Balmer."

"Inspector Balmer said, 'I asked him to account for his whereabouts on the night of the murder,' and did you reply, 'I was at work on the afternoon shift.'?"

"I said I was working around that time. I did not say about the afternoon shift."

"Were you, in fact, on the afternoon shift?"

"Yes. It was only lately I found that out."

Gorman changed the direction of his questioning.

"Did you ever say a word to Mr Balmer about having been at a dance in St Mark's Hall in Edge Lane?"

"No, I did not."

"When did you first remember that?"

"I was in Walton when I remembered."

"You did not remember that until after you were arrested?"

"No."

"Did you say to Graham, 'I don't know why I was foolish enough to have anything to do with the job. There was £15 due to me, some of it holiday pay."

"No."

"Can you think of any other people whom you have told about this £15?"

"Yes. I told it to one of the cleaners in Walton Prison." Connolly was looking in some distress. He turned to the judge and asked if he could sit down. The judge nodded, instructing one of the court ushers to bring him a glass of water. Mr Gorman went on,

"Did you tell it to one of the cleaners in this way? 'I had no need to take part in this thing. I was a fool to do it. I had this money coming to me.' ?"

"No. I didn't say that."

"That was what you told Graham."

"I didn't tell Graham anything."

Judge Oliver addressed Connolly,

"I want you to tell the jury why you should tell a cleaner how much money you had due to you at the time of the murder?"

"There was no reason for me to commit any crime if I had that money."

Mr Gorman continued. "At the police office on September 30th, did Inspector Balmer mention Saturday?"

"No. He mentioned about being in the Beehive with Northam, Dickson and a woman dressed in black."

"Did you say that you didn't know Northam?"

"I did."

"You mean you had never seen Northam to your knowledge until the day of the murder?"

"I had never seen Northam before until I was charged."

"Did you say this to Graham? 'I was with Kelly in the public-house about 7.30. A girl named Jackie Dickson and Stutty Northam were there too.'?"

"I didn't say that to Graham."

"Would Graham know that Northam was known as Stuttering Northam, unless you had told him?"

"Well, Graham was a prisoner in Walton and he had been there apparently before. Other people might have told him."

"Did you ever decide to leave the country?"

"I did put an application in, in 1946."

"On March 31st last year, did you make an application for a free passage to Australia?"

"I made that form up months before I posted it. It was a long time before."

"Did you ever discuss with Dickson that you wanted to leave the country?"

"I never."

"Can you account for her knowing on the Sunday that you were threatening to leave the country?"

"No, that is just a sort of coincidence, because I was going to leave the country a long time before."

Dancing the Rumba

Connolly was followed into the witness box by his wife, an attractive woman with fair hair. Mr Nield asked her to tell the court what she had done on the night of March 19th. Her evidence corresponded with that of her husband. When she had finished, Mr Gorman's first question in cross-examination was whether she had ever seen her husband with George Kelly.

"Never. I don't know him. I think I know most of his associates."

"Did you know Jacqueline Dickson?"

"I've seen Jacqueline Dickson on one occasion before the case. It was in Littlewoods Cafe and my husband and daughter were there."

"Do you know James Northam?"

"I have never seen Northam before the case began, nor has my husband mentioned him."

"Dickson said your husband asked her to go away with him to London. Have your relations with your husband ever been such that you would expect anything like that?"

"It was a family matter. There was trouble between my husband's father and him."

"How do you remember the night of the dance so well?"

"I sang at the dance on March 12th and won a bangle and me and my husband won a half-price ticket for a dance the following Saturday. On Saturday March 19th, me and my husband were in town shopping. We left Lewis's just about six o'clock and went on a 6a tram to Old Swan at 6.30. Charlie's mother had neuralgia and we didn't like leaving the baby. Doris and Irene went shortly after 8 o'clock. Later, Charles just picked his coat off the chair and went. About 8.30, my mother-in-law said she did not mind looking after the baby and I went to the dance too. I got to the dance hall between 8.45 and 9 o'clock and saw my husband within a few seconds. He didn't leave the dance-hall and we were together the whole evening."

"What time was the rumba competition?"

"It began between 9.45 and 10.15, and lasted about 10 minutes. Charley entered with one of his sisters and I was in it with another of his sisters. Two friends of his sisters won the competition and one of them won 20 cigarettes. There were photographers at the dance. They arrived at 10.45pm. We received two photographs that had been taken the previous week. The dance finished at 11 o'clock and we returned to Mrs Connolly's home at Old Swan."

On the Sunday, my husband and I were in our own home until late in the afternoon. My husband got up about 3 o'clock, which is his normal time for a Sunday and later we went to my mother-in-law's house."

"When did you first consider emigration?"

"In late 1946. I knew an application had been made by Charles in March or April of last year. He said no more than he usually did about leaving the country. It was a subject that was in my mind a good deal."

"Where was your husband on Monday, September 26th?"

"He went with me to Littlewoods where I was applying for a job. After lunch, we walked round the town and went into the Scala Picture House about 3.30 to 4pm. The film was 'The Last of the Redskins,' and we came out between 6.30 and 7.0."

"When did you first know about the Cameo murders?"

"On Sunday, March 20th."

Judge Oliver questioned her. "Did you read about the murder?"

"Yes. I talked about it with my husband at my mother-in-law's."

Mr Gorman continued. "When did you first remember about your husband being at the dance on the night of March 19th?"

"It was round about September 31st."

"Your husband is supposed to have said to someone that his wife would have to get him an alibi. Is it you who have acted together on this story of what happened on March 19th?"

"No. I'm telling the truth."

William Gorman's cross-examination was over and Basil Nield rose to re-examine.

"In addition to you having searched your recollection, have you a document in your possession which helped you to remember?"

"Yes."

"May I see the letter?" She handed him a letter which he looked at for a few seconds and then handed it to the judge.

"When did you write this letter?"

"I wrote it to my husband's sister and the date on the postmark on the envelope was March 18th 1949."

Nield read from the letter. (Appendix 21) Although it supported Mrs Connolly's evidence that she had been to the dance on March 19th and mentioned her winning the crooning competition, it was written before the event. Basil Nield looked up at her when he had finished reading.

"Is that the letter which you wrote to your sister-in-law?"

"Yes."

Basil Nield then called Connolly's mother, Mrs Eliza Ann Connolly. He asked her about the night of the 19th March. She confirmed that her son had left the house to go to the dance at about 8 o'clock, her daughter-in-law following him about 9 o'clock. They both returned at about 11 o'clock. She said that she remembered that week particularly because she had caught a cold and was suffering from neuralgia.

Mr Gorman cross-examined, asking her if she was sure she was describing the night of the murder.

"I knew the night of the murder was Saturday March 19th because it was in the Sunday papers. My son mentioned it when he saw the paper and asked me where it was. I said I didn't know. I remember him reading the paper and my saying that I did not know where the Cameo was. He didn't know either."

"When did you first try to remember what took place on March 19th?"

"After my son was arrested. That was some time in September. I remember that after the girls had gone to the dance, one alone and another with her girl friend, I told my son that he could go. About an hour after he had gone to the dance, I told his wife that she could go."

"Are you sure it wasn't as late as 9.30 that your daughter-in-law left?"

"No. I fixed the time when Charley went out of the house, by it being only about ten minutes after the girls went. I could not say exactly, because there was no clock and I was in some discomfort."

"Is it true to say that you have no idea of the time your son went?"

"I am going by the time my daughter came home from work."

The next witness was Connolly's sister Doris who gave evidence about the dance on March 12th when her brother and his wife were photographed. She said her brother's wife sang 'Sorrento' in the crooning competition and won a bracelet. She went to another dance on March 19th, leaving the house for the dance, after her brother and his wife arrived. They had the baby and did not like going but her mother said they might as well. She confirmed that her brother had left before Mrs Connolly.

The judge intervened abruptly.

"Don't tell us what you have been told. Were you there when he left the house?"

"No. I got to the dance about 8 o'clock. My brother arrived there about 9.00 to about 9.30. I saw him arriving. His wife Mary came along in about 10 minutes. There was a rumba dancing competition and I took part in it with Mary as my partner."

Judge Oliver again broke in.

"At what time was the rumba competition?"

"About half-past nine."

"It was a long time after this dance that you began to talk about it at home as to where you had been that night, wasn't it?"

"Yes."

Connolly's other sister, eighteen year old Irene, then gave evidence that she remembered the photographer being at the dance on March 12th and she remembered March 19th because that was the day when her mother suffered with her teeth. Mr Gorman questioned her.

"Have you never tried to remember what happened on the night of the murder?"

"No, sir."

"Do you say you have never, in your family, discussed the happenings on the night of the murder?"

"No."

Mr Gorman commented drily. "Of course you have. Has the discussion been to try and throw your minds back to what happened?"

"Yes."

"As a matter of fact, until the discussion you had in October, you had completely forgotten about it?"

Irene Connolly hesitated before replying. "Some parts."

"And you never tried before to remember about the photographs? You had forgotten all about it, hadn't you?" There was no reply and she was clearly becoming confused. William Gorman continued.

"How long after your brother arrived did the rumba competition begin?"

"My brother arrived at the dance about 8.30. The rumba competition started about 9.30."

"It might have been quarter to nine when your brother arrived that night. One of your sisters has said it was between 9 and 9.30?"

"It might have been that time when I first saw him."

Judge Oliver broke in. "But your sister said she saw him arrive between 9 and 9.30. You say you saw him there about 8.30. Do you really remember those times? It might have been ten o'clock when he arrived?"

"No, it was not 10."

Mr Gorman continued.

"How do you know it was not 10 o'clock?"

"Because he danced the rumba competition with me. He was there well before the dance was over." There was a slight pause before William Gorman continued, almost sorrowfully, shaking his head.

"You haven't any idea when he was there, have you?"

"It might have been 8.30 when he was there."

" If your sister says he arrived between 9 and 9.30, he could not have been there at 8.30?"

"There was no clock."

Basil Nield re-examined, the case was losing credibility.

"In the course of your family discussions did you do your best to remember?"

"Yes."

Other witnesses at the dance then gave evidence of having seen Connolly in the rumba competition. Seventeen year old Teresa McCormack said she knew Charles Connolly and his wife and the whole family. She remembered the dance and said that Charles Connolly was dancing with his sister in the rumba competition somewhere about 10.15.

Another seventeen year old, Elizabeth Dixon, said she arrived at the dance about 7.50. She saw Charles Connolly at the time of the rumba competition. She thought it would be between 9 30 and 10 o'clock. She also saw his wife there.

Thomas Henry Milligan, a photographer said he recognised a photograph of Mr and Mrs Connolly as one he had taken on March 12th. The first opportunity he had of delivering the prints was March 19th but he did not remember who paid the balance of the money for the photograph. It was necessary, however, for him to be handed the ticket and that he usually attended these dances at any time between 10 and 11 o'clock.

Prosecuting counsel cross-examined him.

"If people who had photographs taken on the 12th did not turn up on the 19th, when would they get them?"

"I would take them along again on the 26th."

"These photographs may have been picked up on the 26th?"

"That I can't say."

"The greater part of your business is after 10 o'clock when the public houses closed?"

"Yes."

By now, the eyes of some of the jury were becoming glazed, they were confused by the minutiae of evidence; times, places, arrivals, dances but still they had to sit, patient and mute, trying to be attentive. But in the whole courtroom, everyone paid attention as they listened to the evidence of the next witness which was especially critical.

Charles McBain was the dance organiser at St Mark's Church. He said that on Saturday, March 12th there was a crooning competition and Mrs Mary Connolly sang 'Be mine', which was a popular tune at that time. He continued by saying that he remembered Connolly was at the dance on March 12th and remembered seeing Connolly at a dance very soon after March 12th but that he did not see him at the dance on March 19th before 10 o'clock. He had his hat on and he asked him to take it off.

Michael O'Hanlon, a barman and billiards room attendant at the Vines Hotel and James O'Reilly, a door attendant at the Lime Tree Cafe, both said they had known Charles Connolly for a number of years and did not know Kelly and had never seen Connolly with him.

The final witness for Connolly was Father Thomas Frayne, assistant priest at St Columba's Church, who confirmed that Connolly had consulted him about emigrating to Australia sometime after March 1949.

A curious form of curiosity

For almost everyone in the court room, perhaps even the judge, the high point of the trial was the turn of George Kelly's defence to make its case.

Rose Heilbron's opening statement was meticulous. She had worked hard on it, carefully rewriting and discarding that which would not influence the jury. It was remarkably incisive, identifying and attempting to destroy the circumstantial evidence the prosecution had mustered. She pleaded earnestly, rhetorical questions accompanied by a feminine lift of the chin, her eyes returning to the large printed characters on the sheaf of papers in her hand, discarded pages fluttering in a steady flow to the bench.

She knew it would be a difficult defence to make, the guilt of her client had increased; by headline, by innuendo and by the coverage of the committal proceedings. Everyone in the court, including the judge, believed they knew something. But only Chief Inspector Herbert Balmer knew the whole truth. Rose Heilbron nodded pleasantly to the jury before addressing them.

"All those who are taking part in this murder trial, labour under a very real anxiety, which deepens day by day, that the truth and only the truth be elicited from the mass of evidence that has been heard and will be heard during this very grave case. If justice is to be done, guilt must be clearly proved and then, and then only, will the tragic deaths be avenged.

It is suggested for your consideration that on the night of March 19th of last year, five people congregated in the public part of a well-known public-house on the busiest night of the week in the centre of this town. There, it is said, a bulky gun was produced and loaded with bullets. There, it is said, a handkerchief was tied round a man's face to see if it would fit for a mask and there the details of this terrible crime were plotted.

The story does not end there, the improbabilities thicken and strengthen. You are taken next day to another public-house and there, within an hour of closing time on Sunday afternoon, these people again foregather, not in some dark corner, not in some secret place, not a suggestion that they even lowered their voices, but again in an even more public part of an equally public bar in this same city.

You are expected to believe that Kelly gave to Northam as graphic and detailed an account of the murders as a Somerset Maugham short story.

If this story had been given to you by witnesses of unimpeachable veracity, I venture to say you would have been inclined to disbelieve, but you have had the opportunity now of seeing and hearing Mr Northam and Mrs Dickson, and have heard them on oath. You have had the opportunity of hearing them under cross-examination. I will, at a later stage, deal in some detail with this story, this incredible story and with the truth or falsity of their evidence. To put it at its lowest, they are people who are quite unworthy of belief.

You might think the evidence of Northam and Dickson was fantastic, and that the evidence of Graham was even more improbable. For six weeks, Kelly lay in prison and all that time and even since, he had strenuously denied complicity in the murder. There was little to prevent him talking to his co-prisoner Connolly and yet, on a Wednesday in the middle of November, they happened in there to meet a man who was not only a complete stranger and to whom Kelly unburdened his soul. Not only did he say, I did it, which would have been quite sufficient but he was so minded to confess. Not only did he tell this perfect stranger details of the crime he was alleged to have committed but he went on in great detail to tell him of the plan alleged to have taken place in the Beehive. He didn't stop there apparently, for Graham said he told him of meetings afterwards in The Star and with Dickson.

Is this not a very strange and remarkable story. Is it not inconceivable? And the police, with all their resources and after exhaustive enquiries, in my submission, cannot produce independent evidence."

Rose Heilbron then moved on to review the evidence of what had happened in the cinema, concluding, with emphasis, that the time the shots were fired was 9.40 and that, although there were gaps in Kelly's movements on March 19th, it was impossible to produce witnesses for every hour of the day, ten months ago.

She then dealt with the police evidence, asking the jury if they could rely on the report of Chief Inspector Balmer, as they could upon a verbatim report, if he had written it down at the time when it was said to him.

She went on to refute the evidence of police witnesses who had seen Kelly and Connolly together and that of the witness Dowling who, many months after the incident, could recall that he saw Kelly at a certain spot, at a certain time, on a certain date.

Miss Heilbron continued.

"The case for the prosecution is that Kelly was in the Spofforth Arms just before the murder was committed. It was true he was at the Spofforth Arms without a hat and coat and without Connolly. It was alleged that he went into the Spofforth Arms without his coat. That he donned his coat to go to the Cameo and that he took it off to go to the Leigh Arms. Is that not an amazing thing?

Kelly's house was searched the following day. No overcoat was found, no gun and no bullets. You have heard from Dr Grace and the other police witnesses of the large amount of blood splashed about on the floor of the manager's office and you might think the man who did this, might have had blood on the soles of his shoes.

Northam and Dickson have described the mask as being dark brown, but witnesses from the cinema have said it was black and have gone further and said it was black silk. You might think the overcoat was a very important part of the evidence in this case, but it is a fact that the overcoat was mentioned for the first time on October 9th and that it was eight or nine days after Kelly had been charged with the murder.

You have heard Northam's amazing story about lending the overcoat and the way he got it back. Members of the jury, do you believe one word of it? And there was another peculiar thing, the bullets. The story of Mrs Dickson carrying twenty-three bullets in a handkerchief because she was the sort of person who was even willing to do a good turn for a dog. She said she was not concerned, or had any idea until she got home to Northam, as to what was in the handkerchief. They extracted six for curiosity and because Northam wanted to show them to the police."

There was only the faintest pause before Miss Heilbron continued.

"Don't you think it was a curious form of curiosity? Dickson, when asked about the anonymous letter, said she could not remember details because it was so long back. In the witness box, however, she could come along and give a detailed and substantial story of what took place. You might think about that. If those two people were telling the truth they would be able to tell exactly what they did, but there were discrepancies. These are the two people whose evidence forms the basis of this case. You have these two witnesses who got all the assurance they wanted from the police in that advertisement in the Echo and yet, when they saw the police in May, they only told half the story."

Miss Heilbron returned again to the question of independent evidence.

"Who saw Kelly and Connolly together that night? There is no evidence that Northam and Dickson were seen with them. There is no independent evidence that Kelly and Connolly were in the White Star on Sunday morning. As for Graham, the only matters on which Kelly allegedly spoke to him, were matters which, in my submission, were already known to the prosecution.

And Graham did not ask him any of the vital factors which a guilty man must know. If Kelly was so ready and willing to confide, why not a word about the gun, the mask and the overcoat? Matters which, if the guilty man was ready to confess, one might have thought he would mention, if only out of a spirit of bravado.

You might wish to consider the evidence most carefully. Not only Kelly confesses but, marvel upon marvel, so does Connolly, and the confessions take the same form.

Is this the sort of evidence you can say, without reasonable doubt, is convincing. Are you satisfied, beyond all reasonable doubt, that you know who did, in fact, commit this murder? If you are satisfied of the guilt of George Kelly, you will not hesitate to say so, but if you are not, then your verdict must be one of not guilty."

Her speech completed, Rose Heilbron turned and called George Kelly to the witness box. There was an eager, almost excited atmosphere as Kelly came into view, those at the rear of the court craning forward for a better view.

"Did you shoot Leonard Thomas or Bernard Catterall at the Cameo Cinema on March 19th?"

"No"

"Were you at the Cameo Cinema on March 19th?"

"Never."

"Can you account for your movements on March 19th from about 1.30?"

Kelly looked nervous as he repeated his account of his movements that day, gradually becoming more assured as his evidence continued. (Appendix 22) He related how he had met James Skelly, visited a public house and then spent some time helping his mother on her fruit and flower stall, before going to the Ludo Club. At 5.30, they went to the Royal William and left there, eventually going to the Coach and Horses. Kelly said he left about 8.30 and caught a tram to the Leigh Arms, after which he went to look for Doris O'Malley, calling at the house next to hers to enquire where she was, to be told she had gone to the Spofforth Arms. Kelly then said he called there about 9.15 for a drink. He then went back to the Leigh Arms, getting there about 9.25 and remaining until closing time.

Kelly then went on to describe the visit of Chief Inspector Balmer the following morning and how he had told Balmer everything he had done the previous day and evening. He concluded his evidence-in-chief by describing the visit with the police to Skelly's house, where Balmer was shown Skelly's overcoat.

"Did Skelly say, 'I suppose he was one of the fellows who took me home and I was too drunk to know.'?"

"No. Inspector Balmer just said, 'That's OK.'"

"Where were you on September 26th, four days before you were arrested, in the afternoon?"

"Miss Dutton and a girl I think was Miss Smith, came to Liverpool to my mother's house about 3pm. I saw them there and remained with them. We had tea and listened to the radio and went out about 7 to 7.30. I saw them on to the midnight train to London."

"Do you know Northam or Dickson?"

"I have never seen the two of them in my life before this case. I had been asked by Inspector Balmer if I knew Connolly, Dickson or Northam and when I went into the charge room, Connolly was sitting down in the dock. Although I have never seen Connolly in my life before, I automatically realised he was the man who was being charged with me, because there were no other prisoners there."

"You know it is alleged that you said, 'You have never seen me in your life before, have you? You don t know me.'?"

"I didn't say that, but I said words to that effect. I don't deny it."

"What conversation did you have with Graham?"

"I didn't speak to Graham about the murder. Graham asked me what I was in for and I told him that I was charged with the Cameo murders. I didn't say anything else. My cell in the prison was about ten yards away from Connolly's and we talked every night."

"Did you ever see Connolly in any other connection in prison?"

"Yes, I sat next to him in church."

"Give the court an account of what you said to Inspector Balmer on the occasion of the identification parade, when Sangster identified you."

"I said, 'I won't forget you for this.'"

"What made you say that?"

"I had already been identified by Dickson, whom I had never seen in my life and

Northam, whom I had never seen before, and by this chap out of Lewis's, whom I knew very well. I was boiling at the time, because I was charged with a murder I did not commit."

When Kelly had completed his evidence-in-chief, William Gorman began his cross-examination.

"Why were you going to hold it in your memory?"

"The reason was it was a thing I would never forget, the Inspector charging me with murder."

"Is it because you took the view, 'I am Kelly.'?"

"I didn't say 'I am Kelly'. I didn't adopt that attitude at all."

"Did you, in fact, adopt the attitude that you were something quite different from other ordinary people?"

"No."

"When Inspector Balmer saw you on Sunday March 20th, did you know at what time the murder had taken place?"

"I knew about it. I read it in the newspapers, but I didn't take any particular notice of the time it was stated to have happened."

"What time did the police visit you?"

"I can't swear if it was in the morning or the afternoon. Every Sunday I always got up about 11 to 11.30."

"You have given to the jury a most exact account of what happened on the Saturday, the day before. Can you account for not even remembering whether it was morning or afternoon when the police came the following day?"

"It would be quite easy for me to say morning or afternoon, but I am on oath and don't remember. I remember going to the pub until two o'clock and I thought it was before I went to the pub that Mr Balmer came."

"Balmer says he was there about 11.15. Do you quarrel with that statement."

"I don't know. I don't dispute it."

"Do you agree you had been with Inspector Balmer to Skelly's house and got back to your house before you went in the pub?"

Kelly agreed willingly.

"Could have been."

"Do you agree that Balmer left you by the end of your street about 12 o'clock?"

"I don't think it is much good me disagreeing."

"Did you hear Mr Balmer say that on the Sunday when he saw you, you never mentioned also being in the Spofforth Arms?"

"That is what Balmer says. I told him everywhere I was."

"What Mr Balmer says here is very different from what you were saying now as to your whereabouts that night."

"Yes."

"When did you first meet Jacqueline Dickson?"

"I first saw her at the identity parade in Dale Street."

"Are you saying you had no conversation with her?"

"I did not know Dickson. I could not say anything to her. I don't know any of them in this case. I don't know what I'm doing in this Hall today."

"When you met Connolly in the charge room, did you say, 'You've never seen me in your life before, have you? You don't know me.'?"

"I can't remember the exact words but something to that effect. If the police say I used them, then I must have done."

"The whole object was to let Connolly know beforehand that he had to say he didn't know you?"

"If I had known Connolly before, we could have made up some alibi and not waited until we got to the police station."

"Why did you borrow the overcoat from Northam?"

"I had no need to borrow a coat. I deny everything Graham said in this court. He stood in the witness box and committed perjury."

"But you told him about the shooting."

"Why should I pour my heart out to that man and not to other people?"

"You also told Northam."

"I said nothing to Northam. Northam is a man who seems to know more about this than me."

Prosecuting counsel continued dispassionately.

"What Northam says you said to him, seems to be a fairly accurate account of what other witnesses say happened."

"He knows all the answers. It was all in the papers after that man Johnson was tried. This has been well manufactured against me and Connolly and all I can say is that I am innocent and have never shot any man and would not."

"Did you say to the taxi driver, 'Hello, pal, you can have the best in the house'?"

"I might have done because I'm silly like that. I don't think I said that though, because the best in the house was whisky and that was expensive. I might have said, 'You can have a drink.' I'd treated the man before. I didn't tell him that I'd been having a go and I didn't hear any woman asking the taxi-driver what 'having a go' meant. It might have meant having a go at darts and I might have used the expression, 'on the bevvy', meaning on the booze."

"How should Graham know that you were in the Leigh Arms drinking about a quarter to ten?"

Kelly missed the chance of making a point, the evidence that he was in the Leigh Arms at 9.45 having been given in detail at the committal proceedings, his answer was vague; "Graham talked to a lot of people. I suppose he has read the newspapers. I have told a lot of people in prison. I have spoken to fifty or sixty in prison and to quite a few about the evidence against me."

"Is the Leigh Arms the pub you usually go to?"

"Yes."

"Can you think how Graham should get to know about this pub?"

"He could have got to know through the cleaners. I had told the cleaners about the case and had told them that I was in the Leigh Arms that night."

"Did you also tell the cleaners that your life depended on five minutes?"

"No, my life does not depend on five minutes, because I am innocent."

"Can you suggest how Graham got to know that? Is it not that you, in fact, said that to him?"

"I've had no idea how Graham got to know that and the only suggestion I can make was that Graham was in a jam and wanted to give evidence against me, as he thought that might be the best way to get out of it. I say that because he stood in this witness-box and told lies against me. There is no other way of looking at it and I still say that I am innocent. I don't know anything about this murder."

"Are you suggesting, Kelly, that Graham has invented what he has told us?"

"I am not saying he invented it. He could have been told."

"Did you hear Mr Balmer say that on the Sunday when he saw you, you never mentioned the Spofforth Arms, the Ludo Club, or the Liverpool Arms, and that the only public houses you mentioned were the Coach and Horses and the one near your street, the Leigh Arms?"

"That is what Balmer says. I told him everywhere I was. I disagree entirely with Inspector Balmer's account of the Sunday morning interview. I first began to think about where I was on the night of the murder after I had been interviewed by Inspector Balmer and I might have been seen hundreds of times in the Beehive public-house. After the night of the murder, I was in scores of times but was not there on the night of the murder."

"Is the girl who has been described as dark and heavily made-up, Norwegian Margie?" There was an outburst of laughter in the court and this brought immediate rebuke from the judge.

"If there is any more laughter, I shall have the court cleared."

"I know a Marjory Dawson but I don't know if she was the woman known as Norwegian Margie."

"Do you know she has committed suicide?"

"I don't know."

"Can you account for Graham knowing about Dickson, unless you told him?"

"How could I tell Graham about her, if I did not know her. There are plenty of people in prison who talk to Graham. I deny everything Graham said in this court. He stood in this witness-box and committed perjury."

Mr Gorman read from Graham's evidence about how the man had been shot and how the door appeared to be locked.

"Did you say that?"

"I have never shot anyone in my life. I've never opened any doors or pushed any doors."

"What about these statements you made to Northam?"

"I said nothing to Northam. Northam is the man who seems to know more about this than me."

"Can you could suggest how Northam could give the details of what happened inside the manager's office at the time of the shooting, unless someone had told him."

"Northam is the one who knows all about it, all about the lock business and the spiral staircase. He has told the story. He seems to know more about it than anyone else."

The judge sat forward.

"Do you mean that he could have done it himself or that the real murderer did it?"

"I suggest that if Northam has done this murder, he has blamed two strangers. I don't know Connolly. I have never shot anybody. I am innocent."

Marvel upon marvel

Rose Heilbron then called witnesses for the defence. First to take the stand was George Ross McKinnon, who said he remembered being in the Beehive on the night of March 19th and did not see Kelly, who he knew, in the passage at any time. He was followed into the witness box by Gordon Manson who said that, while he was in the passage that night, there were between sixteen and twenty people there. At no time did he see Kelly, whom he knew by sight.

Miss Heilbron then called John Gardner to the stand. He said his nickname was Yorkie and that he had seen Kelly and Skelly together on the night of March 19th in the Royal William at about 6.40. and that they had a round of drinks, leaving about 7.30.

There was a murmur of anticipation in the court when Rose Heilbron called James Skelly to the stand and asked him to tell the court what happened on March 19th. Skelly recounted the events of that day. They coincided closely with the statement given by Kelly, confirming that they had got to the Coach and Horses about 7.30 and had remained there until closing time, Kelly leaving earlier, about 9 o'clock. Skelly was then helped home by a neighbour named Taffy Roberts. In cross-examination Mr Gorman asked, "What did you have on when the police came?"

"I can't remember. I had a bad hangover. Inspector Balmer asked if I owned a brown overcoat. I showed them mine and the other officer who was with Balmer said, 'That is just the thing'. The inspector then said, 'Where is the gun?' I was surprised when they did not take the coat away."

Mr Gorman commented. "A remarkable thing. They find the coat they are looking for and they leave it with you?"

"I was surprised."

"You have been in the hands of the police on a great number of occasions?"

"Yes."

"Knowing the sort of things the police do, you would be amazed that they would leave behind the very thing for which they were looking?"

"That is why I was amazed."

Skelly's record was then read. It started with petty stealing and escalated to house-breaking and shop-breaking and then on to several cases of unlawful wounding and assault occasioning bodily harm, for which he had spent several years in prison. He was then asked,

"How did you remember that Kelly was with you until 9 o'clock?"

"I looked at the clock at 8.55 and Kelly had left."

"Suppose Kelly says he left you at 8.30?"

"That is probably right, because the clock is usually twenty minutes fast."

Miss Heilbron re-examined.

"It is said that on the Sunday morning of March 20th, you were in the Star public house in Brownlow Hill with Kelly, Connolly and Jacqueline Dickson and James Northam."

"Never. I don't know Dickson or Northam."

Mr Gorman then further cross-examined,

"Were you in the Star at all that day?"

"I go there regularly and was there at 7 o'clock on the Sunday evening. When

Inspector Balmer was leaving my house with Kelly, Kelly shouted out, 'I will see you tonight at Charlie's.'"

Fred Thomalla, the manager of the Leigh Arms, was next to give evidence for the defence. "Kelly came into the bar and asked if I had seen Doris. He ordered a pint. He then left and said he was going across the road to Bramley's."

"Kelly was not in your public house at 9.30 on the night of March 19th?"

"Not to my knowledge."

Mr Gorman read from a statement,

"'I am quite definite that George Kelly was not in my house at 9.30pm on the night of the Cameo murders but he was in the buffet at 9.50pm.' Is that true?"

"Yes."

The judge then questioned him.

"You said you were certain Kelly was not in your house at 9.30?"

"I really meant I did not see him at that time. At 9.30 I was serving customers and there were probably forty or fifty in the bar."

Rose Heilbron re-examined.

"It would be quite possible for someone to be in your bar and for you not to see them?"

"Yes. People were three or four deep and I could not see people sat down at the back."

"What time did he come in on the Sunday?"

"Shortly after I opened at 12.30. He stayed there until 2 o'clock."

"How do you know he was there all the time?"

"I knew he had been interviewed by Balmer. He was very upset. He was sitting in a seat looking terribly worried. I looked at the clock. It was five minutes to one. I don't suppose I looked at it when Kelly came in, but he was there until two o'clock, he was so upset."

Walter Bampton was the next defence witness to be questioned by Miss Heilbron. He stated that on the night of March 19th he was in the Leigh Arms at 9.30 with his brother Charles.

"We went in the side door leading straight into the bar. Kelly was in the bar opposite us as we walked in by the buffet door. I was there about twenty minutes and when I left, Kelly was still there." He said he had fixed the time by looking at the clock in the bar, which is facing the door. Charles Bampton then followed his brother into the witness box and confirmed that Kelly was standing in the bar near to the door leading to the buffet when they got to the Leigh Arms at about 9.30pm.

There was a slight rustle of renewed interest in the court as Miss Colleen Monica Dutton was announced. It was known from the general publicity about the trial that she was supposed to be Kelly's girlfriend. Now the public, and even the lawyers present, were curious to see if this meant the end of Kelly's relationship with Doris O'Malley. She was questioned by Rose Heilbron, who asked her how she came to be in Liverpool on September 26th.

"George sent a money order and telephoned me. I came to Liverpool on September 26th and arrived there about 2.30 to 2.45. George arrived about the same time. We stayed there until about 7.20 and then went out for a few drinks and I got the midnight train to London."

Mr Gorman cross-examined.

"Was your association with George Kelly a very close one?"

"Yes. He is a very good friend of mine."

"Are you in love with George Kelly?"

"Yes, sir."

William Gorman's next question was prurient and even the judge lifted his eyes and frowned disapprovingly.

"Is he the father of the child you are going to have?"

"I am not going to have a child."

"Has George Kelly ever been intimate with you?" There was a gasp to be heard in the court as she answered,

"No." She was reduced to tears as she left the court, assisted by her friend.

The examination of witnesses was over. Now was the last chance for the defence counsels to make their case.

Basil Nield, for Connolly, was first to address the court. His speech was brief; he started by emphasising the sharp and contrasting distinction between each of the cases of the men in the dock.

"If you sought to view in broad outline the case heard so far as Connolly is concerned, you would come to the conclusion that the two accounts of what happened on the night of March 19th, are quite irreconcilable.

This means, that in the course of your deliberations, ultimately you will have to decide where the truth lies and which of these accounts is right, bearing in mind, of course, that the prosecution have the burden passed upon them of proving the charge that they make. In either event, you ought to find Connolly not guilty.

The defence asserts that he was not in any public house, not outside the cinema and throughout that evening he was dancing at St Mark's Church Hall.

The golden rule is that the Crown must prove that which it set out to prove. You must keep in mind that some witnesses were accomplices, whose evidence is suspect. There is no justification to say that Connolly aided and abetted.

And then there is Northam's allegation against Mr Livermore. This is a wicked lie, designed to lay blame even more strongly elsewhere, by a man who was in fear that he might be charged as an accessory and might appear in the dock.

Northam's evidence is not acceptable. There was something said in oath by him which is palpably untrue. He was a witness who did not hesitate to assert that a solicitor acting for the defence of Kelly had invited him, for reward, to change his evidence.

And Jacqueline Dickson presents a tragic figure and we cannot run ourselves away from the fact that she is a woman of loose morals. She is of a class of people, for whom one may have more sympathy than censure.

Graham is man who has a criminal record for fraud. You are then bound to observe the sort of man he is. When, added to that, you have the fact that he was, for a period, in a mental institution, surely doubt is cast upon whether he could say what is actually true.

Connolly's defence is that he has an alibi. I want to make this point as strongly as I can. What was the Crown's attitude at the onset to that defence? This is a lying, concocted story, that you were not at St Mark's Church Hall at all.

I submit that Mrs Connolly's letter helped her to remember what did happen and it would be quite wrong, any more, to suggest that Connolly was not at that dance.

Charles Connolly took no part in the criminal offence on the night of March 19th. In the evidence on the part of Kelly, was it not plain that there was no plot such as was spoken of?"

Basil Nield then completed his closing statement.

"I ask you to come to a conclusion; use this test. Would it not be right, in the years ahead, when you look back on the Cameo murders trial, to be able to say, 'I know that what I did was right'? If you look back and say, 'I think' or 'I hope,' then your verdict will not be right. In the case of Charles Connolly, I submit the just, fair and right thing to do, is to return a verdict of not guilty."

It was now Rose Heilbron's turn to speak in defence of Kelly. She must have been confident of an acquittal. The evidence against George Kelly was circumstantial. There was no gun, no overcoat, no hat and the only evidence was by three convicted criminals. All she had to do now, was to stress these points and emphasise the flaws in the prosecution's arguments.

"I remind you that there is no identification on which you can rely, of the man who did the killing. There was no connection in the sense that, no gun, overcoat or mask, was found on my client. If the overcoat produced in court was the one the man was wearing, then you may think strange happenings were attached to it, because Northam said it was returned to him on Monday September 21st and there it remained. The most remarkable fact is that the coat was not disclosed to the police until October 9th. The fact that no mention of the coat being loaned to Kelly is one of the most curious and strange features of the case, because October 9th was nine days after Kelly was charged with the murder. If Northam and Dickson were out to tell the police the true story of what had happened, they would not have left out one of the most important factors in the case.

I urge you not to rely on the evidence of Northam and Dickson. On the evidence of Northam and Dickson, this particular crime was the suggestion of Connolly and it was suggested that Kelly, who was alleged to have done the killing, was quite unprepared. That, in fact, he had suggested one or two other jobs. Yet this man, who had only planned this murder about an hour or so before its commission, seems to have worked out, according to the prosecution, so neatly, an alibi whereby he gets rid of everything which might identify him.

The prosecution said that it was highly suspicious that Kelly was rolling and excited in the Leigh Arms. But you will remember the evidence, for both the prosecution and defence, that he had been drinking, that George Kelly had a fair amount of drink by 9.45 and started to treat old ladies, the staff and the manger. You may think he was feeling a little generous.

Let me deal with times. Mrs Jackman said the shot was between 9.39 and 9.44. Griffin, the doorman, said the cash was taken upstairs at 9.35 by his watch and that he heard a shot while in the staff room at 9.42. Miss Thornhill put the time of the shots as 9.46 but she may be a little incorrect. Mrs Stevens thought it was 9.30 when Mrs Jackman went through the auditorium and Mrs Watkins said when she heard the shots she saw a clock and said it was 9.35. Mrs Simpson heard bangs which you might think were the actual shots and she put the time at 9.32. This conflicts with the other evidence in the case and perhaps the safest way of dealing with this case, is to come to the conclusion that approximately 9.40 was the time of the murder.

Three witnesses have spoken about seeing Kelly and Connolly together. This is by no means definite. Apparently, they are such complete and utter fools, that they go about town together, after the crime, from time to time in full view of the whole city and the police.

Let us consider the charge room incident. The evidence showed that Connolly was in a little dock or pen surrounded by a number of police. It would be reasonable to believe that if Kelly had known Connolly, there was ample opportunity over many months, when they knew the police were investigating, for them to have agreed, instead of making such stupid remarks at the police station. The only reasonable inference is that Kelly did not know Connolly, but realised after being charged along with a man named Connolly, that the other man was Connolly.

At the identification parade at which Kelly was supposed to have remarked to Inspector Balmer, 'If it is the last thing I do, I will get you for this', I put it to Mr Balmer that it was 'I will not forget you for this.' Whatever view you take of the actual words, are you going to give it very much consideration when trying an issue of this kind? A man in the heat of the moment, might say something for which he might well be sorry the next moment.

The witness, Dowling, said that Kelly was always cutting through Cases Street, but did not remember having seen him at any other particular time. His evidence was given to the police many many months after the incident and he could not even remember how Kelly was dressed when he saw him on the night of March 19th. In my submission his evidence is unreliable.

Concerning Chief Inspector Balmer's evidence and his admission that the notes he made of the interview with Kelly on the Sunday morning March 20th, were written down some time after the interview had actually taken place, you may think that there is room for mistake. If Chief Inspector Balmer had jotted it down immediately, there is less room for mistake. Although no one could be infallible about a conversation written down some three quarters of an hour later, would you like to swear as to its accuracy and say it is so accurate that, therefore, if Kelly says something rather different, he may be right?

The evidence of the cinema witnesses was that the mask worn by the man was not a dark brown apron but that it was a black mask and two witnesses had described it as being a silk mask.

Northam and Dickson said that Kelly threw the gun in the lake in Botanic Park and took a 6a tram car. It might well be if a man was hurrying, as no doubt the killer was from the Cameo, he could get to the Leigh Arms in about five minutes, but could he get to the Botanic Park, throw the gun in the lake, get a car and be back in the Leigh Arms at ten minutes to ten? That was impossible so far as Kelly is concerned, because he was in the Leigh Arms at 9.45.

Graham himself said he sent for the police about the confessions that had been made to him and I asked him why didn't he go to the Governor of the prison and he said it was too important to tell the Governor." Rose Heilbron shook her head in mock disbelief. "The governor of Walton Prison?" She then continued.

"You might be surprised and you might wish to consider the evidence most carefully. Not only Kelly confesses but, marvel upon marvel, so does the other man, Connolly and the confessions take the same form.

Graham is another man in this case with a wonderful memory for conversation but he said he never read anything in the papers about the case and never discussed it, although he was not in prison at the time of the committal proceedings.

According to Graham, Kelly had said that his life depended on five minutes but you might think, in view of the evidence of Northam and Dickson as to what happened to the gun, that his life did not depend on five minutes.

The most important evidence is that of Northam and Dickson. They said there was no one in the passage way the whole time of the alleged planning. Other witnesses said there were a considerable number of people in the passage. Which is the truth at 7.30 to 8.30 on a Saturday night?

You will remember that Northam suggested the gun came from Kelly's hip pocket. If Kelly had entered the Beehive without an overcoat, as the prosecution suggested, you are asked to believe that he walked into the public house with a gun in his hip pocket, which the expert has described as bulky. The police, with all their resources and after exhaustive inquiries, could not and, in my submission, have not, produced independent evidence; evidence of other people quite apart from Northam and Dickson, who could say that they saw Kelly with a gun. There was no evidence of any gun having been sold to Kelly and no evidence from the Beehive of anyone who ever saw Kelly and Connolly together on March 19th.

In my submission every part of the prosecution's case falls down under critical examination and analysis and, you may think, in a matter so great as this, it would be unsafe to rely upon the evidence called before you, to prove that Kelly did the murder.

I trust that, in your deliberations you will be guided by that consideration of justice of which we, in this Crown and the summing up of his Lordship, I trust you will then clear my client from this dreadful charge and allow him to leave the court a free man."

Where, oh where, is Doris O'Malley?

William Gorman stood up, stern of face, staring slowly around the court room, his gaze finally settling on the jury. He ignored the men in the dock, his final speech for the Crown, slow and almost mordant.

"Kelly is guilty of murder and Connolly, the man who planned it, went with Kelly and was there when the shot was fired, is also guilty of murder. I need not remind you that 'reasonable doubt' does not mean the manufacturing of doubt in order to avoid some unpleasant decision.

It is always the province of those who appeared for the defence to attack, should they so desire it, the character of witnesses for the Crown, so that ultimately they could say to you, would you believe this man because this is his character?

Members of the jury, has this occurred to you; supposing I had said in opening this case, that the planning by Kelly and Connolly was done in the presence of the Chief Constable of Liverpool and the Archbishop of Canterbury, would you have believed a word of it? Whatever I said, would you believe that those men would have planned that, in the presence of two men whose whole outlook is above the slightest suspicion?

Mr Nield, in bringing before you the character of Northam and Dickson, has given them the very type of people in whose presence a thing of that kind would be discussed, people who might not be averse to taking part in it, men and women who might not be unduly shocked at some part of the crime.

God knows the character of that woman has been battered about this court, she may earn her living in the streets, she may be unfortunate but it comes ill, members of the jury, to combine sympathy for this woman in her illness, with the case for the defence against that woman, that she is willing to sell the life of these men by going into that box and committing perjury.

You did not hear a single word against Graham's character, or against his honesty, when he was in the witness box but it has been put to you that Graham has been in a mental home. Has it occurred to you that it was not quite the right thing to base the case and the final speech upon considerations of that kind, when not one single suggestion has been made when he was in the witness box?

There is an absence of certain defence witnesses through illness. I remind you that Mrs Doris O'Malley was with Kelly in the house in Cambridge Street when he was interviewed by the police on the Sunday morning after the murder. Where, oh where, is Mrs Doris O'Malley? Is she ill? She was the lady with whom Kelly was living at the time and, therefore, she might have been not unwilling to help, if it had been thought desirable to ask her to go into the witness box, so that you might determine whether the evidence as to her, is in conflict with other evidence and what her version is.

I want now to ask you to consider the events of Sunday March 20th, particularly in relation to Connolly but, of course, it must have repercussions upon the case of Kelly, too. You will remember that when Skelly was called on behalf of Kelly and just before I commenced to cross-examine him the second time, he made use of this expression, 'When Mr Balmer and Kelly were leaving me on the Sunday, Kelly said – I will see you at Charlie's.'

We know that Charlie's is this public house; The Star, in Brownlow Hill. The significance of that is this, that here is a public house known to Skelly and Kelly familiarly as 'Charlie's'. On the Saturday night, Dickson and Northam were told that they would meet the next day at a public house frequented by Kelly in Brownlow Hill. How did they know that, if they were complete strangers to Kelly? They went there and there were Skelly and Kelly. Could you have any doubt that that evidence was right?

Remember the evidence or Mr McBain. If that was right, Connolly did not go to St Mark's Hall until after 10pm and a member of Connolly's family, who said he was at the dance round about 8 o'clock, must be wrong. If they were wrong, and they never started to think about an alibi until September or October, could you rely on their evidence?

You should make every allowance for the fact that a man in Kelly's position must be in a state of utmost tension when giving evidence but how did he strike you? Did he strike you as a bravado? If you accept Balmer's evidence, do you not get a measure of the man? You might remember his denials, and the manner of his denials, the alleged remark in the Beehive, 'I am Kelly'.

Let me deal with the evidence of Mr Thomalla, licensee of the Leigh Arms, who said he was quite definite that Kelly was not in his public house at 9.30 but he was in the buffet at 9.50. Mr Thomalla was an ex-police constable with many years experience and did it avail anyone to suggest that when an ex-police officer says, 'I am quite definite' he means 'I am not at all definite'?"

William Gorman glanced along the line of jurors and, when this had sunk in, he continued; "Mr Thomalla told you that, on the Sunday after the murder, Kelly came in between 12.30 and 12.45 and that he remembered because Kelly looked upset. If he sought to fix the visit by the emotion shown by Kelly, it was in conflict with the evidence of Kelly. Kelly could have spent some time in the Leigh Arms on the Sunday lunchtime and have then got down to the Star between one and two.

Consider the alleged confession of Kelly, with regard to the shooting in the manager's office. Is that the perjured evidence of someone who will seek the death of one whom he knows not, or is it a true account, passed on to you by the witnesses to whom Kelly told it?

Is it not a fact that Kelly's outburst in the box against Graham, was the outburst of a man who knows that that which he has said, has been disclosed and who gives way to blind charges? The hunted hare turns round against his hunters.

Criticism has been directed, on Connolly's behalf, against Northam and Dickson and it has been suggested that those witnesses were lying because, in their letter, they were asking for some sort of protection, or manifestly were suggesting some fear. They themselves denied that they were afraid of anything.

Dickson's life might not have led her in pleasant places but you saw her face up to those men in a crowded court and refer to them by name and tell you what they had said. Out of the whole city of Liverpool, she had chosen two men with whom she had had no contacts of any real account. Was she the sort of woman to do that without any reason?

Northam was a man who might be something of a rolling stone and might not have lived the sort of life that you live. You have seen him in the witness-box. He might be unfortunate, but was he the type of man to swear away the lives of the other two men if, as he said, he never knew them at all?"

There was a slight pause, then, before the court had time to reflect, he continued.

"I urge you not to forget, that Inspector Balmer said that Northam was never suspected. Kelly and Connolly are alleged to have had been seen together, I have not put any witness, police or otherwise, upon a pinnacle, but it could be said about the police, if it was accepted that they were telling the truth, that their work made them exact in recollection and identity. Was there any reason why they should be mistaken?

Why was there this denial that the two men knew each other? It was because, to admit that, would be to knock the bottom completely out of their defence. In the charge room on October 1st, at an identification parade, when Kelly said to Connolly, 'You don't know me' and Connolly replied, 'No, I don't', it has been suggested that it was a stupid and fatuous thing to do. That was the day on which the two men had been found out and you will remember what Connolly was alleged to have said to Graham about the incident, that it stuck out a mile."

Mr Gorman paused, shuffling the papers on the bench in front of him before going on to review the evidence for the prosecution given by Graham and particularly that which dealt with the letter Connolly had written from gaol to Balmer.

"Is it not the truth, that Connolly had said, 'I did not murder the man, I merely stood outside, I did not do the murder,' and he was told, 'Don't be a fool man, why don't you tell the police that if you did not murder this man, you get hold of Mr Balmer.' 'Alright,' said Connolly. 'And I wrote to Mr Balmer and then I changed my mind. My mind went back to the Sunday, after when Kelly had called me yellow and

I made up my excuse about Dennis Barker and, when Mr Balmer came, I told what Dennis Barker had told me.'

In the submission of the prosecution, what he was intending to tell Mr Balmer is what, in fact, he had told witnesses who have been called before us, that he was merely outside the cinema and his hand did not fire that gun that caused the death of Leonard Thomas.

Remember Dickson's account of the conversation she said she had had with Connolly at Central Station in which he told her that he had gone to the cinema with Kelly and had stood outside while Kelly went in and had then run away because he did not think there would be any shooting. Is that evidence invented dishonestly, invented so as to make this woman the most despicable of all creatures, a woman who would swear away the life of her fellow?

Upon you, members of the jury, is a great responsibility, for you have got to decide this; is Graham a man of truth or is Graham, as Dickson and as Northam, a man who will swear to his doom a man against whom he has no conceivable source of grievance and a man who, on the evidence of Connolly, is quite unknown to him?

Let me deal with Connolly's second line of defence – his alibi. As I understand the case for the defence, it was that Connolly could not have been either at the Beehive or at the Cameo Cinema because he was at a dance at St Mark's Church Hall on March 19th. Perhaps the most interesting of the witnesses in support of Connolly was Mr McBain, who organised the dancing. Remember, Mr McBain said 10 o'clock was the earliest possible time for the rumba. Remember when Kelly went to the Leigh Arms that Saturday night he did a most unusual thing. He offered to treat people to a drink and to attract the attention of people that he was there and, in like manner, when Connolly goes to this dance, to impress upon those there that he was present, he adopts the most unusual practice of keeping on his hat.

There has been reference to a letter written by Mrs Connolly to her sister-in-law, but it did not say Connolly went to the dance, it merely said it was his intention to go. If the evidence of Mr McBain is right, Connolly did not go to St Mark's Hall until after 10 o'clock; if Mr McBain was right, then the members of Connolly's family who said he was at the dance round about 8 o'clock, must be wrong. If they were wrong on that and they never started to think about an alibi until September or October, can you rely upon this evidence? You might remember that Mr McBain was called by the defence.

Let us now consider the case against Kelly. It is the case for the prosecution that George Kelly's hand fired that gun that killed Leonard Thomas. You had the opportunity of seeing him in the box. Don't be unfair. The witness box must be a terrible place for a man who is giving evidence on his own behalf and a frightful place for a man who is giving evidence in a case of this kind. Don't set too high a standard. Make every possible allowance for the fact that a man in his position must be in a state of the utmost tension. But how did he strike you? Did he strike you as showing bravado, when he was seeking to explain what he said to Mr Balmer? If you accept Mr Balmer's evidence, don't you get there a measure of this man?

Does Kelly strike you as the sort of man who would say in the Beehive, 'I am Kelly?' Remember his manner giving evidence. Remember his denials and the manner of making his denial.

Patrick Dowling said that on the night of March 19th he had seen Kelly at the Globe public house. Criticism has been made that Dowling did not give evidence before the

101

magistrates and we know he did not want to sign his statement. He was a friend of Kelly and you, members of the jury, have to decide whether he is telling a lie.

You have heard the evidence of the brothers Brampton. They said they took particular notice of the clock in the Leigh Arms when it was 9.30pm. That could not be right on Kelly's own evidence because 9.30 upon the clock in the Leigh Arms was 9.20 and Kelly said he went into the Spofforth at 9.15 and stayed there some three minutes.

Nor could it be right having regard to the statement made in writing and signed by the landlord of the Leigh Arms, who said he was definite Kelly was not there at 9.30."

William Gorman paused, allowing the jury time to absorb his remarks, before coming to his conclusions. "I have tried to suggest to you a fair line of approach to the evidence. It is my submission that Kelly killed Thomas, that Connolly, with full knowledge of what was going on, knowing that Kelly had a loaded gun and the object of their visit to the cinema, went to help Kelly in the nefarious scheme and that he is also guilty of murder."

He looked along the line of the jurors, nodding slowly before sitting down, his submission complete. His presentation had been first class, the sequence of events, the tone of his voice; it must all have improved the credibility of his witnesses.

A man of violent and unrestrained temper

Mr Justice Oliver coughed, he was unwell, suffering from a violent cold and his malaise showed. He took a long drink of water and, on several occasions during his long summing up, he would apologise for having to bring matters to a halt while he regained his composure. He shifted the notes and depositions on the bench before him and then, gazing down from his elevated position, began his address to the jury.

The panelled courtroom had suddenly become almost sinister, there was a tense quiet, an air of expectancy and apprehension, the jury's eyes fixed rigidly on the judge as he leaned forward, his voice thick with cold, his words confidential to them alone, aloof to the rest of the court.

"The law in this case is on the one hand simple and on the other hand not so simple. If Kelly shot those two men, that is as plainly a case of murder as ever came before a court and there is no law on it and you need not waste time discussing it but, with regard to Connolly, the position is different.

It is this. If two persons plan a crime of violence such as robbery, one of them being armed with a deadly weapon to the knowledge of both of them, the common intelligence being that the gun shall be used if necessary to overpower the opposition and, on arrival, the gunman goes in and the other stays outside to keep watch and warn, to aid the escape, then if the gunman uses his gun and commits murder, both are guilty of murder. The man who stays outside is just as guilty as the man who takes the gun in.

Before you convict either of these men, you must be satisfied beyond reasonable doubt that their guilt is proven, the one or the other, or both. It is sufficient, in this case, to tell you that one of the ways of introducing a man's character is for him to attack the character of the witness for the prosecution. Connolly did that and Connolly is a man who had many convictions, including one for violence. Exactly the same sort of thing applies to Northam, Dickson and Graham; they are all people with bad characters but that does not mean that they cannot be believed. You are the judges. In law, they must be corroborated by some other evidence of some other source, although it was not always possible. No one could suggest Graham was an accomplice but Graham was a man with convictions. Particularly, you could look upon a matter of this sort, where Northam was saying, Kelly told him this, or Graham was saying that, could they have got that from someone else? But you can not act without considerable circumspection upon the evidence of Dickson, Northam and Graham."

Judge Oliver's next words caused Harry Livermore's face to whiten, his fists clenching in his lap. He glanced quickly at Rose Heilbron who remained impassive as the judge continued.

"I do not think you need discuss how many minutes elapsed between the time the shots were heard. No one saw the man arrive and the difficulty about getting in by the side door does not matter. The only description of the man comes from Griffin; dark eyes, dark hair and that does fit with Kelly and the only value you may think is that it does not show that it was Kelly, but it does not exclude him.

The judge stopped. His face was drawn and he was obviously in some distress as he decided to adjourn the case for the day, the court waiting as he slowly made his way outside to the car, which would take him to the judges" residence, Newsham House, the restored late 18th century building in Newsham Park. At 6.30 he sat down to eat, and, unusually for him, although there was an excellent cellar of wine at the judge's disposal, he only sipped at his, asking the butler, to bring him something stronger.

When the court resumed the following morning, Judge Oliver seemed contrite. After the wretched start to his summing up the previous day, having had time to reflect, he now reviewed his opening comments concerning the time of the shots and was at pains to emphasise their importance.

"I considered the evidence regarding the time the shooting took place and obviously it is a very important matter. I want to review the evidence about it and then I shall leave you to decide at what time it was. The fireman, Griffin says the cashier left the office about 9.35. 'I looked at my watch and the watch was always right. I carried on changing the advertisement for five minutes and then I took the steps back to the cellar. About seven minutes later there were two shots and screams.' This would make it about 9.47.

Mrs Watkins says that Jackman, the cashier, came in and they heard a shot. They went along to the operating room and looked in. The time was 9.35. That clock, which is specially kept right, shows that the shots were fired at that time. Mrs Simpson was the neighbour who heard the bangs. It was 9.32. The clock was right because she had timed it with the 9 o'clock news half an hour before. Now there is positive evidence of somewhere about 9.32. The telephonist at Sefton Park Exchange says that the call to 999, which resulted in the police being notified, came through at 9.45. That is not an approximate time, because all 999 calls have to be clocked.

Mrs Simpson's impression was that it was ten minutes between the hearing of the first bang and dialling 999. Does that evidence satisfy you, or does it not, that somewhere about 9.35 shots were fired and that there was a ten minute interval before the call went through?"

Again, Harry Livermore frowned in exasperation as the judge continued.

"Was there time for Kelly to get from the Cameo to the Leigh Arms and get rid of the gun and the disguise? Griffin says that when the man ran away he turned to the left, and you may wonder, if he turned to the left, unless he doubled back as he might have done, how he could do it?

According to Northam and Dickson, Kelly was in the Beehive. They don't agree as to the exact time until 8.20. Dowling, the commissionaire, said that he saw Kelly come out of the Globe Hotel between 7.30 and 8 and walk towards Central Station and turn either to the left or go up the middle. He said he was absolutely sure he saw Kelly, but comment has been made on that evidence. It was put that he was not called at the Magistrates Court and it was pointed out that this was, of course, because he had not signed his statement. Afterwards, the police persuaded him to sign his statement and Mr Balmer said he promised Dowling police protection.

The next time is 9 o'clock and, according to one witness, Kelly was in the Leigh Arms at that time. He had no hat and no coat and that means that he could not leave them in the street but if the evidence of Northam and Dickson is correct he had Connolly with him. If the object was to show himself in places where he was well known undisguised, that might help him, if he knew that, when he took the part of the murderer, he would be disguised.

A general topic of immense importance is, did Kelly and Connolly know each other? They had sworn they did not. Connolly admitted having known Dickson but Kelly said he had never known Northam or Dickson. Miss Heilbron had said that all the evidence on that was in the nature of police evidence but the first witness was Sangster and he was not of the police. Sangster was a reputable sort of man and he said he had seen both accused together in the street. There was also Sergeant Richardson who said as a rule he saw them together, but sometimes separately and had seen them certainly eight to nine times together, the last time three weeks after the murder. There was also Constable Nugent, who said he saw them together on September 26th and there was a denial of that by the accused.

Northam and Dickson first gave their statements to the police on September 29th, more than six months after the murder. Dickson, after describing Kelly in her statement, picked him out."

In the back row of the counsel benches, Chief Inspector Bert Balmer sat impassively. The fact that he had shown Kelly's photograph to Dickson, had not been revealed, the conspiracy still intact, only the jury, the last barrier to a conviction. And Judge Oliver's summing up could only help. He listened as the judge continued his summation.

"How was that done? By what mental process do you pick out a man you don't know, having first described him? It might be that Kelly might not know her but that she might know of him. In other words, having made up her mind to bring an absolutely false charge of murder against an innocent man, she must have been studying him unknown to himself, to get his features sufficiently implanted in her mind and then pick him out.

Northam picked out both Kelly and Connolly. By what mental process was that? Had he been studying them to identify them when a charge came and to falsify a charge of murder? He said he knew them perfectly well, and had known them for years. They might have picked out any of 100,000 young men in Liverpool round about the same age, men who were nowhere near Liverpool at the time of the murder. Was it a lucky chance that the two men Northam and Dickson picked out were not only in Liverpool that night but that one of them, Connolly, said that at the crucial time he was at a dance only a mile away and the other one, Kelly, admitted he was within a few hundred yards of the cinema when the murder was committed, within a comparatively short number of minutes of the time.

Dr Grace's evidence, given on October 19th, three weeks after Northam and Dickson had given their statements, said, 'I form the opinion that the man was probably on his hands and knees when the shot was fired.' From there I pass to Northam's evidence and I am going to invite you to consider how Northam could possibly have got this information, unless he himself were the murderer, or got it from the murderer. No-one has ever suggested that Northam was himself the murderer.

Kelly said, 'I shot him, the man went down and started screaming and tearing at his chest and the man got to his knees.' And remember the doctor's evidence, 'I should think that that second wound was when he was on his hands and knees.'"

The judge stared hard at the jury, quoting slowly.

" 'I have seen Balmer and he cannot break my alibi in a thousand years.' Is that an invention? Where did Northam get that from? Not the newspapers. He knew nothing about the doctor's evidence which was not given until three weeks after. Is it too much to suggest that that shows that it is not Northam who was the murderer and if that is not the conclusion to which you come, then it is the account given by the murderer and he said that that murderer was Kelly.

You should remember that the police are trained to observe, listen and record. Inspector Balmer completely denied that Kelly told him of every public house in which he had been on the night of March 19th, including the Spofforth Arms. Who did the jury believe in that matter? Balmer, when he said that the words Spofforth Arms were never mentioned, or Kelly, when he said they were?"

In the well of the court, Balmer's eyes stared, unblinking, straight ahead as the judge continued.

"It might have occurred to Kelly that it would not be very safe after all, to admit he was within a few hundred yards of the place where the murder was committed. Do you think that was deliberately suppressed? Kelly said, 'I got back to the Leigh Arms about 9.25.' That put him there, as the Brampton brothers have said, at half-past nine. The question was; is it true? Kelly had said he remained in the Leigh Arms until closing time and then went home.

You see the importance of the time of the visit to Skelly's house? If it was in the afternoon, Skelly was still in bed and could not have been at Charlie's place at 1 o'clock where Northam and Dickson said he was. If it be true that the officers were with Kelly between 11.15 and 12 noon, he was in ample time, if so minded, to attend the conference alleged to have been arranged at the Star.

At 1 o'clock, or thereabouts, Dickson and Northam kept the appointment and, according to their evidence, found Connolly and Skelly there. According to them, Connolly was thinking about leaving the country and that could have been a reference to the fact that he was already in negotiation. Evidence had been called that he was trying to emigrate to Australia.

Mr Thomalla has given evidence that Kelly was in the Leigh Arms between 12.30

and 2pm on the Sunday. If that were so, Kelly could not have gone to the Star. You would have to consider it. Both Northam and Dickson had said that when Kelly went into the Star, he told them that Balmer had been up to his house. How did they know that unless they had heard it?

Dickson says Connolly said to her, 'I did not go in, I waited outside. But Kelly went in and when I heard the first shot I ran away. He said Kelly had told him he had shot the first man but did not mean to shoot the second man and that the door was closed behind him and he thought he had locked it. The man came for him, so he just had to shoot. Does that sound like something she has invented? Where does it come from, if she did not get it from Connolly, as she swears she did? You will remember that Dickson was in the hands of the police on May 13th and on that day she gave, for the first time, the name of one of the men to Mr Balmer and that name was Connolly.

I refer now to Inspector Balmer's evidence about the occasion when he went to Connolly's house and said that Connolly was then asked to account for his movements on March 19th and he said that which was quite wrong, that he was at work at Bibbys. That happened on May 14th and the murder was eight weeks before. You might think the man might quite possibly be honestly mistaken when he said he was at work at Bibbys because he was, in fact, at work there up to March 18th. You also have to consider the effect on the mind of an innocent man, by the suggestion that he took part in that crime.

But five days afterwards, the officer says to him, 'The information you gave to us is wrong, you were not working,' and the answer is, 'I say I was; you say I was not. If I was not, then I don't know where I was.' If he knew where he had been and if he knew he had been at the Cameo, the less inquiry he had made the better. Can you imagine an innocent man behaving like that?

For some reason or other, Northam did not mention the overcoat until October 9th and on October 10th the police took possession of it. If you think Northam kept that information back on purpose, I must leave it to you to assess whether it was to protect himself and take suspicion from himself. Consider Inspector Balmer's evidence about the incident at the identity parade on October 10th, where Kelly and Connolly were identified by witness Sangster and said, 'I'll get you for this, Balmer.' I have already said you will probably think there is a good a deal of evidence that Kelly was a man of violent and unrestrained temper."

After a fresh start to the morning, Judge Oliver's cold was again taking its grip, his summing up discordant. After lunch he continued,

"It occurred to me that, while dealing with the time of events leading to the murder, I omitted to point out the evidence of Mrs Bore, who said she was in the bar of the Leigh Arms and saw Kelly about 9.45. Later, she said that the manager started to shout time at about ten to ten. They really did not know the time Kelly came in from that.

The witness Currie, who was in the Leigh Arms at ten minutes to nine, said he stayed until round about ten and that Kelly came in at ten to ten. He said that Kelly's behaviour was unusual, and the prosecution inferred it was the behaviour of a man doing his best to attract attention.

You might think it was a far cry that Graham, at large at Preston, should take the trouble to learn by heart great chunks of the evidence of Northam and Dickson, for the purpose of repeating it. I present that for your particular consideration. If it was a matter he could not know about, they were entitled to say, 'We don't care what Graham is, we don't care what sort of a blackguard he is, that must be true."

Chief Inspector Balmer showed no emotion, sitting motionless, neither too relaxed nor too rigid, a man apparently at ease with himself, as Judge Oliver stopped in some distress. He took a drink of water and then spoke apologetically to the jury.

"I must ask you to forgive me. I have a violent cold." He sat quietly for a few moments before continuing. "Connolly's defence was an alibi. Connolly says he was in town on the afternoon of March 19th, going back to his mother's house in Old Swan. He has stated he went to the dance alone, arriving at 9.20. For your consideration, Connolly was supposed, according to Northam and Dickson, to have been in the Beehive somewhere around 7.40. It was common ground that he went to the dance alone. The question really was, what time did he leave Old Swan and where did he go after he left Old Swan? If he left at 7.20, and went to the Beehive, he could be there. That was the question. Did he go alone, and where?

Mr McBain has given evidence that he did not See Connolly at the dance on March 19th before 10 o'clock. He saw him with his hat on and asked him to take it off. It was suggested by the prosecution that, in the same way as Kelly arrived at the Leigh Arms and was trying to draw attention to himself, so was Connolly drawing attention to himself by wearing a hat.

If you accept Connolly's family's evidence as even approximately true, Connolly would not have had enough time to do the things he was said to have done. It was entirely for the jury to assess that evidence. Connolly left the house alone and arrived at the dance alone. The whole question was, 'what time?'

A witness from a cafe was called who told you he had known Connolly for three years and had never seen him with Kelly. Probably you could call three quarter of a million people who had never seen Connolly with Kelly. On September 26th, the policeman Nugent, said he saw Kelly with Connolly and you have the evidence of the two girls who came from Llandudno. You will have to consider whether or not they went out of Kelly's sight from three in the afternoon until seven in the evening.

The only thing left for me to deal with is the evidence of Kelly's alibi. The best thing I can suggest is to read through the times. The early part of the afternoon of March 19th does not matter. The first time we are concerned with is 7.30pm, when the man from the restaurant in Cases Street said he saw Kelly pass. Kelly said he joined Skelly and spent the afternoon with him and, after standing outside the Royal William for three-quarters of an hour, went in at 6.15. There he saw the man called Georgie. If that is so, he could not then have been in Cases Street at 7.30. The man Yorky has said that he left at 7.30 and that meant that he could not help the jury at all about this alibi.

Kelly, if he was so minded, could have gone to Cases Street between 7.30 and 8. In regard to being in Cases Street at 7.30, there was only the evidence of Skelly to support Kelly's evidence. You will give that evidence what weight you think it deserves.

He then went to the Coach and Horses where he remained with Skelly until 8.30. Then he went to the Leigh Arms where he had a drink at 9 o'clock and from there to the Spofforth. According to the prosecution, he has got to be at the Beehive between something like 7.45 and 8.20. You are in a position to decide what happened in the Beehive and I am not. The people who talk about that for the defence are McKinnon and Manson. It is a terribly difficult thing to cast your mind back nine or ten months and think what you were doing. You may remember that a particular day was a

Saturday but do you necessarily remember that it was the very day.

McKinnon said he had a good view of the passageway but he did not see Kelly, whom he knew and he could speak up to the time of 9 o'clock. His friend Manson more than once left the parlour and went to the passage. He knew Kelly and he did not see him there. He saw no gun or a handkerchief being tried on. The question is, whether a man, after nine months, remembers the state of a passage which he frequents certainly once a week. Manson says he did not at anytime see Kelly. Examine Manson's evidence as to how he fixed the time of 9 o'clock. When Manson was asked about it, he first of all said he judged it. Then he said he looked at the clock and it was just before nine. Then he said when he looked at the clock it was 8.45.

You are quite entitled to say that you accept the evidence of Manson and McKinnon as conclusive and that it puts the matter beyond doubt. If you think it shakes the evidence of the prosecution and there is a doubt you will give the accused the benefit of that doubt. If, on the other hand, you think the evidence unreliable, you are quite entitled to reject it.

In regard to the evidence of the Leigh Arms, it was that Kelly was in there having a drink at 9.30. If he was, he could not be guilty of the murder. That was a matter of first class importance to you. You will remember Thomalla's signed statement, 'I am quite satisfied George Kelly was not in my house at 9.30, but he was in the buffet at ten to ten. You have to decide if he was right. It is one thing to say I do not know whether he was in or not and another thing to say he may have been in but I did not see him. But he has pledged himself in writing to the fact that Kelly was not in his house at 9.30.

Members of the jury, one other thing about Thomalla's evidence that I come to, is that, on the Sunday he says that shortly after he opened at 12.30, Kelly came in and stayed until 2 o'clock. If that is true, Kelly could not have been at the meeting in the Star. Do you think anyone would say that, with certainty, he was there from 12.30 until 2, a busy landlord seeing lots of people, the house full of people. Asked 'How are you so sure Kelly was there all the time?' Mr Thomalla said, 'I knew he had been interviewed by Balmer. He was very upset. He was sitting in a seat looking terribly worried.' Thomalla said he looked at the clock. It was five minutes to one, 'I do not suppose I looked at it when Kelly came in, he was there until 2 o'clock, he was so upset.'

Members of the jury, you have seen Kelly and you may describe him as rather a tough individual. You remember when the police went to him and asked him where he was on the night before, what was his reaction? He was not worried. Not much sign of caution about that. There was not much trepidation; I am an innocent man! Can you see that man sitting there for an hour and a half in that public house, cringing, miserable, in despair, because he had been interviewed about this thing?"

This time, it was the turn of Rose Heilbron to show her anger at the judge's selectivity with the evidence. Her face whitened, her eyes blinking slightly as she stared hard at the judge who was now leaning toward the jury. But there was no relief, his comments even more destructive.

"If you don't think that that is the description, what do you think of Thomalla's evidence? Do you think that he could have been serving beer for an hour and a half, while that man Kelly was sitting in that state?

You must first make up your minds about Kelly and if you think the case against him is proved then you will turn to the case against Connolly. I have told you that the cases against these two men are quite different. It is no answer for Connolly, on hearing the first shot, that he ran away. He has helped to arrange a murder and to give the murderer his assistance and encouragement.

You might think that there is a difference in the degree of guilt in this case, but the punishment is no concern of yours at all. The view of our law is that all who take an active part in gang offences of this sort do so at their peril. The sooner the criminal classes realise that, the safer will our society be."

Judge Oliver's summing up was finished for the day and he adjourned the court, his final few minutes kept until the following morning, rather than have the jury sequestered overnight.

By 9 o'clock the following day, January 28th, the crowd outside the Assize Court had become so large, that a queue stretched half way along the colonnade in front of St George's Hall. A group of police officers ordered the queue to break up and shepherded the crowd down the steps, where they dispersed on the plateau.

Inside the hall, it was the same crowded courtroom, only the faces of those who had queued from the early hours different behind the rail at the rear of the dock. There was a nervous and tense silence as, just after 11 o'clock, the judge made a few concluding remarks and the jury retired to consider its verdict.

After they had gone, Kelly and Connolly were escorted from the dock, the tightly-packed court room watching their every move, as they were taken to the cells below the courtroom, the majority of people in the gallery staying in the court, so as not to lose their places.

At 12.25, it was thought the jury was returning but it was a false alarm, it was cold in the jury room and they needed their overcoats and several times the Clerk of the Assizes was called by the jury, creating a ripple of anticipation in the court room but it was not to herald their return.

The period of the jury's retirement provided a convenient opportunity for Chief Inspector Balmer to visit Dennis McLoughlin's small barber's shop in Cheapside, opposite the Bridewell. It was frequented mainly by policeman and staff from the many office buildings in the area. McLoughlin started his usual chatty conversation as soon as Balmer had taken his seat in the barber's chair for his usual military-style haircut.

"How's it going over there, Mr Balmer? You look worried."

"Not too well, Dennis. They could be acquitted."

Balmer was unusually pessimistic, far from certain of success. As McLoughlin was finishing his haircut, Jimmy Morris put his head around the door of the small shop.

"You're needed, Bert. The jury want to ask you something."

Balmer cursed as he stood up, sudden apprehension flooding through him, as he returned to the court.

"Inspector Balmer, the jury here wishes to know the dates of the searches of Northam's house and Dickson's room and was it more than once. Is that correct?"

"Yes, my Lord." The foreman of the jury spoke his agreement.

Balmer was without his notebook but Chief Superintendent Smith and Chief Inspector Jimmy Morris had theirs. They confirmed that Northam's house had been searched on October 10th and 30th and the room occupied by Northam and Dickson in Upper Parliament street on May 14th. Judge Oliver thanked him and then addressed the jury.

"Members of the jury, you have been detained for a very long time. I am very sorry. Do you think this information will help you?"

The foreman stood up. "I do not, my lord."

The judge shook his head in exasperation. He was ill, his cold was worsening and, in his wisdom, he decided that a verdict would not be reached, even though the jury had been out only four hours.

"Very well, if there is no chance of an agreement among you, it is no use me keeping you waiting. I have nothing to do but to discharge you from giving a verdict in this case. The two defendants will be kept in custody and tried again. Take them down."

There was a murmur of surprise from the court, defending counsel and prosecuting counsel glancing at each other in astonishment, as Judge Oliver called an end to what had been, up until that time, the longest murder trial in British legal history. It had taken thirteen days, and was now ordered to begin again.

For the defendants, the judge's decision came as a bombshell. They were confident of acquittal; celebrations had been arranged. Now they sat disconsolately in the dock, Kelly pale and shocked, Connolly shaking his head slowly, disbelievingly, from side to side.

For Chief Inspector Bert Balmer the result was not as bad as he had feared. Later that afternoon, Justice Oliver asked the Clerk to the Assizes to pass some comments to the Chief Superintendent of Liverpool CID. He would later put them in writing. He was anxious that the police should know that had the trial finished in the way he had anticipated, he had intended to pay tribute to the admirable work of the police in the case.

Outside the courtroom, when she heard there was to be a retrial, Jacqueline Dickson collapsed. When she recovered Herbert Balmer had to convince her that she had no other choice but to submit to the ordeal of cross-examination once again.

SEPARATE TRIALS

Kelly goes first

Early on the Monday morning, January 30th, Chief Inspector Bert Balmer approached the Director of Public Prosecutions concerning the impending re-trial. A conviction was becoming increasingly doubtful and Balmer knew that the only chance of a successful conclusion from his point of view, was to try Kelly before Connolly.

The Director of Public Prosecutions was agreeable, accepting Balmer's point and agreeing to drop the 'before' charge to 'after' the act in exchange for a guilty plea on Connolly's part. But Connolly would have to accept that he was part of the crime. This would avoid a capital sentence.

The deal was sealed in Chambers when Connolly's solicitor, Gordon Clover, grabbed at this chance of saving his client's life. To Harry Livermore and Rose Heilbron, this was improper and unfair. The accusation was that it was a joint venture but, in the first trial, Kelly had been the one portrayed as a violent and dangerous criminal, the one alleged to have carried out the murder. In a separate trial his case would be harder to defend.

On January 31st, Rose Heilbron approached Judge Oliver as he was preparing to begin proceedings in the Crown Court at Liverpool Assizes. She requested leave to mention the case of The King against Kelly and Connolly but Judge Oliver was not prepared to hear her application and suggested it should be made in the other court. Rose Heilbron held out her hands in bewilderment.

"I was in the other court and I was told I ought to make the application to your Lordship."

The judge shook his head, his reply brusque.

"I am not going to try the case. Make your application to Mr Justice Cassells."

Judge Cassells was in the Civil Court and Rose Heilbron waited until he had taken his seat. She rose to address him.

"May I mention to your Lordship, the case of the King against Kelly and Connolly? I understand that the case is to be retried and is to be retried separately; that is to say, Kelly is to be tried first. My first point is that, on behalf of Kelly, I object to the retrial separately. My first reason is that the prosecution alleged this was a joint venture and a joint enterprise. That is evidence for the Crown." She then quoted a legal precedent laid down that, where two men were engaged in a common enterprise, it was better that they should not be tried separately. Judge Cassells peered at her over half-moon spectacles.

"Did you say it was improper that they should be tried separately?"

"Yes, My Lord. They have already been tried together once and, in my submission there is no jurisdiction to order a separate trial on the indictment that has already been tried. The retrial should be in the same manner as the trial. In my submission, the discretion which must be exercised has not been exercised in the manner laid down. It has already been decided, I understand, that there should be separate trials."

Judge Cassells criticised her. "Miss Heilbron, I don't know where you got that from. For the convenience of counsel, communication was made to the learned Clerk of Assizes."

Miss Heilbron allowed herself mild sarcasm.

"I did not realise that it was for convenience of counsel."

"It was for the convenience of counsel and, if it had not been done in that way, a protest would have been made that it came as a complete surprise. You are entitled to make the application now and I will hear you. I am prepared to treat it as an application as if it were made at the trial."

"That brings me to my other point, my Lord."

But the judge was not finished.

"In my opinion, Miss Heilbron, this is the wrong course to take, because any such application as this, should be made in the presence of the accused persons. I understood that you were going to make application with regard to the fixing of the case. Now you start by making protests against this separate trial.

"I have to do that for this reason. If the trial was to go on as a joint trial and you were to hear the case tomorrow, I should have no objection. It is only because the trial is going on as a separate trial."

"That is your point?"

"Yes. Tomorrow is too soon for the defence to do justice to this new case which has been put forward. The conduct of the defence may well be quite different. A different situation has to be met and the defendant will be prejudiced if this case is on tomorrow at such short notice and, my Lord, that is only one point. There is another question of witnesses, because one man is now absent from the trial, one man who was alleged to have been present, both when the crime was planned and, when it was committed. In my submission, very great hardship will be caused to the defence if this trial went on tomorrow without some real delay. After all, this trial lasted thirteen hearing days and only finished on Saturday afternoon and it gives very little time for the defence."

"What is it that you would like? Do you mean a postponement of date or a postponement to another assizes?"

"I would like a week or two postponement, in order to get the case ready on behalf of the defence and I would also ask your Lordship to adjourn it to another assize and, if possible to another place, for this reason; practically verbatim accounts have been given in the local press and there can be very few people who do not know a great deal about this case locally. Such extended accounts have not been given in the press of other towns and so it would be fairer to the accused if it could be held in another place."

Judge Cassells nodded and asked the prosecuting counsel if the representatives of the other defendants had anything to say about the application. Gordon Glover stood up.

"I do not support Miss Heilbron's application. I do not feel, without specific instructions, I can say more than that."

When he sat down, Mr Glynn Blackledge, for the prosecution, stood up to say that he had nothing to say with regard to the separate trial aspect. He continued, "So far as the question of postponement is concerned, I have to mention that one of the two principal witnesses for the prosecution, the woman Dickson, suffers from a serious and progressive disease from which her life may be in danger. She is waiting to enter hospital and any delay may be serious from that point of view."

The judge nodded.

"I understand. I see no reason that the date for this trial should be long delayed. If an extra day is required I am perfectly willing for the trial to fixed for Thursday instead of Wednesday, if that is not of assistance, then I think it would be better to bring it on to Wednesday."

Miss Heilbron made one further plea for time.

"Can your Lordship not make it Monday? A few days would be a breathing space and give us time, hurriedly, to do the things that are necessary.

Judge Cassells gave her short shrift.

"When you say 'hurriedly', the trial started on January 12th. Tomorrow will be the first of February. You must, of course, be familiar, Miss Heilbron, with all the facts of the case. It is not as if you have not had your brief for a long time."

"There was the difficulty of a joint trial."

"When was the alleged offence?"

"In March last but the principal witnesses for the prosecution did not see the police until the end of September. It was not the fault of the defence."

"The trial was postponed to the next assizes and the assizes have started today and there is no reason the case should not come on its proper course and it seems to be only right that it should come on at an early stage and if Thursday is any good to you, by all means have Thursday, but I cannot postpone it beyond Thursday."

"Obviously one day is better than nothing."

"Very well, the trial will be on the list on Thursday."

The pipe-smoking James Dale Cassells was then almost 73 years old. Born in York on March 22nd 1877, his was not the traditional way to a senior position in the judiciary. He was brought up in a two up, two down house in a working-class district known as The Groves, just outside the city walls on the east side of the city. His father had previously worked as a butler to Lord Gleneck but eventually got a job as a messenger at Westminster Police Courts. He read books on the law at night, passing on his enthusiasm for the subject to his son, this enthusiasm leading to Cassells senior obtaining a job as an usher at Bow Street, London's busiest and biggest police court, progressing to senior usher and then to magistrates clerk.

When the family moved to London, young Cassells became a grammar school boy, attending Westminster City School, spurning the chance of higher education, when he left school at fifteen, to take up a career in journalism. In 1900, James Cassells married, his bride Jessie five years older than him, and set up home in Kingston-on-Thames. They had no children and four years later, Jessie died.

The interest in the law, instilled in him by his father, then became a passion and, as a journalist, he would discuss with friends the merits of the barristers they had heard. Eventually, and no doubt encouraged by the thought that he could match their oratorical skills, Cassells enrolled as a student at the Middle Temple. In 1906, he married again and, after that, began to study in earnest, finally being called to the bar of the Middle Temple in 1908. His position and name grew rapidly and it was now that his training as a journalist gave him an advantage in court, using his expertise in shorthand to take notes of evidence he thought was important.

This was to be useful on more than one occasion, such as in an early case at the London Sessions when a controversy arose as he was making his final address for the defence, when the judge interrupted and said he was misquoting a witness. Cassells had made a note of what the witness had said and it differed from the judge's. The shorthand writer to the court was consulted and his notes supported Cassells. The learned judge had to allow himself a brief smile at James Cassells's comment.

"There you are, members of the jury, how can you really trust a police officer to make an accurate note of a conversation an hour after it took place, when my Lordship can't make an accurate note of a statement at the time it is being made in the witness box?"

In 1914, Cassells joined the RAC as a transport volunteer and motoring, like cricket, became a lifelong pastime, together with, in later years, bowls. In 1915 he volunteered for the army and was posted to the reserve. A year later, he was called up and, in February 1917, joined the BEF to France as a 2nd Lieutenant, eventually finishing up as a military judge in Cologne at the end of the war.

Like a number of others at the bar, he ventured into politics and, in 1922, won the Conservative seat of West Leyton in London. But he was not to be an active MP, asking few questions, eventually losing his seat in 1928, to the Labour candidate. In 1931, he stood again at North West Camberwell and won with a good majority but three years later decided to retire from politics.

In February 1939, when he was sixty-two, Cassells took the oath of office and allegiance when he was appointed Judge, his appointment late in life, most probably because his educational background had counted against him, the only judge who had not attended a university and who had gone to a grammar school and not, like the majority of his colleagues at the bar, to a public school.

James Cassells was never taken in by mere eloquence. An excellent raconteur himself, he had the actor's ability to raise and lower his voice to make the most of words, with a way of looking over the top of his spectacles at a statement a barrister had made, his great dark eyebrows arching in surprise. But Judge Cassells had a bias, one which would act against George Kelly. Among barristers and solicitors he was known as the 'policeman's friend'. Intransigent in their defence, he was known to punish assaults on police officers very severely and was implacable in accepting the truth of their evidence.

In 1957, when James Cassells had celebrated his eightieth birthday, he sat in the Court of Criminal Appeal with Lord Goddard, the only octogenarian judge in England. In August of that year his wife died and two years later, he again remarried, to one of his oldest friends. In August 1958, he sat for the last time as the Lord Chief Justice of England in the Court of Criminal Appeal. He was eighty-four when he retired.

It was Thursday February 2nd 1950 and at Liverpool Assizes, at the start of the separate trial of George Kelly, the red-robed Judge Cassells gave his opinion on the argument for separate trials.

"A separate trial provides a balanced issue for the jury concerning one person. So far as I read the depositions, they seem to disclose that the two cases differ in some important respects. A separate trial eliminates all evidence which is not directly against the person being tried.

I have come to the conclusion that it is in the interests of justice that the jury, in a long case like this, particularly on a retrial and on a capital charge, should not have to dissect the evidence of individual witnesses and relate it to more than one person under trial.

I don't think that the defence is prejudiced, on the contrary, it may well be favoured by a separate trial, in that there will be before the jury no evidence other than that relevant to the issues being tried, concerning one person.

Witnesses, whether for the prosecution or defence, will be cross-examined once only, and the jury's task and recollection will be simplified. I direct that there shall be a separate trial." Judge Cassells paused before concluding.

"That of George Kelly shall be first."

William Gorman KC, was again prosecuting, the jury again made up of ten men and two women. There was a rustle of papers in the otherwise silent court as the exhibits, maps, plans, and photographs were handed around before the prosecutor mentioned Connolly's role.

He spoke from his usual pace in the rows of counsel benches, slowly and solemnly.

"In the course of this case, you will, of necessity, hear a lot about a man named Charles Connolly. The question of the guilt of that man is not at the moment before you. The question of his guilt is a matter which will be later determined. It would be foolish if I concealed from my mind the fact that you must have heard about the circumstances of the crime of which you are now making inquiry, but I do ask you to disregard anything which you may have read or heard of this case.

Bring to the consideration of this case no preconceived ideas or whims. I ask you to give to this case your consideration and, in accordance with the oath which you have taken, purely upon the facts which will be given before you."

Mr Gorman then planted the time of the crime in the jurors" minds.

"A little after 9.30 on the night of Saturday March 19th last year, Leonard Thomas, manager of the Cameo Cinema, was shot dead in his office. Was the man who shot him George Kelly?"

Kelly sat impassive in the dock, a warder on either side of him, his hands folded together in his lap as William Gorman went on to portray what had taken place in the cinema and to recount Kelly's alleged movements in the vicinity of the Cameo that night, emphasising the appearance without hat or coat as a disguise for the murder.

He then outlined Kelly's interview with Balmer the following day, emphasising Balmer's claim that the only places Kelly mentioned were the Coach and Horses public house and the Leigh Arms.

Mr Gorman continued, assassinating Kelly's character by describing the incident at the identity parade when Kelly was alleged to have said to Chief Inspector Balmer, 'If it's the last thing I do, I will get you for this, Balmer'. William Gorman nodded slowly as he looked long the line of jurors. "You will get a measure of the man from that expression." He then reviewed the evidence of Northam and Dickson and the alleged prison conversations between Kelly and Graham, concluding,

"I submit on the evidence I will produce, there can be no doubt that George Kelly murdered Leonard Thomas."

The hostility of Judge Cassells to the defence was apparent from the onset of the trial when, before prosecution witnesses presented their evidence, Rose Heilbron asked him if she could apply for a copy of the transcript of the shorthand notes of the first trial. "I was not concerned with a great deal of the evidence at the last trial and a transcript would be of considerable assistance."

Judge Cassells was abrupt."This case has nothing to do with the last trial. Suppose you renew your application later. The court has no power to order a transcript and no one knows if a transcript is ready or not. You ascertain first of all whether or not the transcript is ready and, if it is, there are the channels through which you can get it."

Rose Heilbron reddened, more from anger at Judge Cassells's response, than from any sense of embarrassment.

As the trial proper started, witnesses who had presented evidence at the previous hearings, the Cameo staff, telephone operator and pathologist presented their evidence.

Mrs Jackman, the cashier, was cross-examined by Heilbron. She said it was 9.30 by the clock in the cash desk when she left to go up to the manager's office. She thought the shots took place about 9.40.

In the same truculent mood he had used a few minutes earlier towards Rose Heilbron, the judge now commented on the difficulty of hearing witnesses owing to the coughing in court. "There is plenty of time for a real good cough between witnesses. The rest of the time you must keep quiet." His advice to the public was taken literally and there was a barrage of coughing. Cassells allowed himself a thinly-veiled smile.

Mrs Watkins, the cinema supervisor, stated that she was certain that when she looked into the projection room, after hearing two shots, the time was 9.35. She was then shown a brown overcoat and nodded emphatically, "It certainly is the coat."

Miss Heilbron questioned her.

"You were upset when you heard the shots. You could not make certain of that coat, could you?"

"I say it is the coat. It was the only one of that type I had ever seen."

Patrick Dowling repeated his evidence of the first trial, the defence attempting to discredit him but Dowling was not to be moved. "I was talking to a detective who told me Kelly had been arrested and I said that was quite impossible, because he was talking to me that night."

Ellis, the licensee of the Spofforth, then confirmed that Kelly was in his pub between 9.15 and 9.25 and was followed into the witness box by the taxi driver, Currie, who repeated his evidence of Kelly's appearance in the buffet bar at the Leigh Arms.

Edna Bore, the barmaid at the Leigh Arms, then repeated her evidence that she saw Kelly that night at 9.45 and that there would be about eighty people in the bar but, when Rose Heilbron briefly cross-examined her, she was unable to say how long Kelly had been there. Swinburn, the relief manager for the brewery, employed as a barman at the Beehive on March 19th, said he had seen Kelly with Skelly but not with Connolly. He confirmed that the passageway was quite full on a Saturday night, the busiest night of the week.

Those in the court who remembered evidence from the earlier trial, glanced at each other and nodded sagely. They remembered that Northam and Dickson had said that they were alone in the passageway that night.

A cast iron alibi

On the second day of the trial, it was once more the turn of the three main prosecution witnesses to take the stand. Northam was first, Judge Cassells showing him the same consideration that Judge Oliver had shown to the main prosecution witnesses in the first trial, allowing him to be seated anytime he felt like it.

Northam was possibly the most important witness. With some prompting from the prosecution, he repeated, almost word for word, the evidence he had given at the magistrates hearing and at the first trial.

He was far from being at ease and, at times almost inaudible, possibly due to his speech defect and possibly due to nervousness. The judge had been taking verbatim shorthand notes of his evidence and, at one stage, told the jury, who appeared to have difficulty in hearing Northam, that he would read back his notes on Northam's evidence.

It was a moment Judge Cassells delighted in. When first on the bench, he had always made his notes in longhand during a murder trial because, if the accused were found guilty, the judge's notebook was sent to the Home Office, together with the official notification of the death penalty. At that time, the Home Office insisted on longhand because the theory was that, if the convicted person appealed and the judge died before the appeal was heard, the Court of Criminal Appeal could still read his notes. It was a relic from the days before there were court shorthand writers and the judge's notes were the only official record of what was said.

After five years on the bench, it was James Cassells who asked the Home Office if this was really necessary, since the full transcript of everything that was said in court was now available to the Appeal Court. He argued that he could conduct a trial at a much quicker pace, if he were not obliged to write in long hand. As a result of this, the Home Office announced that it no longer needed to see the judge's notebooks and they could make their notes how it best suited them.

Judge Cassells, in a clear, distinct voice, read back his notes, asking Northam if he agreed with what had been said. Northam said yes, some of the reporters breathing out, thankfully, as they had not been able to get every word at the speed at which Cassells had recorded it.

When Northam had completed his statement, Miss Heilbron questioned
"How many people were in the passageway of the Beehive?"
"There were no other people there, although people did pass through."
"Where did you get the overcoat?"
"Off a man in Brampton, Northumberland, about six months ago."
"Did you write the anonymous letter?"
"Yes. It's in my handwriting and Dickson had a hand in composing it."
"You say that you knew the gun used in this murder was in a lake in a park?"
"That is what I heard from Kelly."
"Did you know that on May 6th a man named Johnson was arrested for being an accessory after the fact in the murder and that he was supposed to have received the gun?"
"Yes."
"If your information is correct, that couldn't have been right?" Counsel's voice was

almost persuasive. Northam looked confused and remained silent, staring blankly at her. Miss Heilbron read the passage, " 'I seen the man who had done the job.' Who is that man?"

Northam made no reply for a few seconds and studied the letter. Eventually he replied. "That is Mrs Dickson saying that."

Still reading from the letter, Miss Heilbron continued,

" 'The gun he used he threw it in the lake in the park.' To whom does that refer?"

"Kelly."

"The letter was written two weeks after the murder and yet it referred to some bullets having been handed over six weeks before. What does that mean?"

"I might have meant six days."

Rose Heilbron leaned forward, her voice crackling with sarcasm.

"That is the only explanation you can give?"

"Yes."

"Do you agree, that in May, you did not tell the police anything about the Beehive, the gun, the bullets, the Star public house, the overcoat, the conversation with Kelly, or the confession but said you told the police in September about the Beehive and the Star?"

"Yes."

"When did you first mention the overcoat?"

"About nine days after Kelly had been charged with the murder. I didn't mention it before because I thought the police may have taken it the wrong way."

"How often did the police search your house?"

"On two or three occasions and they also searched the house in Parliament Street in May."

Rose Heilbron finished her cross-examination, confident, as she had been at the first trial, that Northam had been exposed, at best, as a liar, his statements about the anonymous letter so discredited, that it would discredit the remainder of his evidence.

It was now Jacqueline Dickson's turn in the witness box.

She had a heavy cold, her voice hoarse as she took the oath, the judge allowing her to be seated. When William Gorman asked her what she had done on March 21st, she repeated, almost identically, the evidence she had given at the previous trial.

Rose Heilbron picked up on her alleged visit to the Caledonian public house with Kelly."I suggest you never went at all with George Kelly to a public house. You may have gone with somebody else but it was not Kelly?"

"It was Kelly." Dickson replied, in a low voice.

"Why did you go to the trouble of throwing the bullets down different drains?"

"I just threw them down the drains as I walked past."

"Why were you having anything to do with these two men, who you have told us were involved in this murder?

"I knew if I snubbed them, they would know something was wrong and perhaps do something to me, God knows what."

"You were not afraid of Kelly and Connolly, were you?"

"I said I was afraid of Kelly and his brothers but I was not afraid of Connolly."

"Where did you live after the murder?"

"Me and Northam left Birkenhead a few days after the murder and went to live in Parliament Street. We lived there until May and then went to live in Manchester. I have lived there with Northam ever since."

Dickson was nervous and, as Miss Heilbron asked her about the anonymous letter, she breathed deeply, replying with a rather weak show of bravado,

"This letter goes back such a long time, Miss Heilbron. How can you expect me to remember these things?

Rose Heilbron smiled coldly. "Try."

Dickson was less than generous with the truth. On May 13th she had seen Balmer and had then confirmed that the letter came from herself and Northam.

"Me and Northam were concerned in the writing of the letter. On May 13th, I saw Chief Inspector Balmer and was asked by him if I had written an anonymous letter but I did not answer, I don't think I suggested anyone else had written it at that time."

Miss Heilbron commented wryly. "You were not particular whether it was accurate or not?"

"It just told the police what we wanted to tell them. We are not scholars. We just said what came to our minds but the only part that is untrue is the little bit about Brownlow Hill and Dale Street."

"Did you tell the police in May about Kelly, or that he had worn Northam's overcoat, or that there was a meeting on the Sunday morning at the Star public house?"

"No."

"I put it to you, you had three interviews with the police in May, and yet you did not mention one of the vital matters you have told in evidence today?"

"I thought that Connolly would tell everything."

Counsel would not let up, her expression deadpan as she continued.

"You wrote this letter to give information?"

"Because it was preying on our minds."

"You were somewhat nervous about being charged and wanted an assurance from the police?"

"Yes."

"When the letter referred to a man wanting to unload the revolver, who was that?"

"I thought that was Northam."

"When it referred to somebody not being seen since, who was that?"

"I think that was Connolly."

Heilbron attacked Dickson aggressively.

" 'Five days ago, I seen the man who done the job', who was the person who had seen the man?"

"Jimmy, I suppose. Jimmy had seen Kelly."

"Where had he seen Kelly?"

"I don't know."

"Tell the court who the parts of the letter refer to."

"The part about turning King's evidence refers to me, the part about the gun in the pond and the 6a car refers to Kelly and the bit about I am scared of him, he wants me to go away with him, refers to Connolly."

Rose Heilbron's voice was deadly serious as she continued.

"I suggest to you, Mrs Dickson, that the greater part of that letter is untrue?"

"Not the greater part, only that little bit about Brownlow Hill and Dale Street."

"Did the interview you had with the police on May 13th have anything to do with the Cameo murders?"

"No. I did not think anything was said about the Cameo murders at that time."

"At that time, did you say to the police, 'go and see Connolly. He will tell you all about it.' "

"That was after I had asked to see Mr Farragher."

"Why Mr Farragher?"

"Because I did not know Chief Superintendent Smith or Chief Inspector Balmer at that time. I only knew Mr Farragher. What I meant when I told that to the police was that Connolly was there when it was all arranged and I thought perhaps Connolly would have told the police instead of me."

Dickson was followed in the witness box by Robert Graham, his evidence essentially that which he had presented at the first trial. But there was more.

"Kelly told me the police thought the shot was at 9.40 and that he had got rid of the coat and the hat and was having a drink in his own pub at 9.45 and the police would have a job trying to prove he could do that in five minutes. Kelly said that his life depended on five minutes and he had a cast iron alibi."

Rose Heilbron cross-examined him, asking where he had been living at the time of the committal proceedings. He told the court that he was living at Preston and he hadn't take any interest in the proceedings.

"I suggest you had a very good opportunity of seeing what evidence was given in this case because it was very fully reported in the papers."

"I don't remember reading about it. I had read the headlines. It was a case I knew nothing about." Counsel raised an eyebrow and glanced meaningfully at the jury.

"Do you know a cleaner called Marney?"

"Yes."

"Did he not tell you the evidence against Kelly in this case?"

"No, the only persons who spoke to me about this case were Kelly and Connolly."

"I suggest you heard about this case and the evidence against Kelly, from one or other of the cleaners?"

"That is entirely impossible. They couldn't talk to me because, apart from exercise, I was locked up."

"One of the topics in the prison at that time was the murder, wasn't it?"

"I don't think so. The only persons who spoke to me about it were Kelly and Connolly."

Graham's reply was hardly plausible but Rose Heilbron made no attempt to pursue it. "What you are saying today is that Kelly made a complete confession of this murder?"

Graham shrugged. "I don't know whether it was a confession or not."

"In fact, I put it to you that everyone in prison did know the evidence?"

"That I don't know."

"And that, if you did not know before you went into prison what the evidence was, you certainly got to know from the cleaners?"

"I can honestly say I knew nothing about it until I was told by these two people who were charged with it."

"What you are saying is that Kelly told you all the circumstances of the murder, how he had borrowed the coat?"

"Yes."

"And what jobs should have been done instead of the murder?"

"He did. He told me how they had met that night."

"Were you rather surprised at these coincidences?"

"I was more than surprised when he told me how he had done the killing. I thought it was too great a responsibility for me and that was what made me divulge it."

"There was no need for Kelly to use you as a messenger, was there?"

"I don't know. I only wish now I had not met either of them."

"You know that he could have spoken to the other man while in prison?"

"Impossible."

"Do you know he did talk to him?"

"Impossible."

"And while they were in church together?"

Graham hesitated, suddenly apprehensive of what counsel was about to reveal. His reply was muted.

"I don't know."

Miss Heilbron paused, shuffling her papers and staring hard at Graham before changing the line of her questioning.

"Did you, in 1945, offer to go into Whittingham Hospital, as a voluntary patient?"

"Yes."

"And Whittingham Hospital is…?"

"It is a mental hospital."

"And did you go in again, last year?"

"Yes, I did. For nine weeks. I went in on March 15th and came out on May 17th."

"What was your complaint?"

"I was in with anxiety neurosis caused through war service. I was torpedoed in the Mediterranean. I was put into a mental hospital in Algiers and that was the complaint that was diagnosed. That was in 1943."

"And when you went into Whittingham, did you go in suffering from delusions?"

"That I am afraid I cannot tell you. I was seen there by the prison medical officer and whatever the reason was, I don't know."

"Did you hear voices?"

"Certainly not. I was sent there as a sick man. I cannot talk about that, only the medical officer can."

"Did you complain about your mental health between 1945 and the time you went into Whittingham?"

"Like many more, I was suffering from the effects of war service. I don't know what it is you are trying to convey to people. Is it that I am a lunatic?"

William Gorman re-examined Graham. "Did you imagine these conversations?"

"No. I would not be capable."

"It is suggested that, although you may have these delusions, you got this information from a man named Marney, a cleaner. Have you ever had any conversation with him?"

"There is such a man, but not while I was in hospital."

"It has been suggested that Connolly and Kelly spoke to each other in prison from their cells."

Facing his own counsel, Graham had regained some confidence, shaking his head as he replied. "Their cells face entirely different ways."

Once again, it was the turn of Chief Inspector Bert Balmer to give evidence. Calm, composed, immaculately turned out in a dark suit with a dark blue tie, he looked the essence of professional probity. There was no hesitation as he repeated his evidence and responded to counsel's probing.

Miss Heilbron cross-examined.

"How many people have you interviewed in the course of this inquiry?"

"About two thousand."

"And you can remember all that you have been told?"

"That would be impossible." His reply was coolly offhand.

"When you first questioned Kelly, did he tell you that he went to the Spofforth Hotel the previous night?"

"No. I first learned that from the manager."

"When you saw Dickson, after you had first seen Connolly, what did she say?"

"She said, 'You have let Connolly go. I told you to get Connolly. Let him talk. If the gang want to get anybody they can get him, not me. She then told me about someone being slashed with a razor in the Liverpool court, in January, for opening his mouth and she said, 'I am not going to be slashed; get hold of Connolly'.'"

Rose Heilbron frowned; Balmer's embroidery of his statement at the previous trial could only help convince the jury to feel that Dickson's evidence was the truth.

Mr Gorman re-examined Balmer about the letter, asking how he knew it was from Northam and Dickson, Balmer replying with almost nonchalant assurance.

"Dickson said, 'If you think I am telling lies, have a look at that letter and you will find lipstick on it. I am not opening my mouth'. It never occurred to me that it was lipstick, until Dickson told me."

Without a moment's hesitation, Balmer had ignored the fact that the letter had gone for forensic examination immediately it was received and when he had the result, he had immediately initiated a search for a woman.

Rose Heilbron cross-examined.

"But the letter said that the gun was in the Botanic Park lake?"

Balmer replied dispassionately.

"It is quite possible, in seven or eight feet of mud."

"When did you first hear from Northam about the murder?"

"On September 29th Northam telephoned me from Birkenhead, and wanted to tell everything about the murder. He then made a statement. About ten hours after I had seen Northam, I saw Dickson. She said, 'I believe Jimmy has told you all about it'. She then made a statement."

"When did you search Northam's house?"

Again, Balmer twisted the truth.

"On October 30th, at the request of Mr Livermore, we searched for a revolver."

Chief Superintendent Smith was next in the witness box. Questioned by Mr Gorman, he described how, after an approach by Mr Livermore, a search was made of a house in Birkenhead on October 30th. In cross-examination, Rose Heilbron pursued this matter of the search of the home of Northam's parents. She was trying, without arousing the ire of the judge, or alienating the jury, to reveal that the police were lying.

"The search of Northam's residence, on October 30th, was not the result of something told you by Mr Livermore, was it?"

Smith was almost casually dogmatic, unconcerned at his lack of respect for the truth. "It definitely was. Mr Livermore called at the Central Police Office about 5pm on the afternoon of October 29th."

"With the address of a house to search?"

"No, but I knew quite well what he was talking about."

"Oh, it was not on Mr Livermore's information?" Her tone was mildly sarcastic.

"It was the result of what Mr Livermore said." Smith was hedging now and counsel could sense it.

"Mr Livermore called to see you, to say he had some information which might lead to the discovery of the gun used in the Cameo murders? He did not tell you where the gun was?"

"No. He had some information regarding a gun which might be the gun used in the Cameo murders and that he was prepared to give that information on a number of assurances."

There was a brief exchange of words between Miss Heilbron and Harry Livermore before she continued.

"Did he tell you he was doing that under counsel's advice?"

"Yes. And he was told we could not accept those conditions and that if he had information regarding a gun which might be the gun used in the Cameo murders, it was his duty to let us have that information."

"On October 31st, did he write giving you the address?"

"He did."

"So that the search on October 30th was not on Mr Livermore's information?"

"It was the result of what he had said."

"He gave no address?"

"No. But I knew full well what he was talking about, because we had made certain inquiries that afternoon."

"A letter was afterwards sent to Mr Livermore to the effect that when he supplied information, the house had already been searched and that it had been searched on more than one occasion?"

"That is right."

"Every part of the house, including the chimney?"

"Yes, that was searched specially on October 30th. Northam's residence was searched for the first time on May 28th because we were making enquiries regarding the anonymous letter and were very anxious to get hold of Jacqueline Dickson. We knew that Northam was associating with her. Another search was made on October 10th. Northam had told us about the overcoat and we went and recovered it, but we couldn't find the belt and buttons and a search was made for them. We helped Northam to make a search."

"When was the chimney searched besides the 30th? You did not search the chimney for Dickson?"

"We searched the chimney for Northam, because men have been found up chimneys."

Mr Gorman thanked him and sat down. The prosecution's case was completed. It was now late on a Saturday afternoon and the court adjourned until the Monday morning.

This amazing, fabulous story

Two days later, on Monday February 7th, the celebrities were in court. On the High Sheriff's bench was Lord Derby accompanied by the Lady Mayoress. One row behind them, on the bench normally reserved for counsel, sat the show business celebrities, Issy Bonn and Frankie Howerd, who that week were appearing in pantomime at the Liverpool Empire. Alongside them, sat Alderman Arthur Collins, Chairman of the Liverpool Police Watch Committee and his wife, Anne, both good friends of Chief Inspector Herbert Balmer.

Interest had heightened perceptibly, even amongst the seasoned reporters in the press box and along the sides of the court.

Rose Heilbron, in her opening address, appeared confident. She had a genuine sympathy for her client. As if the pressure of the first trial was not enough, he now had to endure it all again and she felt a sudden shame, almost embarrassment, at the cruelty of the English legal system, which would subject a man to such a harrowing experience for the second time. She stood and turned towards the jury.

"This murder shocked everyone, not only in this city, but everyone who heard about it throughout the country. You must have been horrified when you read about it and you must have shared in the hope that the man or men who committed that crime would be speedily brought to justice. There is no doubt that Leonard Thomas was murdered, but you are not here to decide who killed Leonard Thomas, but whether George Kelly did.

The Cameo case has been talked about for a long time and there have been five sets of proceedings in connection with it altogether. It is natural that you should have heard and read a great deal about the circumstances, incidents and the characters in the case.

Forget any preconceived notions. Expunge those natural feelings of repugnance from your minds and deal with this case from the evidence alone. If, at the end of the evidence, you feel yourselves put in the position where you are not sure, or there is hesitation about your decision, you cannot be satisfied beyond reasonable doubt, it will then be your duty to acquit George Kelly.

The prosecution has brought a rather singularly confusing and incredible story before you. It was suggested that five men and women stood in a well-lit passage in a public house on a Saturday night in the centre of the city hatching a plot to rob at the point of a gun. That was the start of the incredible story in the Beehive Hotel.

It has been suggested that Kelly, on March 21st, having already been questioned by the police, was supposed to have gone through the town with Northam's overcoat on his arm and handed it back in Lime Street. He was also said to have confessed to the murder, to a man whom he had told, a few minutes before, to keep his mouth shut. Is not that rather an odd performance?

No item connected with the murder had been traced to Kelly. Neither overcoat, hat, mask, nor gun was found by the police when they searched his home on Sunday March 20th. You might also think, that if a man had been in the room at the cinema committing those horrible murders, there might be some blood on his shoes or clothes.

No ammunition has ever been traced to Kelly's possession. The overcoat was not mentioned until October 10th, after Kelly had been arrested. What was Northam hanging back for then? There was no longer any reason to be afraid.

Having seen and heard the witnesses, what do you think of them? Do you believe them and attach credence to this remarkable story that they tell you. Northam has told you that he could not remember where the anonymous letter was written. That was an astonishing thing, because he was able to remember, six months afterwards, certain other things in connection with the case.

Who was meant to have gone for a 6a tram and to have thrown the gun in the lake in Botanic Park? Northam at first said the reference was to Kelly but that in re-examination he had said Connolly while Mrs Dickson has said it referred to Kelly.

Kelly could not possibly have got back to the Leigh Arms by 9.45 if the evidence of the prosecution is correct and whatever view you may have of the evidence on this case you may think the murders were committed round about 9.40.

Why should Kelly be displaying himself in the Spofforth which was so near the scene of the crime. Was it not, as he himself said, that he was looking for Doris O'Malley?

Chief Inspector Balmer said Kelly told him, on the Sunday morning after the murder, that Kelly had said that he arranged to meet Skelly down town. You might think that if the Inspector was interested in Kelly's movements, it would be a matter of some importance to find out when he was down town, but the Inspector, on his own evidence, had not done so.

Of the incident in the charge room, which, the prosecution alleges, shows that Kelly and Connolly knew each other, you might think it was not an unreasonable assumption for Kelly to know that the other man, Connolly, was the man in the pen and Kelly knew that man was going to be charged with him and was in custody.

As regards the identity parade incident, when Kelly is alleged to have said to Balmer, 'I will get you for this', Kelly maintains that he said, 'I will not forget you for this'. You might think that was a natural reaction of a wrongly charged man who was upset and bad-tempered.

Dickson's evidence was that she went with Connolly and Kelly because she did not want to snub them. There is all the difference in the world between snubbing people and drinking tea and whisky with them and acting as a messenger between them.

You have heard a lot of evidence relating to a search of Northam's house. You heard that in May, Northam's father's house was searched because the police were looking for Jacqueline Dickson. You also heard that they looked up the chimney to see if they could find Mr Northam. You have heard that Mrs Dickson was frightened giving evidence but after September she was obviously going to give evidence because she told a story.

Why wait another ten days to disclose the existence of the overcoat? On October 30th, another search was made and nothing was found. Let it not be thought for one moment that I am making suggestions or implications. All I am dealing with, is the search, but suggestions were made, and I want to deal with those.

The search was at Northam's father's house for a gun and what I do want to draw your attention to, is that you are being asked in this case to rely upon the accuracy of police recollection. I suggest to you that police officers are not infallible as to their recollections."

Miss Heilbron paused, as she waited for her point to sink in. She could comment no more about the police without antagonising the jury and the judge.

She continued her review. "The incident is interesting because you heard Chief Inspector Balmer and Chief Superintendent Smith, both responsible officers of the CID, saying the search on October 30th was made on information given by Mr Livermore. You heard later, that Chief Superintendent Smith admitted that no address was given by Mr Livermore for that search on October 30th. Information was given by Mr Livermore but inquiries were made by somebody else, we do not know by whom and it does not matter but it was from that other source of inquiry, that the address was obtained and not from Mr Livermore.

You heard that Mr Livermore gave the address only on October 31st. Both officers said they made that search because of the information and address given by Mr Livermore." Now she was treading on dangerous ground before a judge to whom the police could do no wrong. Yet Rose Heilbron's voice was firm as she continued. It was the only chance she might have to discredit police evidence.

"They said they had information from Mr Livermore and that that was why the search was made. They agreed that Mr Livermore only gave the address on October 31st and they said Mr Livermore asked, before October 31st, for assurances, the sum total of them being, that he should be present at the search.

At that stage, Mr Livermore and counsel were engaged on behalf of the defence and you heard the question put to the police officer. Mr Livermore, as you know, went to the police and told them about some information he had. He was engaged in defending a man for his life and you may think that he was acting perfectly reasonably, when he wanted to be present at a search of a house for a witness in this case. It was suggested that a gun might be found and you may think that if the defence had any rights in this case, Mr Livermore was wanting to see that those rights were properly looked after." She nodded slowly at the jury before glancing at her notes. There were many pages, her writing so large that each page contained only five or six lines, several pages to be glanced through, before she picked up her next line of argument. She turned her attention to the letter.

"It is an overstatement for Northam and Dickson to say the greater part of the anonymous letter is true. If they were frightened, they had the means of communicating with the police without the police knowing who they were, but it was significant that Kelly was never mentioned to the police until late in September, when the police saw him about something else. It was then that Northam and Dickson told this amazing fabulous story

It was very curious that Kelly should have waited in prison until November 16th before unburdening himself to Graham, this perfect stranger. He not only made a confession that he shot the man at the cinema but, if Graham is to be believed, he told him all the details of the Beehive planning beforehand, all the details of the crime and, all the details of what happened afterwards. That is rather strange because Kelly has, all along, denied to the police, and everyone else, that he was guilty of the crime." Miss Heilbron shook her head in an expression of disbelief before concluding the case for the defence.

"Innocent men have been charged before and I dare say they will be charged again, but while there is a jury system in this country, they will not be convicted. It is your decision on the evidence in this matter that counts. It is your view that will decide this.

At the end of it all, having heard all the evidence, the speeches by learned counsel and his Lordship's summing up, I would submit to you that there is only one verdict you can give with a safe and clear conscience in this case and that is one of not guilty."

George Kelly, flanked by prison officers, entered the witness box, immediately his counsel had finished her opening speech. He was now master of his own fate. There was intense silence as the court waited for him to give his evidence, his chance to speak for himself rather than be represented by others. His appearance, his demeanour, his every word, expression and gesture, involuntary and conscious, would be under scrutiny by the judge and the jury, filed away in their minds, to be recalled later, possibly to influence their verdict. Rose Heilbron glanced purposefully at the jury before speaking to Kelly.

"Did you shoot Leonard Thomas?"

Kelly shook his head, "No."

"Were you at the Cameo Cinema on the night of March 19th?"

"No.".

"Do you know Philip Northam or Jacqueline Dickson?"

"I have never seen them before in my life."

Counsel then asked him to relate his movements on March 19th.

Kelly, in his rapid, almost quickfire, way of talking, recounted what he had done that evening. It was the same evidence he had given previously at the magistrates court and at the first trial, but this time he added to it.

"When I left the Leigh Arms to go to the Spofforth public house, I spoke to Mrs Hilda Kelly, who lived next door to me in Cambridge Street."

"What where you wearing?"

"Brown shoes, a brown birds eye suit, a cream shirt and I had neither a hat nor coat. At no time during the night did I wear a hat or overcoat."

"Were you able to talk to Connolly in prison?"

"Yes. We talked every night in prison through the bars. Although our cells faced different ways and we could not see each other, we could hear each other and there was no difficulty in talking. I could also speak to him in chapel."

"Did you talk to anyone in particular about your case?"

"I talked to a man named Marney, who was an orderly and also with another man. I had exercised with maybe fifty or a hundred people and I've told them the evidence against me. The Cameo was all the topic and Graham had every opportunity of talking to other people. I do remember having a discussion with Graham when I told him I was going down to see Inspector Balmer."

Rose Heilbron's examination of George Kelly finished at 1pm. He had given evidence for almost an hour.

Never threatened anyone yet

After a short lunch adjournment and before William Gorman began his cross-examination, Judge Cassells questioned Kelly.

"Whereabouts would your cell be in relation to Connolly's? Stand up and show us. As you are standing looking straight through the bars, where would Connolly be?"

Kelly was given a sheet of paper and a pencil and drew on it, stepping from the witness box and leaning across the judge's desk to describe what he had drawn to the judge.

"I couldn't see him. It's impossible. I could hear him."

"Apart from exercise, were you in your cell the rest of the time?"

"Yes."

"That would be twenty-three hours out of twenty-four?" Judge Cassells queried.

"Yes."

For George Kelly, his cross-examination was to be a disaster. His natural belligerence, magnified by his sense of injustice, came straight to the fore. Mr Gorman began by asking him what Balmer had done that Kelly would not forget. Kelly was immediately indignant.

"He was the one who charged me with murder. I suppose I was just mad with temper when I said it."

"Did you tell Northam in the Star Hotel on Sunday, March 20th that 'You had better keep your mouth shut, or I'll shut it for you, or my brothers will.'?"

"I could not say that to Northam. I have never seen him in my life."

Kelly was tense, his hands clasped in front of him and he answered some of the prosecution's questions with a quick nod or shake of the head, until the judge reprimanded him.

"You must answer yes or no. The shorthand writer cannot write down a shake of the head."

Mr Gorman continued. "Did you have an interview with your brother Frank, downstairs in this very building, on January 26th.

"Yes."

"Did you say, 'Don't forget, boys, if I do go down, it's up to you to do something about that Northam.'?"

"Yes, I did." Kelly's voice was again indignant. "I didn't know Northam and if I went down it was up to my brothers to do something about Northam, because nobody else would."

Mr Gorman probed deeper. "Is it not strange that Graham should know you had some brothers?"

"I don't know about that. I have never threatened anyone yet.'"

The prosecutor pounced. "Yet? Is that something that is to come?"

"It is just a way of speech." Kelly seemed confused. He looked very tired and passed a hand over his brow. Gorman spoke to him.

"Kelly, if you're tired and want a rest, I will ask that you be given one but I must ask you these questions."

Kelly shook his head. "I'm alright." He took advantage of an earlier offer to be seated.

"Why did you make the remarks to your brother?"

"It was up to my brothers to find out the truth because nobody else would. It was up to the family. It meant to see Northam and get the truth out of him."

"By what means do you think they might get the truth?"

"By speaking."

William Gorman stared hard at Kelly before continuing.

"Are you saying that, 'don't forget boys, if I go down it is up to you to do something about Northam,' means going to see him and trying to get the truth?"

"Yes. I do."

"That was a threat, wasn't it?"

"It was not a threat. I could not threaten anyone because I didn't know the man."

"You are asking your brothers to do something?"

"Yes. To find the truth for me."

"A strange way of asking them to find the truth?"

Kelly's hackles were raised, his reply unthinking.

"Which other way could they find the truth?"

William Gorman's voice was now bitterly sarcastic.

"Do you mean them merely to see Northam and say, 'please, Mr Northam, will you tell the truth?' Is that what you meant?"

"Yes." If the question had stung, it did not show.

Mr Gorman continued, smoothly.

"Do you have any other occupation, apart from going around drinking?"

"I don't go around drinking all the time."

"Have you any sort of regular occupation?"

"Yes. With my mother."

"If you left the Spofforth between 9.20 and 9.25, you very easily could have got to the Cameo Cinema by a little after 9.30?"

"I didn't go to the Cameo Cinema."

Judge Cassells interrupted. "But you could easily?"

Kelly looked surprised at the question, hesitating before replying. "Oh, yes."

"And you could easily, had you desired, have called at your house at 67 Cambridge Street on the way there?"

"Yes."

"And if you left the Cameo Cinema at about 9.35 you could quite easily have got to the Leigh Arms about 9.45 and called at your house on the way?"

"Yes."

"Have you been to the Cameo Cinema?"

"Yes. Once."

Mr Gorman continued his questioning. "How long have you lived in the district?"

"Two or three years, with Mrs O'Malley in Cambridge Street."

"Do you know Fred Thomalla?"

"Yes."

"What time did you get to the Leigh Arms?"

"I got off the tram about quarter to nine and must have got in there about ten to nine. I left to go to the Spofforth and then was back again."

"If you were in the Leigh Arms from 8.45 to 10 o'clock, you could not have been in the Cameo at all?"

"I know I wasn't at the Cameo."

"But if you left the Spofforth at about 9.22 or 9.23, you could have got to the Cameo by 25 minutes to 10?"

"I could, I suppose, but I didn't."

"Was that why you never mentioned the Spofforth Arms when Inspector Balmer saw you on the Sunday?"

"I mentioned everywhere I was."

"You had been drinking that day, in and out of public houses, from before 3.30?"

129

"No. I started about 1.30, just going into a pub, having a pint, talking and playing darts. I would not say I was drinking."

The prosecution would not leave it there, William Gorman's voice mildly sarcastic as he continued, relentlessly.

"Do you not remember very much of what you did that Saturday?"

"Yes."

Under further questioning, Kelly went on to deny that he told Inspector Balmer that there was a note in the sugar basin from Doris O'Malley saying that she was at Bramley's. William Gorman continued.

"Do you know Jacqueline Dickson?"

"I don't know the woman."

"You did not tell Graham that Dickson was living with Stutty Northam?"

"I told Graham nothing." Kelly replied animatedly.

"Did you ever see it in the newspapers that he stuttered?"

"No."

"Did it not say he had an impediment in his speech?"

"Yes."

"Are you suggesting that, from that, Graham might have called him Stutty Northam?"

"It might have been Graham's expression."

"Northam identified you…"

Kelly broke in before Mr Gorman could finish, leaning forward angrily as he spoke, his hands gripping the edge of the dock.

"Northam had difficulty in pointing me out on an identification parade. He gave it up as a bad job. He walked up and down, three or four times and went back over to the police and came back and picked me out." Kelly's outburst was still ringing in people's ears when counsel for the prosecution continued

"The incident in the charge room at Dale Street, that was when you were free?"

"I'll still be free." Kelly banged his fist down on the rail.

"How many times have you been in the White Star public house?"

Kelly's belligerence continued.

"I will say I was in there every night if you want me to."

William Gorman stared hard at Kelly before picking up some of his papers and reading quietly.

"There was an old man there sitting down and he said to me, ' What do you want here?' I said ' I want the takings,' so I went to take the bag. The man stood up and said, 'You cannot take that it belongs to the company. Put that toy away, you can have some of my own money. He tried to push the gun away, so I shot him.' Kelly, is that description familiar to you?"

"No, it is Northam's, Northam knows."

"Have you heard your counsel say that there is no suggestion being made about anyone else in this case? Allow me to remind you that she said that." There was slight pause before counsel continued, solemnly.

" 'Another man came in and stood by the door with his hands behind his back. He said – What is going on here? – and came towards me. He knocked the bag out of my hand and the money scattered all over the floor, so I shot him. He fell on his hands and knees and started to tear at his shirt and was crying. He made a move towards me so

I shot him again.' " Mr Gorman paused and looked up at Kelly. "That seems rather familiar to us."

Kelly shook his head vehemently, his face pale with emotion.

"Not to me. I was never at the Cameo."

"Dr Grace said that Thomas was apparently shot while his arm was raised. That does seem to fit in very well, doesn't it?"

"My conscience is clear."

"Did you hear Dr Grace say that the wound that caused the death of Mr Catterall was either when he was on his knees or standing with his back to you?"

"Yes."

" 'So I shot him and he fell on his knees. I shot him again?' "

"I have never shot a man. I can face God with a clear conscience."

"The description of what happened in that room fits in rather well with what the other people say?"

"Only the man who had seen it would know."

"Let me put this to you, 'I shot both men and when I shot the assistant manager I thought the door had locked itself behind him, so I shot the lock off and then found the door opened inwards.' Do you remember saying that to Graham?"

"No."

"It does, at any rate, seem to fit in rather well, doesn't it?"

Kelly clenched his fist, his voice shaking as he replied.

"I did not say that to Graham."

"Can you think why Dickson and Graham should know about some of these incidents?"

"I told everybody in prison the evidence against me. I have been foolish."

"Did you tell Graham?"

"No, I would not trust Graham."

"Are you suggesting Graham has made this up?"

"No. I was told he was mental. A mental man is not safe. You are liable to tell him something and he will say something else."

"Are you suggesting you told Graham something and he mentioned something else?"

"I was told not go round with him. Graham, McBride and Johnson were in prison together but nobody knows that, do they? They don't tell you that McBride was to give evidence against Johnson, now Graham is giving evidence against me."

"Are you suggesting that someone called McBride told Graham what Graham has said in the box?"

"No."

"Are you suggesting Graham has gone into the box to give evidence against an innocent man?"

"Definitely and Dickson and Northam." Kelly leaned forward, his voice again shaking with emotion. "I have been been persecuted for months all through these people, mostly Dickson and Northam."

Gorman quoted: "Don't forget if I go down, it's up to to you to to something about that Northam. What do you mean?"

"Well it is up to my people to see Northam and get the truth out of him."

"Merely to get the truth out of a man who for five months has persecuted an innocent man?"

Kelly was fighting for control as he replied. "If he was a Catholic, he would tell the police the truth like I have done. I have been to confession and received Holy Communion for sixteen weeks and knelt at the altar rails because I am innocent. That is more than Northam and Dickson could do."

" 'If it is the last thing I do I will get you for this.' What does that mean?"

"I would not say that. I was hot-tempered at the time."

"Is your bitterness against Northam and Dickson because they changed their minds and turned back on you?"

"I have got no bitterness against them because I don't know the people."

"In spite of the fact that you just said that for five months they have persecuted you?"

They have, but what can I do about it. If I am convicted for it, I cannot do anything about it. I have just got to take the blame for somebody else's doings."

"George Kelly, you went to the Beehive on the night of 19th March last and you shot Leonard Thomas at the Cameo."

"I did not shoot anyone." Kelly seemed in despair, almost shouting as he replied, the terrible strain of yet another cross-examination telling.

"And on the Sunday and other days, you told Northam and Dickson what you had done?"

"I told you I don't know Northam or Dickson."

"You told them because, as you said on the Saturday, 'I am Kelly'?"

"I did not say that."

William Gorman nodded to the judge and sat down, his examination of Kelly over.

It was a brutal examination in which Kelly had been successfully portrayed as a man more than likely to lose control. And George Kelly had damned himself.

The evidence of the remaining few defence witnesses took less than ten minutes.

McKinnon and Manson, the street photographers at the time of the Cameo murders, said they were in the Beehive on that night and definitely did not see Kelly

They were followed by Reginald Bampton who said he was in the Leigh Arms at 9.30 by the public house clock. He noticed Kelly standing in the bar by the buffet door. He left after twenty minutes and Kelly was still there. Gorman cross-examined him.

"Did you tell a man at work that Kelly came into the pub at about 9.40 on March 19th and was white and shaking?"

"Definitely not." He stepped from the box to be followed by his brother, Walter, who also gave evidence of having seen Kelly in the Leigh Arms that night.

Again, William Gorman attempted to throw doubt on his evidence.

"Did you tell a workmate that Kelly had done it and got back? The man asked you why you did not tell the police and you said something to the effect that the police had had Kelly for questioning and had let him go and that had they kept him, you would have gone to the police."

"No."

"Why are you giving this evidence?"

"I think that Kelly has been wrongly charged and I know the time I saw him."

The next witness for the defence was Fred Thomalla, the landlord of the Leigh Arms. His time in the witness box was to be disastrous for George Kelly. Thomalla told the court that he was in the bar at 9pm and was asked by Kelly if he had seen Doris.

Kelly said he was going to look for her. The next time he saw him was at 9.50 in the buffet.

He then repeated his evidence of the previous hearing, that he had seen Kelly the following day at lunch time from 12.30 until 2pm. Kelly told him he had been questioned by Inspector Balmer and was very upset. William Gorman cross-examined.

"You made a statement and signed it, that said, 'I am quite definite that George Kelly was not in my house at 9.30pm on the night of the Cameo murders but he was in the buffet at ten to ten.' Is that true?"

"I could not say it is true. I said, 'not to my knowledge.' "

"Look at the statement. Read it to the court."

Thomalla slowly read the statement he had signed.

"Is that true?"

"That is not true."

"Why did you sign it?"

"At the moment I signed, I did not notice the word definite."

"What did you think you were signing, you a police officer of twenty-three year's service?"

"I signed that statement going along in a motorcar. I didn't read it."

"When did you decide Kelly may have been in at 9.30pm?"

"When I saw Mr Balmer."

"Why did you not say; I am not sure, he may have, or may not have been?"

"I understood Mr Balmer had put in, 'to my knowledge.' "

"Have you seen Doris O'Malley recently?"

"She has only spoken to me for an order since Kelly was arrested."

"When did you last see her?"

"Last night."

"Did she bring any message to you from Kelly?"

"No."

"What did Mr Balmer ask you?"

" 'Was Kelly in the house at 9.30pm?' I said 'not to my knowledge.' "

"Did you look at what you signed."

"I did not. I made a mistake by not reading it."

"Did you say that Kelly was wringing his hands and was very concerned?"

"He was."

"How did you fix the time that Kelly was in your house on the Sunday?"

"I looked at the clock because he was really upset."

Miss Heilbron re-examined.

"Did you know then, that the Sunday had anything to do with the case?"

"No."

"Who has brought you here?"

"Mr Livermore. He saw me the next day, or two or three days after the Sunday night when Balmer saw me."

Judge Cassells intervened, his heavy eyebrows arching up in astonishment.

"Mr Balmer saw you on the Sunday night?"

"Yes."

"Mr Livermore came to see you to give evidence. When was that?"

Thomalla hesitated.

"He did not ask me to give evidence until about three or four weeks later."

"What do you mean by your reference to two or three days after the police visit?" Cassells demanded sternly.

"I saw him three days after the Sunday." Thomalla appeared confused, he shifted his position and leaned against the side of the dock and looked around the courtroom as if seeking refuge.

"Are we to judge your general evidence by the accuracy of that answer?"

The ex-policeman's answer was almost a whisper. "Yes, my Lord."

Thomalla's evidence was a disaster for the defence. If he had wanted Cassells and the jury to disregard his evidence that Kelly had been in his pub on the Sunday, it was the perfect answer.

Rose Heilbron now had to repair and minimise the damage done in cross-examination, her next question giving an impression of fairness, as she attempted to restore Thomalla's credibility.

"Can you remember if it was after Kelly was arrested that you saw Mr Livermore?"

"I can't remember. I have no idea. If Balmer had asked me about Kelly, I would have told him."

Judge Cassells intervened, leaning forward, his voice almost kindly.

"Has this been rather a worry to you?"

Somewhat brokenly, Thomalla replied."No, my Lord."

"You have never been at all nervous?"

"No, my Lord."

The final witness for the defence was Colleen Dutton, who repeated the evidence she had given at the first trial, that she was at Kelly's house in Trowbridge Street on September 26th and it was impossible for him to have been seen in Lime Street that afternoon. William Gorman cross-examined her.

"Is Kelly your boyfriend and are you in love with him?"

"Yes."

"When were you first asked to remember what had happened on September 26th?"

"Around January 12th."

A very serious, terrible adventure

Rose Heilbron knew now that her summing up would be critical. In the witness box her client had been a disaster. William Gorman had been ruthless and now she had to attempt to undo the damage which had been done and restore George Kelly's standing in the eyes of the judge and the jury. But this could only be done by discrediting prosecution witnesses. It was a daunting task.

She glanced at Kelly. Still innocent until proven guilty, her client would never, in the world's eyes, be innocent, even if acquitted. There would never be official redemption or compensation, except perhaps, for the sheer relief of an acquittal. But she knew that if acquitted he would survive, feeding on his time in court and his sudden fame.

But first she had to win the acquittal and, although nervous, she was still confident that she would win her case. The prosecution's case was flimsy, the evidence circumstantial, the witnesses' evidence conflicting and the main witnesses had been exposed as liars.

She stood up slowly, arranged her gown around her and started to speak.

"I will remind you that it is not easy for an accused to gather evidence together when he was not charged until six months after the alleged offence. Kelly has brought such evidence as was available after such a long time.

Defence witnesses have been asked how they could remember months back, but that also applies to prosecution witnesses. It might be wondered how Northam and Dickson could remember what happened on a day so far back as March and give a record of conversations. Are you satisfied that the evidence the prosecution has given you to prove this man's guilt is the sort of evidence upon which you can truly rely?

You might think that without the evidence of Graham, Northam and Dickson, you would have very little upon which you could convict Kelly. No coat, gun, mask or bullets were ever found in possession of Kelly and, except for Northam and Dickson, no one has said they ever saw Kelly in possession of bullets, gun, overcoat or hat. Whenever Kelly was seen, either before or after the time it was said the murder was committed, he was never seen wearing a hat or coat.

Kelly said, and repeated on oath in the witness box, that he did not know Connolly but the prosecution invited you to come to the conclusion that he did and that they committed the murder together. The prosecution called the evidence of two police officers and a store detective to say that they had been seen together.

But you might think that it would have been possible to have called someone from the district where Kelly or Connolly lived, or one of their friends, to say that they had been together.

Constable Nugent said he had seen Kelly in Lime Street on September 26th but Miss Dutton said Kelly was with her in his mother's house that day.

Does it matter that Miss Dutton was in love with Kelly? Miss Dutton had no doubt that it was September 26th as she had caught a train to London that night.

The note of the interview which Kelly had with Inspector Balmer on the Sunday after the murder was made some three-quarters of an hour later. That might not be a very long time in some matters but there had been a lot of conversation and a lot of words, and you might think that it was not entirely easy to remember accurately all the words that were spoken and, in a matter of this kind, every word was surely important.

You cannot attach much importance to the incident in the charge room when Kelly was alleged to have shouted to Connolly, 'you don't know me, do you?' As Kelly has said himself, 'If I had known Connolly I could have ignored him altogether.'

You heard Northam and Dickson say that on Sunday March 20th, Kelly and Connolly agreed between themselves that they would say they did not know each other. Yet it was suggested that, after that, they were seen together as late as September 26th. Even if they did know each other, do you think it would be a good policy on their part to go about in public in Lime Street and associate together, if they had agreed earlier that they did not know each other?

Another incident is put forward and what you are asked to deduce from this is a matter for you, but you are asked to believe that Kelly said, 'I will get you for this, Balmer.' Kelly says he said, 'I will not forget you.' Whatever was said, do you not think that could be the natural reaction of an innocent man? He admits quite frankly, 'I was mad.' Because he is a prisoner on trial, is he not allowed to have a temper?" Miss

Heilbron looked up at the jury as she discarded more of her notes, her voice low and earnest as she continued.

"Then there is the evidence of a man called Dowling. It is suggested that because things happened some time ago, a man's memory might be inaccurate. With what tremendous force you may think, does that apply to the evidence of Dowling. Here is a man who comes a long time after and tells the police, 'I know on March 19th I saw George Kelly in Cases Street.'

Dowling could not remember any of the other days he saw Kelly and he saw Kelly a number of times before and since. Do you not think that he might be mistaken, or is a mistake impossible on the part of a witness for the prosecution? Dowling said he remembered the date because he saw Kelly the following week. He could not remember whether it was the Monday, Tuesday or Wednesday and you may think that is some measure of his memory and Dowling says he remembered because Kelly told him he had been questioned about the Cameo.

The prosecution suggested 9.32 might have been the time of the murder. If that was right, Mrs Jackman's time must be wrong. At the lowest, her estimate was 9.39 and at the highest 9.44.

If the man who committed the murder left the Cameo at 9.40, or thereabouts, he had first to do over 900 yards to Smithdown Road, dispose of his hat and coat in his house, and be back in the Leigh Arms at 9.45. And there is the curious hesitation of Northam in not telling the police about the overcoat. Why was it not disclosed to the police until October 10th?"

There is no dispute that, at 9.45, Kelly was in the bar. You have heard, and Kelly himself has also said, he was there at 9 o'clock and, allowing for some discrepancies in time, it seemed reasonably certain that he was at the Spofforth between 9.15 and 9.25.

You will have to consider the evidence of the Bampton brothers who had said that they saw Kelly in the Leigh Arms because, if you thought the evidence in the case to matter, if their evidence cast doubt in your minds, then you may think you will have difficulty in accepting the prosecution's story.

Mr Thomalla told you that on Sunday, between 12.45 and 2 o'clock, Kelly was in his public house and he had reason for remembering, as he was so upset. That evidence is very important, because Northam and Dickson said that Kelly was in the Star public house in Brownlow Hill at that time. Kelly could not have been in both public houses at the same time.

Graham came to court from Walton Prison. You may think that the only matters Graham says Kelly told him about, are matters already known to the prosecution and as having been given in prosecution evidence. Graham alleges that the first time Kelly spoke to him was November 16th and you must remember that the murder took place on March 19th and the committal proceedings at the police court on October 19th to 22nd, were fully reported in the newspapers.

The only difference between the story that Graham tells and the story that everyone else knew, except Graham, is the fact that instead of saying this is the evidence for the prosecution against me, Kelly says, 'This is how I did it.' Kelly says he did not tell Graham and Graham did not ask him because Graham says, 'I had no interest whatever in the case.'

Graham does not say, ' What did you do with the gun, or the overcoat, or the mask?'

and Kelly does not tell him that information, although he has confided and poured out his heart and soul to this man Graham; although he is pouring out all that is known to the prosecution.

Kelly was in prison approximately six weeks up to November 16th and, therefore, you may think he had ample opportunity, when he was exercising, to talk with lots of people and discuss the evidence given against him and he says he did and he says; 'I talked to the cleaners,' and he says, 'I had no need to talk to Graham. Why should I give a message to Graham to give to Connolly, because I could talk to Connolly. Although I cannot see Connolly, because of the way the cells faced, I could talk and we could hear each other.'

Graham's alleged statement of what Kelly had told him was the prosecution's case and I will remind you that, from the beginning to the end of that case, Kelly had all along denied any complicity in the murder and yet Graham has come along and suggested that Kelly told him all the details in a long confession.

You will remember that Graham himself admitted, that in 1945, he applied for admission to Whittingham Mental Hospital. You know it arose through war service and that it was indeed very unfortunate but the fact remained, that Graham admitted he was mentally ill between 1945 and 1949 and that, in 1949, he again entered Whittingham for a period of some weeks and that he was discharged as recovered. No one suggested that Mr Graham was a lunatic. He was, however, the man whose evidence, as to a confession, you are asked to accept."

Rose Heilbron stopped, glancing along the line of jurors before continuing, speaking slowly to give emphasis, asking the jury to remember that Dickson and Northam had said no one was in passage drinking at the Beehive, but other witnesses said there were about fifteen or twenty people.

"Why did they say that? You might think they were saying it because if there was no one in the passage, the goings-on they alleged, could have happened without anyone noticing them.

And what about this dark girl who was supposed to be with Kelly. I ask you to consider that, although she apparently was in the group for a time on the Saturday night and quite a time on the Sunday, no one appeared to have given her a name.

You might think that Northam and Dickson would pause to consider before having anything to do with what they knew was a very serious terrible adventure and you will remember that, according to Northam's evidence, the man put his overcoat on and he was planning go to Webster Road and do a hold-up, whatever the outcome, a terrible crime. The only explanation he could give for not asking for the overcoat back, was that it had slipped his memory.

There are certain discrepancies between the contents of the anonymous letter and the evidence of Dickson and Northam, who wrote the letter. There was no mention in the anonymous letter of the Beehive Hotel and there are other things which might cause you to ask yourselves, 'What are they talking about?'

You are asked to believe that Northam has come to court and given in detail, the account of something six months previous, without the aid of a note. Why did the man, who did not like guns, keep six bullets out of curiosity and because he wanted to hand them over to the police. They never were handed to the police.

It was a fact that could not be overlooked that the bullets were handed to Northam six weeks before the letter was written. That meant four weeks before the murder was committed. You might think that was a very curious thing. You are being asked to rely on Northam and Dickson and yet, when Northam was asked why he had put six weeks in the letter, he said he didn't know."

Another tranche of Rose Heilbron's pages were fluttering to the bench, another batch ready for recital, when the judge adjourned the court for lunch. An hour later, she reappeared in the court, looking refreshed and more confident than earlier.

"I will remind you what Northam and Dickson had said in the anonymous letter to the police, about the assurance they sought from the police, that they would not be involved if they gave further information. Despite that assurance, when Dickson was seen by the police in May, she did not reveal herself as being a party to writing that letter. When she was asked why she had not indicated certain things in the letter, she replied that she was afraid the police, or others, would discover that they were living in Birkenhead. If that was the case, why was it that, within a short time after the murder, Dickson and Northam removed from Birkenhead to Liverpool, where they remained for four to six weeks?

Northam has declared that he knew that the gun had been thrown into the lake. It was because of that, that I asked Northam about the case of Robert Johnson and you might think you could not entirely divorce that case, from the statements made by Northam. If Northam was speaking the truth when he said that he knew the gun was in the lake, why did he not come forward with that information when he heard that Johnson had been charged with being an accessory after the fact to murder? Northam had that knowledge and he kept it to himself, knowing the other man was being tried and that the information would have been of value in that trial.

The only clue the police had as to the writer of the anonymous letter was the lipstick on the envelope. It would have been a simple matter, you might think, for Northam and Dickson to have put in the letter the details which they had given in evidence and there was nothing to stop them mentioning Kelly's name. You will not overlook the fact, that Northam and Dickson made no mention of any of the matters they had given in evidence, until September. The police said Dickson was afraid but if she was, what had happened to remove her fear in September, that was present in May?

You may think the anonymous letter is a rather important document, because it is the first documentary evidence in this case. The letter contained admitted lies, but Northam and Dickson were two people on whom the prosecution are asking you to rely, in this very grave matter.

You are asked to rely, for instance, on the memory and the accuracy of Northam, but in the witness box, although he could remember what happened in such great detail six months before he told the police, he could not remember what he had done on the afternoon of March 19th. He could not remember where he lived in Upper Parliament Street and he could not remember where he had written the letter."

Defence counsel paused, discarding more of her notes, some of them fluttering to the floor under the counsel benches. She glanced swiftly along the line of jurors before continuing.

"You have heard the brothers Bampton say they saw Kelly in the Leigh Arms between 9.20 and 9.40. You have heard Thomalla's evidence and you might still feel he was a witness of truth, although he became confused under cross-examination. If you do not believe Northam and Dickson are telling the truth about the Sunday, can you believe them about the Saturday? You have to look at their evidence as a whole.

I have no intention of making suggestions about Northam. I am not suggesting he ought to be charged. Nor could he be. Supposing, however, Northam had been charged on the basis of the evidence that the murderer was wearing a coat that belonged to him; that bullets were afterwards found in his possession; that the overcoat had been discovered at a later date; that he had gone away from Liverpool rather hurriedly and that the police searched up the chimney for him.

Supposing he had given an account of his movements in a document, which was completely different from what he afterward said really happened. Supposing the roles were reversed and he had been in the dock and Kelly in the witness box. Supposing he said, 'I lent that coat to Kelly,' and supposing Kelly denied that.

Of those two stories, does one give you more difficulty than another or perhaps do not both give you equal difficulty? If there was no evidence for the defence, would you convict a man of murder on the evidence called by the prosecution? Is there no room for doubt?

I trust you will come to the only conclusion to which, in my submission, the evidence must give you and that is, that there must be a verdict by which George Kelly will leave this court a free man."

When she sat down, Rose Heilbron looked drained, her statements now appeared inadequate against the weight of the witnesses for the prosecution. And the oratory of the counsel for the prosecution.

Perjury of the most hellish kind

It was almost mid-afternoon when William Gorman started his closing speech for the prosecution. He had a stronger presence than Rose Heilbron, his voice more commanding, his demeanour almost arrogantly confident. It was an echo of his opening speech as, rationally and forcibly, he summarised the prosecution's case.

"You have heard many times that the burden of proof is upon the prosecution. You have been reminded of the consequences of finding him guilty. In this case, members of the jury, you are here to decide if the evidence called by the prosecution satisfies you beyond reasonable doubt, that Kelly killed Leonard Thomas.

Miss Heilbron has said it is difficult, six months after, to get witnesses. I want to examine that, before I come to discuss anything else. There are two people in this case, one in particular, who could have provided complete corroboration for the alibi of Kelly from 7.30 until 8.30 that Saturday night.

That was James Skelly. You have heard it suggested and, it was the case, that James Skelly was called before, as a witness for his friend George Kelly. Where is James Skelly at this moment? Is he still in Liverpool? So far as I know, my friend Miss Heilbron says, 'I did not call Skelly because he was drunk.' With respect to Miss Heilbron, that was not the evidence that George Kelly gave yesterday afternoon, 'When I left James Skelly at 8.30, he was not drunk.'

Skelly could have told you what happened until 8.30 on that Saturday night, or maybe later. The last witness for the alibi, the man named Yorkie, said he knew nothing after 7.30, because that was when he left the public-house and left Skelly. Skelly could have told you what Kelly did on that Saturday. Skelly could have told you whether Northam and Dickson were speaking the truth when they said they saw Skelly with Kelly in the White Star Hotel on the Sunday afternoon. Skelly could have told you what happened on that Sunday afternoon, when he was interviewed in his house by the police, or on that Sunday morning. Skelly was the man who could have satisfied you, or helped to satisfy you, that it was quite impossible for George Kelly to be at the Beehive at 7.30 or 8 o'clock.

Where is Skelly today?

Another thing is the whereabouts of Mrs O'Malley, the woman with whom Kelly is living, the woman who was seen the night before last by Mr Thomalla, the licensee of the Leigh Arms Hotel, the woman about whom I asked certain questions.

Mrs O'Malley was the woman who could have told you where George Kelly was on that Saturday night, or the time he got home, what time he got up next morning and where he went, whether he went to the Leigh Arms at lunch time. She could have told you whether Inspector Balmer's account of what took place at that house was true and could have told you of the interview with Kelly in prison and whether the police have given a full account of that. That is the woman with whom Kelly was living and who, two nights ago, went to the Leigh Arms and yet the defence says it is difficult, after six months, to get alibi witnesses.

James Skelly and Doris O'Malley were two persons who could have told you a lot about that weekend and who could have helped to fill a gap in Kelly's alibi. There is no evidence of any kind to support Kelly as to what he did on the Saturday night, between 7.30 and 9 o'clock. None at all.

You might think that the attitude of the defence towards Northam and Dickson is 'willing to wound but afraid to strike.' You saw Dickson in that box for two hours and thirty five minutes. You saw that creature taken by some frightful disease. You saw her there, heard her, hour after hour, being questioned and maybe you saw her look at this man and call him Georgie Kelly and refer to Charlie Connolly.

Do you think, members of the jury, that woman could have stood the cross-examination she was subjected to, if she were telling a pack of lies to send a man to his doom? Do you think she had the physical or the mental energy to stand up for one hour and forty seven minutes in the cross-examination of my learned friend, if that what she was telling was not, in fact, the truth?

Yesterday, members of the jury, you saw her counterpart in that box, George Kelly. You saw two people. You heard what they said. You heard how they said it." William Gorman paused. He gave a grim smile, one eyebrow quickly arched before continuing, shaking his head sympathetically.

"Dickson may be a prostitute, God knows her life may not have been lived in very pleasant places, but I don't think it is as illogical to say that every prostitute is a liar, as to say that every liar is a prostitute. You would not, in my submission, be justified in saying that because this woman has been treated harshly, physically, at the hands of some men, that she is a woman who cannot be believed when she goes into the witness box.

You will decide whether that woman has gone into that box and, with full consciousness of what she is doing, has sworn on oath on that which she knew was true, not against a friend of hers, a former acquaintance who has treated her badly, not against someone whom she knew well but, on the defences submission, against a man she had never seen in her life before, or had any contact with. Of all the thousands of young men of Kelly's age in Liverpool, this woman picks out George Kelly and says it is he who took part in this murder. Do you believe that?

You have this to consider. The police had never made any made any imputations against Northam or Dickson of being liable for this murder. I don't know whether it was suggested in some strange way that Graham was involved, because Miss Heilbron has lumped them all together as people against whom there were made no imputations.

The police have never suggested that Northam or Dickson took part in killing the two men. Does it not strike you as being remarkable that, if Dickson and Northam did not know Kelly, that of all the thousands of men in Liverpool, they should choose Kelly, who was within three minutes of the scene of the murder, on his own evidence?

Is it not remarkable, that they should have the devilish foresight to seize upon the man who happened to be, at 9.20, at the Spofforth Hotel, that they should have gone to an identification parade weeks after to identify that man, a stranger to them, that they should speak to him by name and that he should turn out to have been a few minutes walk of the murder?

Is it not remarkable they should seize upon the very man who said to Graham in prison, 'I shot that man.' By what wonderful imagining did Dickson and Northam seize upon that man? By what mental process did people identify people in those circumstances, unless their mental process was the process of truth? Can you think of any other than the truthfulness of those people, that would allow them to pick on that man by name and, that the whole circumstances should show, quite apart from the evidence, how right they were?

What was the inference behind the questions about the searching of Northam's father's house? On October 29th, the solicitor said he could give information about a gun in a certain place but it is well that you should not be left with any idea in your minds, that the police searched because it was suspected that Northam had the gun.

Consider the right way to approach the evidence of Graham, as I see it. Three things have been said about Graham; that he read it in the papers, that he spoke to a cleaner by the name of Marney in Walton Prison and that, because of being torpedoed in the war, he was for a time in a mental hospital. Let us consider these separately.

You see, members of the jury, the defence must of necessity, counter, or try to counter, the evidence of Graham. Graham was in prison but you saw him in the witness box. First of all, will you ask yourselves this question: did Graham seem the sort of man who would stand there and commit perjury, in a capital trial, against a man whom he had never seen in his life, until November 16th of last year? Is there on earth a lower type of being than the man who would dishonestly swear away the life of a complete stranger to him? You are up against that.

It is said by the defence here, that that which Graham has said in the witness box, is perjury of the most hellish kind. Will you consider this fact; that he belonged to Preston and the paper he read was possibly a Preston paper. Assuming that, do you think that a man, seeing the papers in October, would cherish in the innermost recesses of his mind, all the details, as he saw them, of this case, months before ever he knew Kelly, so that if he ever met this man Kelly, he could perjure himself against him by using that which he had read?

Many times, in the course of the case, you have heard it said that Kelly maintained his innocence throughout. That is not true. If you accepted the evidence of the prosecution, he has disclosed to both Northam and Dickson the whole of what had happened. Miss Heilbron has said that that was the most incredible part of the whole of this incredible story.

When you heard, yesterday afternoon, the outburst in the witness box by Kelly against these people, was that not the outburst of a man who had been thwarted by the disclosure which he had not expected?

You might think that there is no doubt of the time when the murder took place. Mrs Simpson placed it just after 9.30. The witnesses in the cinema saw the clock in the projection-room showed 9.35 and the 999 call was put through at 9.45. Is there the slightest doubt that the murder took place a few minutes after 9.30 and before 9.35?

The point has been raised that Kelly could not have got into the cinema through the side door, but someone got into the cinema, someone shot the man and someone cut the telephone wires. The witness Dowling has been criticised for remembering what happened on the Saturday night but it is natural that he only remembered the important night." Mr Gorman stopped, picking up his sheaf of papers, about to continue when Judge Cassells stopped him. It was late, he supposed Mr Gorman still had a lot to say and he adjourned the hearing for the day.

On the following day, February 7th. William Gorman resumed his case for the prosecution. He nodded to the jury and launched directly into his delivery, reviewing the evidence of Kelly's interview by Balmer on the morning after the murder, commenting on the absence of Skelly as a witness.

"It would not have been without interest to have had some sort of confirmation from Skelly as to where he was. Do you think Kelly was with Skelly all that night? Are you satisfied George Kelly was ever with James Skelly? If the whereabouts of Kelly could have been fixed to 8.30, Northam and Dickson said it was about that time he left the Beehive. If there was evidence that he was anywhere but the Beehive at 8.30, you could say that they could not both be right."

Mr Gorman then reviewed Kelly's alibi which centred around the Leigh Arms.

"It has been suggested, by the defence, that Kelly was in the Leigh Arms at 9.30 and it was abundantly clear why that time has been put forward. Kelly could have committed the murder and could still have been in the Leigh Arms at 9.45. The Bampton brothers, who have been called by the defence, have said that Kelly was in the Leigh Arms at 9.20. That was nearly half an hour before any one else saw him there. The fact remains that at 7.30, Kelly was a few minutes from Cases Street and, at 9.45, he was a few minutes from the Cameo Cinema.

It would not be unfair to ask you to consider the events leading up to the identification of the people who wrote the anonymous letter. You will remember Dickson seeing Mr Balmer on May 13th and saying, 'Get hold of Connolly' and remember her saying on May 18th, 'You have let him get away. Get hold of Connolly.' Getting a little more careless, on May 23rd, when she was told Connolly would tell nothing, she said, 'look at the envelope and you will find lipstick,' gradually being driven into the position that the police were tracing the letter to her.

View the letter in its broadest sense, not meticulously with a microscope and say that, substantially it is true.

Much has been said about the absence of Connolly at the scene of the murder, but was that surprising? Have you any doubt, that between 8.45 and 9.35, the position was observed and nicely sensed by these men, who had gone to the cinema with a specific object. Was it to be wondered that Connolly was not seen. Of course he was not. His being there would have excited comment. Could they expect any man, who had gone there, if merely to rob, to hang around the front of the cinema, while there was a man there sticking up bills."

Mr Gorman paused, taking a sip of water before nodding to the judge and then turning back to the jury.

"I am now finished and I am relieved, for no man can take with pleasure, the submission on behalf of the Crown, that I feel it now my duty to make you. You have heard the whole of the evidence and you will, I know, fearlessly and regardless of the cost, give your verdict.

It is my submission, with the full responsibility of leading for the Crown, that George Kelly shot and killed Leonard Thomas and that, members of the jury, by the law of this land, is murder.

William Gorman sat down. The final prosecution speech, in the longest murder trial the country had ever seen, was complete.

Sometimes people want to talk

Many members of the bar disagreed with capital punishment and it was the unfortunate task of a judge to hear a murder trial for which, if the accused was found guilty, there could only be one result.

James Cassells had already made the decision that Kelly should be tried first, which had affected the whole tenor of the evidence the jury had heard. With only Kelly's evidence, there was every chance they would reach a verdict.

It was terrible burden, especially as he was sharing accommodation with Judge Oliver at Newsham House, where they dined together and no doubt discussed the case together. It would have been unlikely if some of Roland Oliver's opinions had not transferred to James Cassells.

Before Judge Cassells began his summing up at eleven o'clock on the morning of February 8th, there was a gradual drop in conversation, until an almost awesome silence settled on the courtroom. Counsel for the defence and prosecution, their supporting entourage, their juniors and the solicitors, waited quietly. Their task was done, now they sat with hands folded on their laps, or on the bench in front of them.

Judge Cassells stared around the courtroom, shuffling his notes and then laying them carefully on the bench in front of him. He stared over his glasses at the jury, before outlining their responsibilities.

"I will remind you that the burden of proof rests upon the prosecution and you must be satisfied beyond reasonable doubt. If there is reasonable doubt created by either the prosecution, or defence, as to whether a prisoner killed a deceased man with a malicious intention, the prosecution could not then be said to have made out a case and an accused man was entitled to be acquitted.

If, on the other hand, the evidence satisfies you beyond reasonable doubt of the guilt of the accused, then conviction must follow. These facts are for you. You are the judges of the evidence. If, in the course of my summing up, you think I have expressed any view on the facts, you are entitled to ignore what I said. You make up your minds.

It is right I should say something on the subject of accomplices. Two of the witnesses for the prosecution might be described as accomplices. A person who took a part, however small, in an offence, should be regarded as an accomplice. On their own evidence, two of the witnesses might be said to have some associations with the accused man on that night; the man Northam and the sick woman, Jacqueline Eva Margaret Dickson.

Let me warn you that it is dangerous to convict a prisoner on the uncorroborated testimony of accomplices, although it is within your province to do so if you choose. Corroboration merely means that the evidence is strengthened by independent evidence. It is not necessary you should look for corroboration of everything the accomplice said, because if that was so, the evidence of the accomplice would not be necessary. What is required is independent testimony, direct or circumstantial, which affects the prisoner by tending to connect him with the crime and confirms any material particulars that the crime was committed and that the prisoner committed it.

Evidence between accomplices cannot be corroborated by another. Northam's evidence cannot not be used to corroborate Dickson's and vice versa. But the prisoners conduct in the circumstances of the case might be corroboration. Graham's evidence, if you accept it, might be corroboration, because you might think that it strengthened the other evidence.

Is this the man who killed? Put out of your mind anything that you might have read and apply yourselves entirely and solely to the evidence which has been given in this case. The prosecution submits that Kelly was the man armed with a gun who shot Leonard Thomas, that his appearances, before and after the crime, were designed and carried out to frustrate identification and that his subsequent conduct and talk point to his guilt.

The defence submits his denial throughout; denies the association with and all knowledge of the persons Northam and Dickson and submits an alibi which means, at the material time, he was not where the witnesses for the prosecution say that he was.

Let me remind you, in order that you may keep them in your minds, of some of the dates." Judge Cassells referred to his notes, reviewing the sequence of events, from the night of the murder, to Graham's exercising with Kelly in Walton Prison. He then reviewed the evidence presented, particularly what had happened in the Beehive according to Northam and Dickson's testimony, emphasising that, according to Dickson, Kelly had used the phrase, 'So what, I am Kelly'.

He then compared the estimate of fifteen to twenty people in the passage, by the barman at the Beehive, with that of Northam and Dickson, who said they were the only ones there.

He went on to review Kelly's evidence of his afternoon and evening and then what happened inside the cinema, giving a graphic description of the murderer.

"Out came a man wearing a brown overcoat, a mask over his face and with a trilby hat pulled down over his head. He has dark eyebrows and dark hair and pointed the gun at these people and said; 'stand back or I'll let you have it,' and down the spiral staircase he rushed."Judge Cassells peered at the jury over his half moon glasses as he continued. "An armed robber who has killed does not move leisurely."He then discussed the time element.

"Times might be of some importance in this case. In considering the evidence of times, you must bear in mind the opportunities and means that those who spoke of those times had, of being accurate."

At this point, the judge's summing up strayed from the impartial – his times not bearing any close comparison with those given by witnesses, the very positive evidence of the fireman ignored completely.

"Miss Thornhill thought it was 9.25 when Mrs Jackman got there and Miss Stevens said it was 9.30 when Mrs Jackman gave her the papers.

There you have the position of one person up on the first floor saying 9.25 and someone downstairs saying it could not be before 9.30. Mrs Jackman gave 9.30 as the time she took the money to the office and the bangs were at 9.40.

Mrs Evans gave the time of the bangs as 9.32 and she said her clock was put right by the nine o'clock news. Mrs Watkins fixed the time by the clock in the projection room and said when she heard the bangs it was 9.35. You might take it that the first shot was fired at 9.35 and the others within seconds."Judge Cassells then reviewed the evidence concerning the overcoat, before commenting that the gun had never been found.

"The pond had been dragged by the police with no result. There was a special search at Northam's house on October 30th, as a result of a visit to the police by Mr Livermore, Kelly's solicitor, of whose efforts in this case, the prisoner, at any rate, can have no cause to complain."

The judge again returned to discussing Kelly's attitude.

"Currie said Kelly seemed very excited, putting his clenched fists on the counter and saying 'You can't take liberties with Kelly.' Does that link up with Mrs Dickson's piece of evidence, that when the gun was being shown at the Beehive and she said he should put it away, Kelly remarked; 'So what, I am Kelly'?"

Judge Cassells then remarked on the importance of public house clocks in the case, "That in the Leigh Arms is ten minutes fast and the Spofforth twenty minutes fast. The brothers Bampton declare they saw Kelly in the Leigh Arms at 9.30. And if that is the position, it is quite obvious that Kelly could not have been shooting the manager at the Cameo Cinema at 9.35.

The manager of the Leigh Arms said he saw Kelly at nine o'clock when he was looking for Doris and the next time he saw him was at 9.50. When Mr Thomalla came to be cross-examined, he had to agree that he signed a document which was shown to him, in which he said that he was definite that Kelly was not in the house at 9.30. That is a very important time and Mr Thomalla is an old police officer with twenty-three years service and, as licensee of a public house where there can be, at any rate, one night of the week, as many as eighty people, can be quite a busy man.

He says he signed that document without reading it and he says he thought instead of the word 'definite', it was, 'to my knowledge' and if he had seen the word 'definite', he would not have signed it and that Mr Balmer had put into the document the word 'definite' when he ought not to have put it in.

Let me remind you about the events of Sunday March 20th and the suggestion that Connolly had said something about leaving the country. Skelly said he would find him a ship. Kelly called Connolly a yellow..." Cassells refused to use the word, merely

145

nodding his head meaningfully.

"Remember what Kelly was alleged to have told the others about the interview with Inspector Balmer on the Sunday. Of his suggestion to Connolly that the inspector was likely to visit him, 'if he does come to see you, remember, we don't know each other.'

Dickson's account substantiates that. Kelly said it is all invented, he was not in the Star public house at all on that Sunday and that he was in the Leigh Arms from 12.30 until 2 o'clock.

It is strange, you may think, it is a matter for you, that Northam and Dickson should pick on a public house which Kelly does visit.

Northam and Kelly met in Lime Street a few days after the murder, when Kelly went to fetch the overcoat. You might think it would be difficult for Kelly to have made the journey from there to his home and back in fifteen to twenty minutes. If the incidents happened, which was denied, you might think, from the time Kelly was away, the coat could not have been at his home at that time.

When Kelly came back, he told, according to Northam, the whole story of what happened at the Cameo and about shooting the man. If an interview took place, if that statement was made by Kelly to Northam, you may think that it is a piece of very important evidence. Kelly denies the interview. He denies that he saw Northam on that day. He denies that he knew him or ever saw him.

The anonymous letter arrived. We know now, if the evidence of Northam and Dickson is to be accepted, that they were responsible for it. What was the object? Why was it written? Why was it anonymous? You may think the answer to that is the answer given by Northam, that he was scared of Kelly.

When, on May 13th, Dickson spoke to Inspector Balmer, her only comment was, 'get Connolly'.' Later, she was complaining to the police that they had let Connolly go and the message was, 'get Connolly and make him talk. If the gang want to get anyone, they can get him, not me.' Dickson was scared of the gang. On May 23rd, the police saw Dickson again but there was still no word about the Beehive, or Northam, or the overcoat. Dickson said, 'If you think I am telling lies, you will find lipstick on the envelope'. Still Dickson was preserving her attitude, 'I am not opening my mouth'.

Why? What was the reason for that attitude? It came out in the cross-examination of Inspector Balmer. Dickson referred to someone who had been slashed with a razor in the Liverpool Courts, Inspector Balmer told the whole story of how Dickson had said that while a man was giving evidence against a gang in the Liverpool court, a woman went out and bought a razor blade in Dale Street and slashed the witness across the face and got four years penal servitude. Was that the reason which kept Dickson and Northam in the background for so long?

The anonymous letter was the composition of illiterate people. Northam and Dickson both took a hand in it, although the hand that actually wrote it may well have been Northam's. It has been admitted that some parts of the letter were true and some untrue. Dickson seemed to be scared of Kelly. About the time of the anonymous letter, when she was with Kelly at the Caledonian, she said she was scared of somebody called Woolerton and that Kelly tapped his pocket. She also said that Kelly remarked, 'If you mention anything about this, I will knife you. If I don't someone else will'.

Did that interview take place? Dickson said she was frightened when she left Kelly on that occasion and she also said she had been attacked in Manchester. Were these people scared by the possibility of what would be done to them if they gave information?

Constable Nugent said he had known them for three years. He had known them to be associates with each other. On the one hand, Constable Nugent says that he saw them together at 5.30 on September 26th and, on the other hand, Miss Dutton says that on that afternoon, they were together.

Sangster says he had seen them together about five or six times and Sergeant Richards says that he has seen them associating before and after March 19th. But Swinburn, who knew Kelly, said he had seen him often with Skelly but never with Connolly.

The judge then reviewed the evidence of the identity parade.

"Kelly was alleged to have shouted out, 'If it's the last thing I do, I'll get you for this, Balmer'. But Kelly maintained he said, 'I'll not forget you for this'.

I now come to one whom you might regard as important in this case; Robert Graham. He was a stranger to Kelly and Connolly and they were strangers to him. He has purported, in the course of his evidence, to give you his account of what he said Kelly told him, in the course of talks during prison exercise. 'The only evidence against him, was the evidence of a prostitute named Jacqueline Dickson and a man named Stutty Northam.' Northam, you will remember, had something of an impediment in his speech."Judge Cassells then paused before continuing, with emphasis. " 'Said Graham, a man named Stutty Northam.' Graham said he did not know anything about Northam and his stuttering and did not even know him. Graham also said that Kelly told him he had shot both men and of how the door opened inwards into the office. How true was all that? Kelly was supposed to have told Graham that he had a cast iron alibi, and that he had got rid of his hat and coat and was in his own pub at a quarter to ten and that his life hung on five minutes.

Another thing put to Graham was that he had been a voluntary patient in Whittingham Hospital, which was a mental institution. He had a great deal to say about that. He told you he had been torpedoed in the course of the war and had suffered a great deal from anxiety neurosis and was invalided from the service. He denied that a proper description of him would be that, either then, or at any time, he suffered from delusions, or that he heard noises. He said he was sent there as a sane man. He said he certainly had fits of depression.

Let's see what Kelly has to say about the so-called interview between himself and Graham. Kelly said he did not have any of these long conversations with Graham and that everyone in the prison knew what he was there for and that everyone was talking about the Cameo murders. He denies absolutely that he said anything to Graham which could justify, in the slightest way, any of the evidence which Graham has given.

That is a matter for you. It was suggested to Graham that he could have read it all in the newspapers. It certainly comes after the whole of the proceedings in the Magistrates Court because Graham did not go into the prison until November 14th.

But Graham said the case did not arouse any special interest in him and that he did not follow it in any great detail and it was not until he got in the prison, that he became the recipient of this information from Kelly, who, by that time, had been in the prison, on remand, ever since September 30th.

There are one or two recollections you may have about this. Twenty-three hours a day is a long time to be in solitary confinement. Sometimes people want to talk. You have to ask yourselves, is Graham's evidence worthy of consideration in this case? It certainly cannot lightly be left out. You may think it provides you with some extra evidence in regard to those matters about which Northam and Dickson have spoken. There is no suggestion that Northam and Dickson, or either of them, has ever seen Graham in their life. They were as complete strangers to Graham, as Kelly himself was, until he met Graham in the prison.

Later on, two things came out in cross-examination which you may think very important. The first was on January 26th, in this very building. Kelly said to his brother, Frank, 'Don't forget, boys, if I go down, it's up to you to do something about that Northam'. You will remember cross-examination brought from Kelly the answer, 'All the time I have been in prison, my brothers have not threatened anybody, yet'. Counsel for the prosecution said, 'What do you mean by 'yet'?' Kelly said it was just a way of speech and that he maintained his sole object was that he wanted his brothers to find out the truth from Northam. That was one significant word.

If you are satisfied that Kelly did know Connolly, Northam and Dickson, you may ask yourselves why was he denying it. Could Northam have got the story from anyone but the murderer? That is a question for you. Three persons were present in that room when those fatal shots were fired, the manager, the assistant manager and the killer. The killer only survived. According to Northam, Kelly said to him, 'The man fell on his knees and I shot him'." The judge paused, as if to let the jury recreate in their minds, the picture Northam had drawn, of what had happened in the manager's office. He continued,

"Dr Grace's evidence was that Catterall was probably on his knees when he received the fatal shot." Cassells paused again and then put another question.

"Who knew that?" There was a longer pause before Cassells answered his own question. "Only one person. Is Graham imagining his evidence?"

Judge Cassells stopped, removing his glasses and leaning forward toward the jury. His hands were clasped in front of him as he concluded.

"If you have any reasonable doubt, you will find George Kelly not guilty. If you come to the conclusion that he is the man who shot Leonard Thomas, you will find him guilty. You may now go and consider your verdict."

He had finished his summing up, the jury leaving the courtroom at 3.25.

The atmosphere in the courtroom had changed. It differed from that at the first trial. Then, the jury's adjournment had been accompanied by a tense, expectant, almost excited atmosphere. Now, it was unnerving, a sense of foreboding overshadowing the expectancy. The prosecution's closing statement and the judge's summing up, had been portents of a grim verdict and there was an absence of hushed comment, people reluctant to speak, almost embarrassed to be waiting in that place, for a young man to be condemned to be hanged.

Their wait was not to be long, an ominous thing in itself, the members of the jury filing back in and sitting self-consciously in their places, the eyes of the court upon them. They had been out only fifty-five minutes.

Outside the courtroom, the police were holding back the crowd of hundreds who had waited on the St George's Plateau and now tried to force their way into the court for the last moments.

Rose Heilbron glanced back at Harry Livermore. Her face was white, the tension showing. He shook his head slightly in despair. They knew what to expect.

Mr Justice Cassells sat, a human but remote presence, isolated on his throne in the centre of the high, polished, wooden bench. On it, to his left, hidden from the view of the others in the court, was a square of black silk, which had figured in many ultimate sentences. It had been given to him when he was first appointed judge, on February 10th 1939, when the clerk to the late Mr Justice Avory, had presented him with Avory's black cap.

Judge Avory was a figure of fear in the courts. His cold eyes and wrinkled skin were said to make him the embodiment of legal retribution. He was noted for his merciless treatment of the guilty, the black cap used on numerous occasions before Judge Cassells became its unfortunate heir.

For James Cassells, it was a moment he dreaded but which he had faced before. He turned to the foreman of the jury.

"Have you reached your verdict?"

"We have, your honour." The wrong form of address attributed to the man's terrible nervousness.

"What is it?"

The foreman spoke in a loud, clear voice.

"Guilty, my Lord."

There were loud moans and muted screams from the public gallery and, in a row at the rear of the well of the court, Chief Inspector Herbert Balmer threw both hands into the air in jubilation, fists clenched.

The tension in the court was now almost unbearable, the atmosphere unreal, ghostly, the quiet almost frightening as the judge gazed across the court to the dock and addressed Kelly.

"On that night of March 19th, you committed a cruel and brutal murder for which the jury have rightly found you guilty. A man who uses a gun to assist him in a robbery can expect no mercy. Have you anything to say before the sentence of this court is passed on you?"

Kelly shook his head slightly, almost in disbelief. He swallowed hard and opened his mouth to speak but was unable to do so. He got as far as a mumbled, "I am..."

Judge Cassells paused but that was all Kelly said before the square of black silk was placed on the judge's head, the weighted corner carefully placed at the back of the head, to prevent the cap falling off when the judge bent his head to look at his papers, or when the chaplain said 'Amen', when the death sentence was passed.

Kelly regained his composure, pale-faced but now showing no other sign of emotion, standing with his hands clasped in front of him, as they had been during most of the trial, as the judge pronounced sentence.

"The sentence upon you, is that you be taken from this place to a lawful prison and from thence to a place of execution, there to suffer death by hanging and that your body be buried within the precincts of the prison in which you were last confined before your execution. And may the Lord have mercy upon your soul."

At a word from a warder, Kelly turned and left the courtroom for the last time. The public were made to remain in their seats for several minutes, until Judge Cassells had joined Judge Oliver, who had been presiding in an adjacent court and together they left the court to be driven to the Judge's residence. Outside the court, the large crowd which had gathered pushed forward to hear the verdict. There was no demonstration but the crowd remained in place for almost half an hour, until they were moved on by the police. Near the iron doors from which the car carrying Kelly would emerge, the photographers were waiting, standing on the plateau and leaning over the railings to take their pictures of the condemned man.

It's just a formality

On February 13th, five days after George Kelly was sentenced to death, Charles Connolly appeared in the same court. His morale was rock bottom. The news had reached him quickly in prison, passed almost sadistically by one of the warders, who warned him that he was next. It destroyed any hopes of acquittal which Connolly still harboured. He was devastated, so convinced was he that they would both walk free. And he was confused. The evening before his trial, his solicitor had came to see him in Walton Gaol and introduced him to his new counsel, Edmund Rowson KC.

Mr Rowson was straight to the point. "It's not going to be easy, Mr Connolly. You know what the law says; if two men plan a crime of violence and one has a weapon he intends to use, then the man who stands outside and keeps watch, even if he runs away, is equally guilty with the man who fires the shots." Edmund Rowson paused, waiting for his words to sink in. Connolly made no comment and Mr Rowson continued to try to persuade him.

"But I've arranged a deal. If you plead guilty to robbery, the murder charge will be dropped."

Connolly shook his head, failing at first to understand the significance of what his counsel had said, until it gradually began to sink in.

"No way. I'm innocent."

Mr Rowson leaned forward. "Think, man. It's your life that's at stake here. You won't be the first innocent man to be hanged, and certainly not the last. Now, the court has said it will consider a change of plea. If you plead guilty to the lesser charge of robbery, you'll only have to serve six years and eight months, the same length as the war, after all."

"I can't plead guilty to something I didn't do. What will my parents do? What will my wife do?" Connolly looked unsure and Edmund Rowson pressed home his point.

"You have no other chance except the offer of the court."

"But how will it affect Kelly's appeal?"

"That's nothing to do with you. Any appeal will not be on the facts, possible misdirection of the jury and any other legal arguments that can be used."

Still Connolly was unsure, asking his counsel for time before he made his decision, spending the remainder of the day in a torment of emotion until, later that evening, his family came to see him. He sought their advice. His mother was tearful as she spoke to him. "I don't have the right to tell you to plead guilty but I would rather have you alive."

The next morning Connolly was brought to court from Strangeways Prison in Manchester, where he was being held. He was escorted by prison warders and, next to him, in the back of the police car, sat Bert Balmer, who ordered the driver to go as slowly as possible. He offered Connolly a cigarette as he attempted to persuade him to plead guilty and accept a prison sentence to avoid hanging. It would have been the final triumph for Balmer, George Kelly's conviction justified.

But, despite all Balmer's eloquent persuasion, Connolly still protested his innocence. When they eventually arrived at the court, Balmer shook his head ruefully as he spoke to his murder squad colleagues,

"We've done no business. It's a full trial. Just hope for the best."

But the pressure was having its effect, Connolly's resolve flagging. When the driver asked the escort whether he should return in the afternoon to take Connolly back to prison, Connolly answered for them.

"Make it half past ten. It'll be all over by then and I'll have been given ten years."

"You hope." The driver did not smile.

Judge Cassells again sat in judgment. After the jury were sworn in, the Clerk of the Assizes read the indictment.

"Charles Connolly, the charge against you is murder, in that you, on March 19th 1949, at Liverpool, murdered Leonard Thomas. How do you plead?"

"Not guilty."

"And you are further indicted that on March 19th 1949, you robbed Leonard Thomas of £50. How do you plead?"

"Guilty."

"There is a further charge of conspiracy to rob, in that you, on March 19th, conspired with George Kelly and other persons unknown, to rob Leonard Thomas of £50. How do you plead?"

"Not guilty."

Edmund Rowson rose in his seat, glaring at Connolly, who immediately crossed the dock, leaning forward to speak. There was a brief exchange.

"It's just a formality, man."

Connolly returned to his place. He looked apprehensively at the judge as he changed his plea.

"Guilty, my Lord."

Bert Balmer, again at the rear of the benches usually reserved for counsel, half rose in his seat, raising his hands in the air above his head, clapping them together once, his case against George Kelly now secure.

William Gorman, again prosecuting, reviewed the case against Connolly.

"Your Lordship has, I know, read the depositions of this case. You have also heard certain evidence given in the recent case of George Kelly which, while that was not in fact evidence against Charles Connolly, did give a picture of the part played by Connolly in the tragic events of March 19th. In all the circumstances, if your Lordship thinks it just, on behalf of the prosecution I take no objection to proceeding on the charges to which Connolly has pleaded guilty."

Judge Cassells nodded.

"In view of the evidence disclosed in the depositions in the case I tried last week, I think that it is the proper course to adopt in the case of Charles Connolly. Do I take it then, that the prosecution offers no evidence on the first indictment, which relates to Leonard Thomas?"

"That is so, my Lord."

"We find Connolly not guilty, therefore, on that indictment."

Connolly bowed his head, his shoulders slumping in sudden relief as Gorman gave a very short summary of the prosecution's version of events of the night of March 19th, in which Connolly was now inextricably written. The list of Connolly's previous convictions was then read out, before Edmund Rowson addressed the court on behalf of Connolly.

"The difficulty for Connolly has become obvious from the moment the jury accepted, as one must assume they had accepted, the evidence of Northam, Dickson and Graham. Under these circumstances, Connolly has accepted my advice and pleaded guilty to the charge of robbery.

When Connolly came out of the navy he got into what I might call 'an unruly set'. Examination of the evidence of Northam and Dickson, made it obvious that Connolly never intended a gun to be used in carrying out the robbery. You also have the evidence of Graham, to whom Connolly had said he had nothing to do with the chap who did it.

Connolly had not the slightest indication, or knowledge, that violence was to be used. Somehow, and perhaps tragically, between the time of the shooting and later, Connolly became frightened, not only of the part he had taken in the venture, but in view of the threats made against him by Kelly. It was from this time that Connolly took the line that he did and supported the evidence of Kelly, with regard to not knowing him and not being in the Beehive Hotel on that night.

To some extent, I venture to think the events with which Connolly was fixed are not really the outcome of his own desire and he expresses his very deep regret with regards to them. In Walton Gaol he told Graham what a fool he was to have been mixed up with the job. I ask your Lordship to deal leniently with Charles Connolly."

Judge Cassells peered sternly at Connolly over his half-moon glasses.

"Charles Connolly, you have pleaded guilty to robbery and to conspiracy to rob. The evidence in this case discloses that, with another man, to your knowledge armed, you went to the Cameo Cinema, on the evening of March 19th last, with the object of robbing the manager of the takings. Your part was to wait outside. You were as guilty of robbery as if you had been by his side, although, in fact, you were lurking in a side street to give the alarm and, if need be, to aid his escape. When you heard the shots, you fled. The man with whom you associated yourself on that night has been convicted of murder, upon a second and separate trial.

Though the position of the law is clear and though you may have had a narrow escape, I think, that in view of the disagreement of the jury at the first trial and the fact that yours was not the hand that fired the fatal shots, the prosecution have adopted a proper course in offering no evidence against you on the indictment for murder and accepting your plea of guilty to the offences of robbery and conspiracy. You were there to lend your aid to an attack on a place where men were following their lawful occupation, in order that you might put into your pockets some share of the proceeds. Such conduct must be followed by appropriate punishment.

For the offence of robbery you go to prison for ten years. For conspiracy you go to prison for two years, the sentences to run concurrently; ten years in all. I direct that the indictment relating to George Kelly, charging him with the second murder of the man Catterall, shall remain upon the file of this court, not to be proceeded with, except by leave of a judge or upon an order of the Court of Criminal Appeal."

There was an almost uniform sigh of relief from many in the court, from the prosecution and the officers of the court. Only those for the defence remained silent. It was the end of a long and bitter sequence of trials. But James Cassells was not finished.

"The court desires to commend the police officers engaged in the investigation of this terrible crime. For six months their efforts never relaxed. I particularly desire to mention Chief Superintendent T Smith, who has been responsible for directing the inquiries throughout the whole of this case and to his other officers, Chief Inspector H Balmer, who may be said to have had charge of the case, Chief Inspector James Morris and Chief Inspector Hector Taylor. They all deserve the thanks of Liverpool for the efficient manner in which they have discharged their different duties. I hope this recommendation will be brought to the notice of their superior officers and duly entered on their record.

The evidence of James Philip Northam and Mrs Jacqueline Eva Margaret Dickson was accepted by the jury in the trial of George Kelly and, by his plea of guilty on the indictment just heard, Charles Connolly has acknowledged the truth of what these witnesses said on oath. But for their evidence, these two dangerous criminals might never have been brought to justice. Dickson's case seems to be one where some Liverpool organisation, or perhaps some Liverpool lady or ladies, could show a real act of kindness. There is an old act of Parliament, which came in one hundred and twenty years ago, which enables me to order £20 compensation to be paid to these people. It does not, however, enable me to make any direction with regard to the witness Robert Graham, although I will forward a recommendation to another quarter.

The Judge summed up for the prosecution

It had been the longest murder trial in the history of the English courts and left a number of questions to be asked of the judiciary. Was it right that the two defendants should have been split up in a major murder trial? It had never happened before and has never happened since.

Judge Cassell's decision that there should be two separate re-trials no doubt pleased the prosecution almost as much as Connolly's counsel, because, with Kelly's guilt alone to be decided, there was every chance that this time the jury would reach a verdict. But was it legally right to divide the trials? Or just?

And what was the legal right that George Kelly should be ordered to go first? Was it because it would be easier to convict the one who was alleged to have held the murder weapon? And why was there such an unprecedented haste to stage the trials, despite a serious plea by Rose Heilbron, before both the first and second trials.

The harrowing ordeal to which the two men were subjected, after Judge Cassells had refused to allow the case to be heard in Manchester, after a short period of time for the defence to fully prepare their case, was highlighted by James Cassell's comment concerning the time Kelly and Connolly spent in their cells; '23 hours a day is a long time to be in solitary confinement. Sometimes people want to talk'. It is a terrible indictment of the English judicial system at that time, that Kelly and Connolly were held in such circumstances for six weeks.

There are many questions to be answered but perhaps these decisions, wrong, even sinister as they may seem to us now, should be put into the context of national opinion at the time.

Two decent men came back from the war, started to raise families and were cruelly and brutally murdered. It is hard now, when such crimes are more commonplace, to envisage the sense of outrage that the murders caused at the time. There was a need for punishment, even revenge, by the God-fearing residents of Liverpool. People who had no real awareness of the criminal mentality and for whom the police could do no wrong.

When questioning how the jury failed to reach a verdict of not guilty, through reasonable doubt, the background to the jurors of that time must also be considered. They were people who owned their own houses and who knew little, and understood less, of the sordid and petty criminal fraternity which infected the city. They were part of a society unaccustomed to murder by the gun and living in a time when peace was sought by all, after the brutality of the recent war. George Kelly and his lifestyle would seem light years away from them.

To the jury, the police were sacrosanct, protectors of the peace, Chief Inspector Balmer a major crime fighter in their cause, held in high regard and not expected to deviate from the course of righteousness in his enquiries, or to lie in the witness box.

To attack the police, whether from the witness box, or from the well of the court, was unwise. It would mean immediate prejudice against the defendant by both judge and jury. Defending counsel had, therefore, by necessity, to tread a very thin line when arguing against evidence presented by the police.

Rose Heilbron, after her success in defending Johnson in the first Cameo trial, when she had criticised police methods, must have prepared her brief in great confidence, the confidence of youth and inexperience, with a degree of certainty that the lack of any real evidence must allow the case against Connolly and Kelly to be dismissed. But she was unaware of the cruel summing up to come.

Even allowing for the virtual impossibility of a summing up not leading a jury one way or another, Judge Oliver's summary of the evidence in the case should have brought but one verdict. That it did not, is an indictment in itself of the paucity of evidence, much of which lacked credibility. This selective choosing of evidence made the judge's summing up severely flawed. It is incomprehensible that the judge should choose to discharge the jury after only four hours and this when they had returned to ask for further details from Chief Inspector Balmer.

One possibility is that Judge Oliver knew that if he had not halted the trial, a verdict of not guilty would have been recorded. As he stated in his post trial letter to the Chief Superintendent, Liverpool CID, this was not the verdict he had anticipated. This was certainly the view of the foreman of the jury, a man by the name of White, who later became chairman of a Labour Party Ward in the south of the city. He affirmed, after the trial, that he would not bring in a conviction for murder, come what may.

One reason for Judge Oliver's precipitate action, may be that he realised that his bias towards the prosecution, shown throughout the trial and manifested strongly in the summing up, would allow Connolly and Kelly to win an appeal if, in fact, they were found guilty. The case was prejudged, and it is relatively easy to select examples of the judge's bias. Judge Oliver said.

"Consider Inspector Balmer's evidence about the incident at the identity parade on October 10th, where Kelly and Connolly were identified by witness Sangster and said,

'I'll get you for this, Balmer'. I have already said you will probably think there is a good a deal of evidence that Kelly was a man of violent and unrestrained temper."

Another description of Kelly, in the summing up, was pure conjecture when Judge Oliver discussed the evidence of Thomalla. "Members of the jury, you have seen Kelly and you may describe him as rather a tough individual. You remember when the police went to him and asked him where he was on the night before, what was his reaction? He was not worrying. Not much sign of caution about that. There was not much trepidation. Can you see that man sitting there for an hour and a half in that public house, cringing, miserable, in despair, because he had been interviewed about this thing?"

There was a selective choosing and disregarding of evidence by both the judge and the prosecution, who also manipulated the evidence of the licensee of the Leigh Arms. Thomalla's signed statement was presented as evidence for the prosecution, 'Although I saw Kelly at about 9pm and again just before closing time, I cannot say whether or not he was in the house between those times. I am quite definite that Kelly was not in my public house at 9. 30, but he was in the buffet at 9.50'.

It was a statement Thomalla had been fooled into signing, his actual comment to Balmer being, 'He may have been in the pub at that time, I was too busy serving to notice'. Mr Fred Thomalla, the son of the licensee, years later recalls his father's bitterness towards Balmer. He recounts how, after visiting the Leigh Arms and talking to Thomalla, Balmer then offered him and his wife a lift down town. In the gloom of the police car, Balmer asked Thomalla to sign a statement, 'just to keep things official'.

Quoting the signed statement and extolling the virtues of the ex-policeman, Judge Oliver commented; "Mr Thomalla is an ex-police constable, with many years experience and did it avail anyone to question that, when an ex-police officer says 'I am quite definite', he means, 'I am not at all definite'?"

Yet Thomalla's very positive evidence regarding the day after the murder was disputed, the judge showing a remarkable inconsistency in his summing up,

"Members of the jury, one other thing about Thomalla's evidence that I come to is that, on the Sunday he says that shortly after he opened at 12.30, Kelly came in and stayed until 2 o'clock. If that is true, Kelly could not have been at the meeting in the Star. Do you think anyone would say that, with certainty, he was there at 12.30 until 2, a busy landlord seeing lots of people, the house full of people?"

This contrasts with evidence given by Thomalla that there were about eighty people in his pub on the night of the murder, standing three or four deep at the bar, yet the judge dismissed Thomalla's evidence in court that Kelly may have been there.

What was the reason for both judge's selecting only parts of the anonymous letter as evidence? Northam and Dickson lied about it and in examination could not agree on it.

In Mr Gorman's closing speech and in the summing up by both judges, the detour to the lake and the catching of the 6a tram was not mentioned. It was simply stated that Kelly could have left the Leigh Arms, called at Cambridge Street for the hat and coat, after showing himself at the Spofforth pub, then revisited Cambridge Street after the murder, to dump the hat, coat and gun and then back to the Leigh Arms.

Surely if the evidence from Northam and Dickson as to what happened on the Saturday and Sunday was accepted, then the evidence of the letter should have been accepted in total.

There are other examples of selectivity. Why did both judges fail to point out to the jury the contradiction between the statements of witnesses at the cinema and those by Northam and Dickson. The cinema employees described the gunman as wearing a black silk mask, whereas Northam and Dickson said a brown apron was used.

The presentation of evidence for the prosecution was also highly selective and it can be argued that, in more enlightened times, if it had reached court, the case would have been rapidly thrown out. Circumstantial evidence, based on the word of known criminals, convicted thieves themselves, together with that of a prison informer, was all the prosecution had. It is worth reflecting on the role of some of these witnesses.

During her final defence statement, Rose Heilbron commented that the only other witnesses, were police witnesses. This is true. They have an uneasy knack of fitting into that special category of people used by the police; doormen, taxi drivers, store detectives, many of them ex-policemen, prostitutes, informers and others who were well acquainted with what was happening in the city at the time and who were in a position to pass on information or gossip which may have been of use to the police.

Almost every prosecution witness had a record, which would make them tend to curry favour with the police. Or they were serving sentences, in which case their evidence consisted of conversations with the accused men in prison. Others were informers and Balmer was known to have a range of people he could use, sometimes through a hold he might have on them, sometimes for simple gain on their part.

It was only police witnesses who said that Kelly and Connolly had been seen together. It would surely have impressed the jury if the defence had brought forward a number of witnesses, friends of the accused, who could say that they had never seen Kelly and Connolly in each other's company.

James Daniel Sangster was a police witness and no friend of Kelly. Contemporary comments by those who knew Sangster make him out to be an unsavoury character. One person, a member of a shoplifting family of that time, accuses him of taking female shoplifters up to the male toilets on the top floor, where he would demand sex, in return for releasing them. Charles Connolly has affirmed that Sangster was a police stooge and would say whatever Balmer wanted him to say.

The taxi driver, Currie, stated with conviction, that Kelly came into the buffet from outside, at about 9.50. This error, if it was an error, was easily made. The layout of the Leigh Arms is such that the bar and buffet are served by a common vestibule, the door to the bar facing that to the buffet and Currie could not be certain that Kelly had not come into the vestibule from the public bar. In other words, Kelly moved into the buffet by the shortest route, rather than work his way around the crowded horseshoe-shaped interior of the crowded pub. Currie was with a woman, Mrs Butterworth, who would have been a witness to what Kelly may have said, 'I've been having a go' or 'I've been on the bevvy'.

The prosecution made a great play about the absence of defence witnesses; 'Where, oh where, is Doris O'Malley?' yet neither they, nor the defence, were able to produce Mrs Butterworth, either to confirm or refute his evidence. Although both judges commented on the absence of defence witnesses, highlighted by the prosecution, some of these, if of benefit, could also have been called for the prosecution, as could Mrs Butterworth.

Constable Nugent, a young policeman, gave evidence that he had seen Kelly and

Connolly in each other's company on several occasions. He had last seen them together on September 30th. However, police then were very much subject to their superiors and there may be many reasons why the police make a statement which is not always the truth. If we accept, however, that Nugent may have believed he was telling the truth, there is a sound reason for this. Connolly and Skelly were remarkably similar, in height and build and appearance. Kelly and Jimmy Skelly would frequently be seen in Lime Street in each other's company and it would be a simple error for Nugent, shown a picture of Connolly, to think he was the man seen with Kelly.

The only other evidence that Kelly and Connolly were ever in each other's company, is that of Northam and Dickson, corroborated by Graham.

McBain, the compere at St Mark's Church Hall, who gave the only evidence to contradict the alibi given by members of Connolly's family and others, was, according to Charles Connolly, drawing dole money while working at the church hall. Connolly claims he would have been easy prey for Balmer to pressurise as, at that time, a gaol sentence was the punishment for claiming dole unlawfully.

Judge Oliver failed badly, in his summing up, to point out a flaw in the prosecution's presentation of the evidence by the photographer who took the pictures of Connolly and his wife at the dance. The prosecution made a great play of the fact that Connolly wore a hat while dancing, McBain, the organiser, asking him to remove it. Mr Gorman affirmed that Connolly did this to draw attention to himself.

However, Judge Oliver failed to point out to the jury that the photograph taken a week previously and produced in evidence, showed that Connolly was wearing a hat on both occasions. Moreover, he drew an analogy with Kelly's appearance, without hat and overcoat, in the Leigh Arms and the Spofforth, before and after the murder.

Dowling, the doorman at the Primrose Cafe, had taken Kelly's job. According to Jimmy Skelly there was little love lost between Kelly and Dowling, Dowling having been a Sergeant Major in the army, with little respect for deserters and there had been an altercation between the two when Kelly was sacked and Dowling got his job. Dowling would certainly have reason to be less than careful with the truth in giving dates and times when he saw Kelly in Cases Street.

Were the prosecution aware that the so-called 'Livermore incident', when Northam accused Mr Livermore of attempting to bribe him, was going to be introduced? Basil Nield was disparaging of it and the judge would not allow Harry Livermore to take the stand in his own defence. However, such an accusation must have had some effect on the jury's thinking.

There are other examples of judicial inadequacy. In Kelly's cross-examination by William Gorman, he was asked how Graham knew that he had been in the Leigh Arms at 9.45 on the night of the murder, if Kelly had not told him. Both judges failed to point out that this could have easily have been obtained from press reports of the committal proceedings, Mr Gorman skating over this fact, by emphasising that Graham was in Preston at the time of the Magistrates Court hearing.

But George Kelly's natural belligerence was to be as damning as any of the evidence presented against him. In reply to a question by William Gorman concerning a visit to him by his brothers, Kelly said, 'All the time I've been in prison my brother has threatened nobody yet'. Gorman pounced on this. 'What do you mean by 'yet'? Is that something that's yet to come?' It was just a manner of speaking, Kelly explained confusedly, but it was a slip of the tongue which would have terrible consequences. That 'yet' was 'a significant word, or one you might think significant,' said Judge Cassells in his summing up.

In the Beehive

The scenario presented in the build up to the murder and the underlying conspiracy and from information gleaned from a number of sources, is of four people, Northam, Dickson, Johnson, who drank at the Beehive public house and one other acquaintance of Dickson's, planning the robbery together.

Johnson's statement to the police suggests that the third man was involved. 'I went with him on the Monday before the murder. He asked me to look around the place and weigh up the woman who worked there, while we were supposed to be looking at the pictures.'

Were Johnson and the unknown man, the two reported to have visited the manager's office at 6.30 on the evening of the robbery when, incidentally, Kelly was still with Jimmy Skelly? Was this a visit to survey the scene and cut the telephone wires?

Did Kelly take the place of Johnson? The Beehive was used by Kelly and it was known that Connolly was often in the vicinity. And the other intended corroborative witness, Norwegian Margie, frequented the pub.

Johnson was certainly, by his own admission, an avid picture-goer, perhaps the sort of man who would use the actual words which Mrs Watkins said in her deposition the murderer used, but which were not given in any of the evidence in court, 'stand back or I'll blow your head off'.

Johnson admitted that he had been to the picture house earlier that week. Was the fact that he was a regular, one of the reasons why, according to his statement to Graham, he was scared of the fireman recognising him?

It is an ironic fact of this case that, if Rose Heilbron had not defended him so successfully, at the same time destroying police credibility, Johnson may have been persuaded in court, under threat of a major sentence, into revealing the whole truth of the affair.

The evidence casting Johnson as the actual murderer is compelling. Of all those involved in the case he was the only one who can be confidently placed near the scene shortly after the crime had been committed.

He admitted his involvement and was even able to draw a picture of the type of gun used in the crime. Various statements made by him, his letters and statements by his mother, girlfriend, brother and the prison officers who were involved with him (Appendices 3-11), all point to his guilt, the confession he made to Graham fitting the facts of the actual murder exactly.

It is surprising that the evidence of Northam and Dickson was even considered credible.

According to them, a number of jobs were discussed in the Beehive. How did they remember in such detail after a time lapse of over seven months? Was it because, under police tutelage, they would establish Kelly and Connolly's readiness to carry out a robbery and shoot if necessary?

Is it not all beyond the realms of belief and coincidence? Was it not all too convenient that when Connolly suggested the Cameo, adding that it would have to be a stick up and a gun would be needed, Kelly pulled a gun from his pocket?

Dickson's statement says that she, Northam, Connolly and Kelly stood in the passageway of the Beehive discussing various robberies and one mentioned the Cameo Cinema, when it was said that a gun was necessary and Kelly produced one and loaded it. All this, when they were within sight and hearing of the licensee and barmaid in a passageway which, at that time on a Saturday night, was always busy.

Vindication for the conspiracy theory and that Northam was primed in what to say, can be seen in the fine tuning of the evidence of Dickson and Northam. On September 29th 1949, they gave statements which differed dramatically from those given in evidences. Was this the first run at scripting the evidence to be used in court?

Perhaps the most significant points in these original statements are the facts that both Northam and Dickson agree that, on the following day, they stayed in Birkenhead. They both state that Kelly was wearing a dark raincoat or overcoat with a belt and Northam says that Kelly told him that the gun was hidden in the soil in Wavertree Park. Kelly is also described as pulling the mask out of his pocket. There is no mention of it being supplied by a dark girl.

The robbery was supposed to have only been suggested in conversation during that meeting in the Beehive but, according to Northam, Kelly had come prepared; in his pocket there were pliers, to cut the telephone wires, and a gun. Did Balmer realise that this just was not believable and removed the description of the pliers from the script?

The statements concerning these events were not made in just one document. In a later statement, dated October 10th, Northam and Dickson added to their statements to describe the loan of the overcoat. The final statement, on October 26th, introducing the meeting in the Star pub on the Sunday after the murder.

It is worth recalling Kelly's response during cross-examination by Mr Gorman.

"What about these statements you made to Northam?"

"I said nothing to Northam. Northam is the man who seems to know more about this than me."

"Can you could suggest how Northam could give the details of what happened inside the manager's office at the time of the shooting, unless someone had told him?"

"Northam is the one who knows all about it; all about the lock business and the spiral staircase. He has told the story. He seems to know more about it than anyone else."

But there was only one way Northam and Dickson could have known what happened in the manager's office; it was all part of the role tutored by Balmer. Balmer had the basic substance of what had happened from Johnson's confession to Graham, before which details of what had happened in the manager's office were only conjecture, but the statement fitted the facts and the pathologist's evidence, almost exactly.

The manipulation of facts continues. Dickson and Northam said Kelly and Connolly took a number 8 tram to Wavertree, Dickson accompanying them to the stop. But the number 8 tram went along Renshaw Street, around the corner from Mount Pleasant where the Beehive was located. The simplest and most convenient route to

Wavertree was by the number 4 or 5 bus, both of which stopped practically outside the Beehive. But this bus went to the end of Webster Road which is furthest from the cinema. A more convenient route, to impress a jury, would be to take the 8 tram along Smithdown Road to the Cameo, which was at the Smithdown Road end of Webster Road.

In their statements, both Northam and Dickson claimed that Dickson travelled to Birkenhead to visit Northam at his parent's home when he arrived home from prison. This is unlikely, as his train would have arrived at Liverpool Exchange. They then claim to have gone to the pictures before travelling to Liverpool in the evening.

Was this because they did not want to make public the fact that Dickson's flat in Parliament Street was in walking distance of the Cameo Cinema? Is it not more likely that Northam, after a sojourn in prison, having being briefed by Dickson to collect the gun from his parent's home in Birkenhead, the journey a simple change of trains at Exchange Station, would then want to spend the afternoon in bed with his girlfriend, before going to the local pub?

And is it not possible that Dickson, having planned the robbery with Johnson, would have met Northam in the Beehive, where Northam passed the gun to Johnson?

There is other evidence that Balmer was prepared to make the facts fit the crime. Blackie, the barmaid at the Beehive, saw two people, a man and a woman, handling a gun in the pub. Although her evidence about the date is vague, this evidence was of such significance to Balmer, that he pressurised Blackie into leaving Liverpool until after the trial. Why was this? Did Blackie prejudice the carefully planned conspiracy that Balmer had orchestrated?

After the crime, did Johnson return the gun to Northam at Dickson's flat, after first staying around to see what was happening? Out of curiosity, he had walked down Smithdown Road and, after being accosted by Police Constable Thompson, panicked and made his way through the cemetery on his route to the flat, just as he described in his statement to Graham.

Kelly's alleged admission, on the Sunday, to committing a double murder to two people who had backed out at the sight of a gun the night before, is extremely unlikely, as are the actions of two people who had backed out but then turned up for a meeting the next day, all the way from Birkenhead? Is it likely that Connolly, so terrified after hearing the shots that he fled the scene, would travel some miles from his home in the suburbs of Liverpool to keep an appointment with his murderous accomplice? Might he not be afraid that Kelly might try to silence him? And Kelly's alleged reception of his partner in crime, in the Star Hotel, was strangely complacent for a man who had deserted him. It seems rather surprising that there was no real anger or recrimination from someone described by Judge Oliver as 'this man of violence'.

Corroboration

In the A6 murder Case, for which James Hanratty was charged and convicted, he had always denied the murder, the case weak until, at the last moment, a fellow prisoner, Langdale, on remand for serious offences, claimed that Hanratty had confessed to him and subsequently got off with a suspended sentence. Hanratty was hanged in 1962, the judge at his trial being the same William Gorman who prosecuted Kelly and Connolly.

In the Carl Bridgewater murder case, Brian Sinton said that Michael Hickey confessed to him, in detail, to the murder, in the prison shower. Years later, Sinton admitted that this was a fabrication to get him better treatment in prison. In the same case, Mervyn Ritter claimed that Jimmy Robinson, one of the accused, had made a complete confession to the murder. Ritter got a Queen's Pardon and was soon released. However, at the appeal in 1988, Ritter was show to have a lifetimes history of lying, despite which, the three appeal judges described him as 'a witness of truth'.

There are many other similar cases. The journalist Paul Foot, in 1990, claiming that there was increasing evidence that professional grasses are moved around the prisons to meet remand prisoners and report their confessions.

The ruse of using someone inside prison to obtain a so-called confession is not new. It has been used by the police many times. In most cases, these witnesses had prison sentences reduced or commuted after giving evidence and all were publicly acknowledged to have been helpful to the police on a number of occasions., as was Robert Graham.

Northam and Dickson were both accomplices testifying in exchange for immunity. But this was not enough on which to base a case. Independent corroborating evidence was needed. This was the role for Norwegian Margie. She was to be the dark, heavily made-up girl in the Beehive talking to Kelly and who was supposed to have brought him the apron, her part of the conspiracy that she would come forward to corroborate the story of Dickson and Northam.

Why then was she not called to the witness box? The answer, according to the police, although not submitted at the trial, was that she was dead. Margaret Taanevig had committed suicide. Was this because she could not bring herself to sell the life of a man she did not know, or have her family know her real profession?

A police report, from the Chief Superintendent CID, to the Chief Constable, dated 16th February 1949, presumably not revealed to the defence, states that: 'Margaret Taanevig, twenty-seven years, otherwise known as Norwegian Margie, a prostitute, committed suicide by gas poisoning at her home. This woman answered the description of the unknown woman who was in conversation with the prisoner, George Kelly at the Beehive Hotel, Mount Pleasant, on the night of the murder.'

She had been interviewed by the police about a month before her death but had denied all knowledge of the incident referred to and unfortunately she could not be identified by the witnesses Northam or Dickson.

It has been freely acknowledged among prostitutes, that Joseph Kelly, brother of the prisoner George Kelly, had spoken to Taanevig shortly before her death and had threatened her, that if she did not keep her mouth shut, she would be 'attended to'. No confirmation of this, however, could be obtained and it was strenuously denied by Joseph Kelly. There is little doubt, however, that the unknown woman was the deceased. Was the truth that Balmer attempted to coerce Taanevig into giving evidence in favour of the prosecution but she refused after being threatened by Joseph Kelly.

Is it not likely that Balmer, without Margie Taanevig as a witness, then approached Graham whom he had interviewed in Preston, taking the statement about Johnson's confession. This seems particularly likely, given Graham's late entry, on November 19th, into the case, just one week after Taanevig's suicide. After his report of Johnson's confession, there was now an opportunity for Balmer to use Graham, in exchange for remission or reduction of his sentence.

The credibility of Graham's evidence was based on a simple premise; that Connolly and Kelly were unable to communicate while held in the hospital wing of Walton Prison. This was based on yet another premise; that it was against regulations for them to talk to each other. However, it can been proved beyond any doubt, that they could freely communicate. Examination of the plans of the prison and the location of the cells in which they were held, show that these cells were only ten yards apart, out of sight from each other but within easy speaking distance. Furthermore, Connolly has asserted that both he and Kelly were able to use mirrors, to see when the warder was approaching on his fifteen minute rounds and were able to talk in confidence, if necessary.

Rose Heilbron questioned Graham,

"Is it not a fact that it is quite possible for Kelly and Connolly to talk to each other through the bars of their cells?"

"Absolutely impossible. Where they are situated it is impossible."

At this point, Kelly drew a quick sketch of the relative position of the cells before

"I suggest to you, that not only is it possible, but at night they are able to talk across the corridor with one another."

Both Kelly and Connolly went to Mass in the prison chapel. Sitting next to each other, were they really so devout as not to converse freely? During exercise periods also, they were able to meet and there is no indication, anywhere in the prison records, that they were deliberately kept apart. Strong confirmation of this was given during the proceedings when Connolly was purported to have held Kelly against a wall during an exercise period, accusing him of dragging him into the Cameo murders investigation. Connolly agreed that this did happen and it was allegedly witnessed by a cleaner called Mahoney, erroneously called Marney during the hearings, who warned them that everyone was trying to hear what they were saying to each other.

But Graham lied about not knowing Mahoney. He said he was not in the prison at the same time as Mahoney. This contradicts later police evidence which confirms that Mahoney and Graham did meet in prison.There was, in fact, no need for them to use a go-between and Graham's evidence can be dismissed as a fabrication, so remarkably similar in form and substance to that of the witnesses Northam and Dickson, it could only have come from the same script.

Balmer, of course, added the fine details, the comments by the murdered manager which made Kelly's behaviour even more deplorable, 'You can take some of my money'.

The attempt to use corroborating witnesses did not end with Graham and Taanevig. There were other witnesses waiting in the wings, if Balmer felt they were necessary. Statements were taken from four women, the profession of each given as prostitute, all of which are to the effect that they had seen Kelly and Connolly and Dickson together. This was not used as evidence. (Appendix 23)

Doris Campbell alleged that she saw the three together in the Beehive on the night of the murder and it is interesting that, in Campbell's statement, the arrogance of Kelly is again stressed. She mentions the fact that Kelly again uses the expression, 'I am Kelly'. Campbell's statement is supported by that of Jane Henderson, who also said she was with Campbell in the Beehive on the night of the murder.

Campbell and Henderson lived at the same address, 107 Oxford Street. Their description of events that night in the Beehive are almost identical. The main body of the statements is unclear as to which day they saw the events take place but, in riders to their statements they both state; 'I remember now it was definitely Saturday that I saw them all in the Beehive and that was the Saturday of the murders at the Cameo Cinema.'

Another prostitute, Lucy McLarney stated that she had seen Kelly, Connolly and Dickson together on many occasions in the city, as had Doris Mellor. McLarney's statement is interesting, in that it goes further to cement the relationship between Connolly and Dickson. 'I have also seen Charles Connolly, whom I have known the same length of time as Kelly, with Jacqueline Dickson. When I have seen Connolly and Dickson together, they have been in the Lime Tree Cafe, the Marigold Cafe and Littlewoods Cafe.

Defence

Why was George Kelly treated so cruelly by the police and the judiciary? The descriptions of his contemporaries all follow the same theme: 'A little wild and inclined to drink too much but not the sort of man who would commit a brutal murder', 'A robber but one of the lads', 'Not guilty of murder', 'No angel but no killer', 'An innocent man, he was set up'.

Others remember Kelly as 'Quick of speech, very happy go lucky, who loved a song. He had a pleasant light tenor voice which added to his charisma. The women liked him.' 'Happy go lucky, a spendthrift always with money, he lived above his means but was always generous to a fault when in funds.' Others who knew him and members of his family, say that he made regular money from a variety of activities; working on the barrow for his mother and as a doorman but also as a petty criminal, able to distribute stolen and black market goods through the markets and clubs of the day.

He was also, according to Balmer, a police informer, but this is uniformly disputed by those who knew him. Did Balmer describe him thus, in court, as a further way of casting a slur on his character? However, it was certainly not unusual for criminals operating in one part of the city, their patch, to willingly give information on those from other areas, whose activities intruded upon their own.

Why was Charles Connolly precipitated into a major role in the drama? What was his crime, that Balmer would want to convict him of a part in a capital offence? There could be several reasons. Johnson, in his statement, referred to Charley Duggan, a man he was in Walton with in 1946. And Jacqueline Dickson told Balmer; 'go and see Charles Connolly'.

A search of the records would reveal to Balmer that Connolly had a record for violence, some of it against the police. An accomplished amateur boxer, he regularly played snooker in the city clubs and, by his own admission, was frequently in fights, often with visiting soccer fans. During one of these melees he fought against police officers who were trying to break up the trouble, not realising they were police. For this, he was sentenced for violence against the police.

To Balmer, the police were sacrosanct and any violence against the members of the force would result in severe retribution.

Connolly certainly knew Jackie Dickson who, according to his own recollections and his evidence in court, he would often see walking the streets around the city centre. Connolly tells how he would wait outside the St George's Restaurant in Lime Street for his wife, who was working there. He knew many of the women who worked Lime Street and would also meet them when he played snooker at The Vines pub ('The Big House') or in the Marionette Club.

Is there some truth in the assertions of people who knew them both at the time, that Connolly would sit in the window of a cafe, signalling to Dickson? The evidence of the prostitute, Lucy McLarney, supports this when she states that she had seen Connolly and Dickson together in various cafes. Did Dickson have a grudge against Connolly? Shortly before the Cameo murders, Connolly was in Littlewoods cafe with his wife Mary and daughter Tina and when Tina approached the table at which Dickson was sitting with her head bandaged, Connolly pulled his daughter away. Did this create, in Dickson, an antipathy towards him?

Connolly has described her as a scruffy, unhealthy-looking prostitute and has attested to her, 'taking men down the back of Skelhorn Street...' and he is less than gracious in his further description of her as, 'the lowest of the low, a woman who would even pick cigarette stumps up from the gutter, always filthily dressed and dirty-looking'. Could there have been more in the relationship than one would expect? Connolly, tall, good-looking, well-dressed, hardly a drinker with a respectable home life, a wife and child, does not seem the sort of man to fall for the charms of a young prostitute. But it would not be the first time a presentable, perhaps naive, family man, would fall for the guile of a woman of the streets.

Is there some truth in Dickson's statement in the anonymous letter, 'I'm scared of him. He wants me to go away with him and I cannot go down the town.'? Did Connolly draw his holiday pay and leave his job because he was going to London with Dickson, as she claimed. Was the Cameo robbery intended to supply further funds for the visit to London?

Donald Johnson, in evidence submitted at his trial, said that Charlie Duggan was knocking about with a whore but also had a decent girl. There were hints, during the trial, and from others, that Connolly had been associating with Dickson and that he had had domestic problems with his wife. Was this over the relationship with Dickson? Was Charlie Connolly the man Johnson referred to as Charlie Duggan? Was there bitterness in Dickson. Did Connolly promise things to Dickson that he could not deliver. And did she, the woman scorned, find a way for the ultimate revenge?

Northam stated that Connolly had talked about fleeing the country. The prosecution seized upon this and asked Connolly had he applied to emigrate? Connolly agreed that he had, in fact, first filled in emigration papers in 1947, when he got married. He had a brother in Australia, who was married there after the war. A letter from the Australian Immigration Office confirms that his sister-in-law, in Sydney, had at that time, acted as nominee for Connolly. Connolly's defence even brought a priest to give evidence concerning his long-standing wish to emigrate. But the inference was there; a suspicion placed in the jury's minds.

Connolly's alibi depended upon his being at a dance at St Mark's Church Hall. He claims that many of his friends made statements about him being at the dance but they were never called to give evidence. One must ask why? Was it that they did not come up to proof? Certainly the prosecution chose only to concentrate on the evidence of Connolly's family, witnesses who the jury would see as being ready to lie, in order to save their brother and husband.

On the basis of the evidence, it is reasonable to assume that Connolly was guilty as charged and that, through his relationship with Dickson, he helped in the crime as described by Dickson and Northam. Was he, in fact, the third man in the meeting in the Boundary Hotel prior to the murder? Were he and Johnson the two men who visited the cinema earlier that night on the pretext of looking for work?

Many years after the trial, in 1965, in a letter from Sydney Silverman MP to a member of the Kelly family who was attempting to have the case reopened, Mr Silverman wrote; 'A statement in full detail by Connolly would provide further evidence'. (Appendix 28). In another letter in 1967, Mr Silverman comments; 'The key to the whole story now, is the willingness of Connolly to come forward and tell the whole truth, so far as he knows it'. (Appendix 29)

Later in 1967, Sydney Silverman continues; 'if Connolly will sign a statement which could be used in evidence, something further could be done. In the absence of such a statement, or the refusal of Connolly to make one, I am afraid that I cannot take the matter any further. I myself can do nothing more. The Home Secretary, in the absence of new evidence, will not do anything to re-open the matter'. (Appendix 30)

Do these letters suggest that Sydney Silverman was convinced of Connolly's guilt?

At Kelly's second trial, the defence were able to call only six witnesses. Others were not revealed by the police, or were not called.Donald McDermaid, who had been to the cinema that night, states that, at about 9.30 he left the cinema and was stopped by a woman in her twenties, who asked if the cashier had gone up. His evidence, although reported to the police the following morning, was either ignored or suppressed. But Judge Oliver commented in his summing up, 'The murderer must have been a man who knew about the light in the cashier's office going out at 9.30'.

What happened to other witnesses for the defence? Both Harry Harrison, who claimed to be drinking with Kelly at 9.30 that night, and Doris O'Malley, were subpoenaed, Harrison waiting to be called throughout the trial. In particular, it is rather surprising that O'Malley did not give evidence to support Kelly's denial that he had said, 'I was with Skelly and then I was with you'.

Another potential witness to the time of Balmer's visit to Doris O'Malley's house, on the day after the murder, was the Mrs Mathews who Kelly claimed was present when Balmer arrived. Where was she? It must be born in mind, however, that counsel are always extremely cautious of bringing witnesses to court who could, inadvertently, or in cross-examination, destroy the defence. Did O'Malley and Harrison fit into this category?

Barbara Blore, a witness for the prosecution, in her statement says, 'I noticed that Kelly was wearing the same suit that he always had on when I had seen him in the public house. It's a brown birds-eye'. The relevance of this is in considering other evidence which, if introduced, could have thrown further doubt on Kelly's involvement. A statement taken by the police, presumably not disclosed to the defence, is from two witnesses who saw, 'a man, about 5'7", with dark hair swept back with a lock falling over his eyes, run along Garrick Street into Smithdown Road, his impetus taking him out into the roadway. He then ran back along Tunstall Street. He was about twenty-two to twenty-three years old and wore a blue pinstripe suit'.

Elizabeth McDonald, the wife of the licensee of the Coach and Horses stated, "About half past eight, I was in the lounge and I saw Skelly. He had some drink and was very noisy and wanted to sing. Another man in a brown suit, thin dark hair brushed back, thin build, was with him. They had been there for half an hour at least. This would make them come in about eight to a quarter past.

At about quarter past nine, the man who was with Skelly went out and talked to me about the weather as he went. He was still very quiet and no trouble. I don't think I would know the man again, because I've never seen him before or since."If this was Kelly, Mrs McDonald must have been wrong about the time, as were many others who gave evidence.

Kelly stated that he had never had a gun in his life. He would not know how to fire one. Balmer claims that this was untrue and that Kelly would have been familiar with firearms from his service in the Royal Navy. However, Balmer overlooked the fact that the Royal Navy only use rifles, if anything, and that Kelly's time in the navy was spent either on the run, or in prison. Balmer's comment is, to say the least, not convincing.

Did Kelly help Balmer to schedule the setting of the Sunday meeting when, in leaving Skelly's house on the Sunday morning, he shouted, 'See you later at Charlies.'? Charlie Mathews, the licensee of the Star, in evidence, stated that he did not recall Kelly or Skelly in his pub on March 20th, yet he knew them well and Bridget Skelly, who also was not called to give evidence, said Jimmy Skelly never left home during the day on Sunday March 20th.

Dickson and Northam claimed that when they arrived at the Star, Connolly was already there talking to a man called Skelly. Yet Jimmy Skelly swore that he did not know either Dickson or Northam. The only people to say there was a meeting there were Northam and Dickson and, presumably, the dark-haired girl. But she committed suicide on November 10th, which was about two weeks after the final depositions had been taken from Northam and Dickson. It was also ten days before Balmer said he took his first statement from Graham. Was it now too late to write Margie out of the script?

Kelly was convinced that Balmer would try to frame him. His sudden fear of Balmer, is reflected in the fact that he went to see Harry Livermore within a few days of Balmer's visit, on the Sunday morning after the murder. His solicitor then visited the Spofforth Hotel and the Leigh Arms to confirm Kelly's alibi. This, however, acted against Kelly when it was picked up by Judge Cassells when Thomalla declared, in answer to a question, that Harry Livermore had asked him to give evidence on Kelly's behalf only two or three days after that Sunday. Judge Cassells interrupted in astonishment. 'When was that?'

If what Thomalla had said was true, it meant that Kelly was preparing his defence, six months before he was even charged with the murder.

Time and distance

The time factor was important, but tended to be obscured by many other factors in the trial and, perhaps inadvertently, as the hearings progressed, earlier and earlier times for the firing of the shots were introduced by the prosecution and accepted by the judges.

Kelly's alibi was based on time, yet Judge Oliver's initial comments concerning the time the shots were fired, shows a remarkable failure to appreciate the importance of time in the sequence of events that night. In the Magistrates Court, the cashier gave evidence that she had remained at the cash desk until 9.30, when she put out the light and took the money to the manager's office. She then went to the staffroom and, after talking to her supervisor for about 10 minutes, heard a bang. It would be between about 9.45 and 9.50. At the trial, she modified this to between 9.40 and 9.45.

The cinema fireman was then called to say that he saw the cashier leave the cash desk at about 9.35, when she switched the light off. He then heard bangs and screams between about 9.45 and 9.50. The staff supervisor gave in her evidence at the committal proceedings, that she heard shots and gave the time for this as about 9.40 but, at the trial, stated that the shots had been fired by 9.25.

A sales girl at the cinema also stated that she thought the bangs occurred at 9.40 and Phyllis Stevens, an usherette, said she thought it would be about 9.45 or 9.50 when she heard the bangs. At the trial, she reaffirmed these times. Finally, at the trial another usherette, Edna Ashby, stated it was about 9.55 when she heard two bangs. Contradicting these times were Mrs Simpson and her husband, who were in their house in Garrick Street and had put their clock right by the BBC. Just a little after 9.30 by their clock, Mrs Simpson heard a noise.

Could she really have heard the noise from the shots, with thick chapel walls intervening? And could they be distinguished from the sounds emanating from the film itself, even customers in the cinema itself not realising anything amiss was going on.

In marked contrast to the statement by Mr and Mrs Simpson, is that of Mr and Mrs Evans, also of Garrick Street, which was not used in court. William Evans said that at 9.45pm on the night of March 19th, he was in the kitchen of his house which overlooked the exit door to the Cameo Cinema, when he heard two or three loud bangs. When he went out, he heard the sounds of scuffling coming from inside the Cameo and somebody shouting, 'let me go,' before a man, wearing an overcoat and hat, ran out and up Bird Street, turning into Garrick Road toward Smithdown Road. His wife, Elsie, stated that at about 9.45, she joined her husband at the back door of their house. She had just heard loud reports and she saw a man wearing a light-coloured trilby with a wide brim and an overcoat, running past.

What is not in question, is the time recorded by the telephonist at Sefton Park Exchange, who received a 999 call at 9.45pm on March 19th.

The time of the shooting, critical to Kelly's defence, on the balance of the evidence, was not before 9.40pm. In the light of these conflicting reports, it would have been more realistic for both judges to have fixed the time the shots were fired as 9.40pm. It was a misinterpretation of facts to unequivocally state that the shots were fired at 9.35, a time given by only two witnesses. If 9.40 had been allowed as the time the shots were fired, it would have considerably weakened the prosecution case, but William

167

Gorman, during the second trial, planted a time of 9.30 in the mind of the jury, even though Judge Cassells, in his summing up, defined the time as 9.35.

The next major inconsistency, vital to the defence but, surprisingly, not fully exploited, are the time-distance relationships involved in Kelly's alibi. Neither judge explored these relationships satisfactorily, their relevance minimised and relegated in importance. During the examination of expert witnesses, a police sergeant gave evidence about distances concerned between the Cameo and the Leigh Arms. Judge Oliver, a sick man at the time of the trial, obviously did not appreciate the vital importance of the time-distance relationships involved, 'I do not think the times it took one to walk certain distances matters very much, or benefits the jury'.

The time to walk briskly from the Cameo to the Leigh Arms, is eight minutes.

The prosecution argument was that, after the shots were fired, the gunman ran down the spiral staircase and then along Garrick Street, into Smithdown Road and then back again on a route parallel to the Cameo. This would add at least two minutes to the journey.

He would have then had to go at no more than a brisk walk, rather than attract attention to himself, particularly when passing the Spofforth Arms and turning into Cambridge Street where, according to the prosecution evidence, he dumped the overcoat and hat. This would add at least another minute to the time. Adding a further two and a half minutes each way, for the detour to dump the gun in the lake, gives a total time of sixteen minutes. Added to this, if the evidence of Northam and Dickson is accepted, is the time Kelly took in catching a tram before arriving back at the Leigh Arms.

Allowing the decision of both judges that the shots were fired at 9.35, and the fact that there is no dispute that Kelly was in the Leigh Arms at 9.45, it would be remarkable indeed if he could have been in the Cameo Cinema at any time after 9.30. He had enjoyed a long afternoon and evening drinking, at a time when beer cost less than one shilling a pint, and, according to the evidence of Mrs Blore, Thomalla and Currie, was somewhat the worse for wear. Unless he had a remarkable constitution, he would not have been in any fit state to run down the spiral staircase in the manner described and then manage the distances involved in these time intervals. We must ponder why both judges did not consider this more in their summing up.

The evidence of Currie, the taxi driver, is relevant. In his testimony, Currie stated that Kelly did not look ruffled or disturbed. In other words, his demeanour was not that of a man who, after drinking for most of the day, then had to sprint to the Leigh Arms, with several detours on the way, in order to establish an alibi. Kelly showed none of the behavioural symptoms which would be expected of a man who had just carried out a double murder and was in such a state of panic that he had attempted to shoot the lock off the door of the manager's office, when it had refused to open for him. There were none of the outward signs to be expected; breathlessness, fear, agitation.

The post mortems on both victims were carried out on March 20th at Smithdown Road Hospital by Walter Henry Grace, the pathologist to the Home Office for the North Western region. Dr Grace was also a lecturer in forensic medicine at the University of Liverpool.

The doctor's reports were concise. For both Thomas and Catterall, after reporting on the bullet wounds, Dr Grace states; 'There was no further evidence of external marks of violence or of fractures'. This statement, made by a prosecution witness, goes towards the defence of Kelly. It refutes the alleged confession by Kelly to Graham, 'the man moved towards me as if to put his hands around me. I then butted the man'. Was this remark about the butting, intended to further indicate the vile and brutal character of the murderer? Was the murderer right or left-handed? Does the pathologist's report help?

Thomas was hit from the left side, his hand outstretched and the bullet passing under and wounding the arm, as if the arm was raised at ninety degrees and in a line parallel to the projectory of the bullet, which damaged the spinal vertebra before exiting at the right side of the chest. This trajectory implies that the assailant was standing alongside Thomas, in which case, the gun may have been fired either left or right-handed. The position of Thomas's arm, when wounded, as if striking out, also agrees with Johnson's confession to Graham:, 'When I asked them for the cash, one of them went for me, so I let him have it right away'.

The post-mortem on Catterall shows he was shot once through the hand, a second time in the right shoulder, the bullet being deflected and emerging at the right side of his chest. The third bullet entered the right upper side of his back, when he was in a kneeling or crouching position, the bullet finally lodging inside his right thigh. If the gunman was standing immediately in front of Catterall, the shots could only have come from a weapon held in the left hand.

Conflicting reports were presented, as to which hand the gunman held the gun in. Evidence given by Northam states that Kelly allegedly said to him, 'The bag was in my left hand then and my right hand was free and, taking the gun out of my pocket, I shot him in the chest'.

It seems surprising that the gunman had time to place the weapon back in his pocket. However, of more significance, is the undisputed evidence of the usherette, Mrs Stevens, who said that while the gunman was fumbling with the door and the panic bar, he used his right hand, his left hand remaining in his overcoat pocket. Is it reasonable to assume that the left hand still held the murder weapon, that the man was left-handed and that he was having difficulty using the brass push bar to open the door with his less facile hand? George Kelly was right-handed.

The police forensic team, of which Sergeant Farragher was the fingerprint expert, took many fingerprints and examined the scene shortly after the murders took place. This included prints from the outer and inner knobs of the lock which was subsequently shot off. As the murderer had escaped through the fire exit door, it is reasonable to expect that fingerprints were also taken from the polished brass bar.

Nineteen different fingerprints were found and photographed and prints were also taken from the employees at the Cameo; the cleaners, cashiers, usherettes etc. Obviously, these fingerprints did not match those of George Kelly and all but two were eliminated, one on the door of the safe and the other, on the back of a chair where a hand may have rested. These unidentified fingerprints were even sent to the Provost Marshal of the Burtonwood US Air Force Base for identification, but no match was found.

Although a fairly detailed description of the gunman was given by witnesses, even down to the colour of his black shoes, nowhere in the pages of testimony is there any mention that he wore gloves.

Police evidence and photographs of the scene of the crime and the evidence of the cinema employees, show that the victims were bleeding badly and lying in widening pools of blood. This was emphasised by Rose Heilbron, 'You have heard from Dr Grace and the other police witness, of the large amount of blood blood splashed about on the floor of the manager's office and you might think the man who did this might have had blood on the soles of his shoes'.

It would have been impossible for the murderer not to have had blood on his clothing and particularly on his shoes. Despite this, there is no forensic evidence linking any of Kelly's clothing, or shoes, with the crime and, when Balmer visited Kelly at Doris O'Malley's house the following morning, convinced, according to his evidence, that Kelly was the guilty man, nothing was taken from the house for forensic examination.

Much was made at the trials of the overcoat said to have been lent by Northam to Kelly. It is a strange affair and of damning importance. Is it likely that a man who is so horrified at the prospect of a gun being used in a robbery that he wants nothing to do with it, offers his own coat to help in the crime and thus incriminates himself in a murder? If an overcoat was such an important piece of evidence, why did Balmer not take Jimmy Skelly's overcoat for forensic examination? This would make Balmer grossly incompetent or, more likely, he never really believed that he would find any evidence against Kelly. Perhaps it was because, at this early stage of the investigation, some seven months before the overcoat was introduced as evidence, the conspiracy involving an overcoat had not yet been devised.

Rose Heilbron, in her final speech for the defence of Kelly, pointed out that if the overcoat produced in court was the one the man was wearing, then strange things were attached to it, because it was not disclosed to the police until October 9th. This, of course, was the date of Northam's final statement.

A coat was finally found at Northam's house. However, this coat, produced at the trial, was never proven to be the overcoat worn during the murder. But witnesses, employees of the cinema, said it was very similar to the coat the murderer wore. Mrs Watkins was quite emphatic that it was the coat worn by the murderer. Yet no forensic evidence was presented linking the coat with the murder, despite the fact that Balmer alleged that he had sent it for forensic examination.

There was no reason for the jury to accept that this was the coat and surely this should have been pointed out to the jury by both judges. Northam's father, who was supposed to have been wearing the coat the first time the police searched his house for it, was not called to support this in evidence.

What was the true purpose of the anonymous letter? Possibly the truth will never be known. When was it written? Who wrote it? The letter is an enigma.

Both Northam and Dickson, at various times, claimed to have written it. Although Northam claimed it was in his handwriting, it was actually in a crude print, very similar to the loose, uneducated writing used in Dickson's signature. Dickson, as the author and writer of the letter, more readily fits the facts and one must wonder why a hand writing expert was not used.

The likely reason for the letter is that Dickson was panicking. Armed robbery had turned into a capital offence and there was disagreement between her and Northam.

She then wrote the letter in an attempt to obtain immunity by turning King's Evidence. The letter does appear to be from a woman who is frightened and is turning the tables on her partner in crime; 'Dear Sir, This letter is not a crank's letter nor suchlike, nor am I turning informer for gain. I know three men and a girl, not including myself, who heard about the plan for the robbery. I would have nothing to do with it'. Minimising her own role, she uses the expression; 'heard about the plan'.

When questioned extensively about the letter in Rose Heilbron's examination, Dickson appeared to be cracking, 'Did you write this letter?' But, before she could reply, the judge let Dickson stand down because she did not appear well.

Did Dickson play into Balmer's hands by sending the letter and admitting Northam's complicity in the death of the woman on Lime Street? 'I can also tell you who ran the stolen motor lorry through the pub and killed the person some time back.' A car was driven down Skelhorn Street into O'Connors pub and a woman was killed.

Northam was fanatical about cars and could drive, Kelly and Connolly could not. Did Northam drive the lorry and did Dickson reveal this to Balmer, who then used it as a lever for Northam to do as he wanted? Parts of the letter would then be make believe; the gun in the lake, the 6a tram, etc., all part of the conspiracy designed to to detract attention from herself but, with no knowledge of, or intent at that time, to implicate George Kelly in the crime.

Is it possible that Dickson and Northam had made up their differences by the time the reply was published in the personal column? If so, it would explain Dickson's reluctance to give any further information when she was arrested on May 14th. Balmer then supported her application for bail, in the hope that she would give further information and she gave the first name she could think of, someone who had angered her, 'Go and see Charles Connolly'. There was no mention of Kelly until September.

Then, rather than tell the whole story and implicate Northam, Dickson fled to Manchester where she was found on September 26th – Chief Superintendent Tiffany of the Manchester Police personally informing Balmer that they had traced her. Could it be that Balmer then persuaded her to help in the conspiracy to frame Kelly, at the risk of being accused herself, alongside Northam, with the Cameo murders and that of the woman in Lime Street?

Bring back the cat

Chief Inspector Balmer was mistaken with his evidence. Not once but a number of times. If he did this, is not the rest of the evidence presented by him suspect? On oath, Balmer stated that the first time he heard about Graham was on November 18th and he first saw him on November 19th at Preston, taking his statement on November 21st.

In fact, he interviewed Graham on September 15th and obtained from him the statement which, if it is to be believed, was Donald Johnson's admission of guilt. At that time, Graham had nothing to gain, as Johnson had been acquitted. Balmer, however, after the death of Norwegian Margie, took the opportunity of using Graham for the corroborating evidence he needed to convict Kelly.

Balmer was also incorrect when confirming when the statements were taken from Northam and Dickson. In cross-examination by Miss Heilbron at the committal hearing, she asked Balmer how many times he had seen Dickson. He replied; "between May 13th and September 24th, I saw her twice and took her statement on September 29th." The statements on record show this to be untrue, Balmer changing and consolidating the original statement on October 10th and October 26th.

Balmer did not offer evidence, including the October 2nd statement by Hilda Kelly, which described Kelly's visit to her house at 9.30 and also included the contents of the note in the sugar basin which mentioned the Spofforth Arms. The latter, in Balmer's description of the note, becoming Bramleys, another local pub. Was this slight change an attempt to make Kelly appear to be lying? It can be argued that Hilda Kelly's evidence might well have been the catalyst for the jury to bring a not guilty verdict.

The evidence of Rowlands and Smith, the police informers from Birkenhead, was that Northam had had a gun available for sale a month before the murder was committed. Does this explain the expression in the letter, 'I will give you both their names also some of the bullets he left with me about six weeks ago. I can also tell you where he got the gun.'

When questioned about Harry Livermore's request that a house in Birkenhead be searched for the murder weapon, Chief Superintendent Smith claimed that he guessed where Livermore meant, although he was only told the address two days later. In reality, he had already been told by the police informer Smith, on the same day that Mr Livermore had made his request. This gave him time to make his own search, without involving the defence team. But on the witness stand, Balmer stated that the first time he had heard that the gun might be in Northam's house, was when Harry Livermore told him on October 31st.

Balmer contradicted himself when he said he did not know it was lipstick on the envelope until Dickson told him. When he received the letter, he claimed to have sent both it and the envelope for forensic examination, when the stain was confirmed as lipstick.

Chief Inspector Herbert Balmer was known to be ruthless. He had already established a reputation among the law-abiding community and, as his career developed, it was for the conviction of murderers that he became famous. In his memoirs, he claimed to have dealt with over one hundred murders, although a number of them, including the Cranbourne Road murder of an elderly widow, for which two young men were hanged and the Old Curiosity Shop murder in Aintree, for which John Todd was hanged, all carry evidence of corroboration given by a third person, the prosecution depending on the evidence of convicted persons.

Balmer was a firm believer in the deterrent effect of capital punishment. He frequently gave talks on the subject of corporal and capital punishment at venues in the city and beyond, finding fault with the court's leniency. He argued that for crimes in which knives or other weapons were used, the courts should;

"Inflict the penalties which the law permits, instead of paltry fines, whenever a man or young hooligan is found in the possession of a gun or a knife. This would do much to eradicate crimes of violence. I am well aware that well-intentioned citizens refer to the 'terrible' sentences passed a hundred years ago, for much lesser crimes but any suggestion of more severe punishment to the thugs and hooligans is frowned upon."

Balmer was equally unequivocal on the subject of corporal punishment; "I speak from knowledge of men who have suffered it and also men who feared having to undergo that punishment. We should try, to the best of our ability, to bring home to the violent man, the hooligan, the thug, that the game is not worth the candle. Too often, in this day and age, the miscreant is depicted in the courts as being a model son, known for his kindness to animals, or some such alleged virtue. I do not advocate the 'cat', as it once was used, for many and sundry offences. I think the mistake was made in the total abolition of the cat. It would not matter if a judge were to order the sentence of the cat once or twice a year. It is the total abolition that has done the damage and put so called bravery into the craven hearts of the most vile of all types of criminals."

He was also a firm supporter of capital punishment. After hanging was abolished he said; "As with the cat, so with the No Hanging Bill. The minority who, as usual, are the most vociferous, had their way and capital punishment was abolished. Here again, to my mind, this should not have happened. The argument often used by advocates of the No Hanging Bill, is that the wrong person might be hanged. Despite all the publicity that has been given to such an argument, I know of no case in my forty-one years in the police force, where a man convicted of murder and sentenced to death, has been mistakenly hanged."

A bold and, in his case, cynical view. He expounded his views further in a later talk; "Abolition of the death penalty is just plain silly. Why should innocent people be killed because capital punishment is barbaric? The Government has made an absolute mess, if the job of capital punishment is to deter. Crimes of violence have gone up 40%-50%. It was now the rule rather than the exception for violence to be used in the pursuit of crime. Criminals do not hesitate to carry a knife, a cosh or a gun. Thirty years ago, they carried none of these and looked with disdain upon those who did. In abolishing the death penalty, the Government is saying it does not matter how brutal a murderer might be, he could not be hanged. Use the deterrent, have it there, and if you only save ten lives a year of innocent people, it is well worth it. I've dealt with about one hundred murderers and I know, from what they say, that they will fight for their own lives. Capital punishment is a deterrent. Life imprisonment is a complete misnomer, with discharge after about ten years."

Why should Chief Inspector Herbert Balmer conspire to convict Kelly? In trying to interpret Balmer's reasons, we cannot separate his role completely from that of the police in general at the time.

In those days, the police were tough on criminals, with far more latitude to treat them harshly than today's force. To the police, criminals were, in Balmer's words, 'the scum of the earth'. Rational and libertarian thinking did not really exist and, if it did, it could be a massive barrier to advancement.

The police had human frailties and many among them, although they saw themselves as protectors of society, were not above acts of dishonesty themselves. Chief Inspector Balmer was one who, more than many others, had the opportunity to be involved in questionable activities. He was also, by the standards of that time, a good, if severe, policeman. Convictions were expected and necessary and the Cameo case would not be the first or the last in which victims of a police conspiracy were made to fit the crime. With no results, following the acquittal of Johnson, the pressure was on him; in the local press, from the Watch Committee and from the Home Office.

But little of his early activities in the case point towards George Kelly. Balmer claimed that in the early hours of the morning, after the murder was committed, he had decided that Kelly was the culprit. Hours later, he went to where Kelly was living in Cambridge Street, claiming, in his memoirs, that, 'Kelly's alibi bridled with suspicion'.

Yet there is nothing in the account of that morning's meeting, as reported in court, which would suggest that Balmer had strong suspicions. If he knew Kelly was the guilty party, why then did he widen the murder investigation to become the greatest manhunt the country had seen, with 9,500 houses visited and more than 75,000 people interviewed over the following six months. A massive waste of police resources, if he knew Kelly was the murderer.

The relationship between Kelly and Balmer is hard to interpret. Sometimes it would appear that it was on a friendly basis, particularly if Kelly was of use to Balmer. But the relationship broke down. Was this when Balmer's infatuation with Doris O'Malley deepened, O'Malley becoming the catalyst for the fall of George Kelly?

Kelly had, for years, and despite his usefulness, been a thorn in Balmer's side, insolent, quick in repartee and with a charisma and charm which Balmer, a dour man, lacked. And Kelly had, too often, offended Balmer's dignity at a time when his criminal activities, although minor, were escalating.

Johnson had been acquitted, Balmer had a blemish against his name and George Kelly was not only involved with Doris O'Malley but he also treated her badly. Was this the reason why Kelly fitted the frame vacated by Johnson? Is it conceivable that Balmer's hatred of Kelly, a rival for the affections of Doris O'Malley, was so pathological that he would have him convicted of a capital crime?

Contemporaries say that Doris O'Malley idolised Kelly, despite his oafish behaviour when worse the wear from drink. Balmer was alleged to be besotted by O'Malley and seldom away from her house, having adopted a habit of dropping in to see her almost daily, neighbours becoming accustomed to his black police car parked outside the house in Cambridge Street, their relationship common knowledge to local residents in the vicinity of Cambridge Street and the Leigh Arms.

It is significant that Balmer, in evidence, stated his surprise, on arriving at Cambridge Street the morning after the murder; 'When I went to his house on the Sunday morning, unusually, he was up and dressed'. This was something Balmer could only have known if he was a frequent visitor to the house.

Was Rose Heilbron aware of the relationship between Balmer and O'Malley? Is it possible that she feared that, if she introduced the enmity between Kelly and Balmer due to their relationship with O'Malley, it may have been looked upon with disfavour, even disbelief, by the jury?

Why was Doris O'Malley not called? She would have been an important defence witness, the prosecution referring scathingly to her absence. Was her illness an excuse? Did Rose Heilbron have a reason for not putting her on the stand? Was she aware of the incident between O'Malley and Kelly that evening but could not introduce O'Malley or Harrison as witnesses in case Kelly's bullying, drunken behaviour was drawn out by the prosecution?

Perhaps the most telling testimony to Balmer's infatuation with O'Malley is given by Kelly's close friend, Jimmy Skelly, in a letter written from his death bed in 1994, in Walton Hospital;

"...after Kelly had been convicted and was awaiting his fate in the condemned cell, Connolly *was offered a lifeline by accepting the offer to plead guilty, thus saving his neck, although innocent himself of any offence and wanting to live, he sealed the fate of the other innocent man (Kelly).*

The man in charge of the case investigation was Chief Superintendent Tom Smith, aided by his right hand man Chief Inspector HR Balmer. This is the man that seemed to find the answers to this case but did he find the answers without any double dealings? Only vague descriptions were given about the fleeing murderer; both accused were never recognised. The killer had a brown belted overcoat (Kelly never owned one) but the main prosecution witness (James Philip Northam) did own one. No firearm was ever found but Stutty Northam (Stutty was a nickname because of a speech defect) at one time admitted he had revolver bullets in his possession, which were put down a sewer by his fellow conspirator and crown witness Jacqueline Dickson, a convicted prostitute and thief.

Northam, too, had convictions for theft among other things, they even lived in a room not far from the cinema at the time of the murder (I state this because a lot was made at the trial that Kelly lived in the area of the murder). After the convictions, Northam wrote in a Sunday newspaper of how he used to drive along Lime Street in flash cars (which he had probably stolen – Kelly never drove a car).

Was there a conspiracy? If so, by whom and why? ...I was a defence witness (I had numerous convictions as well as almost all the principals in the case) and I know that Balmer lied in his sworn testimony. He did not investigate for six months and decided that a certain George Kelly was the culprit. He knew Kelly well before the murder.

He used to visit Kelly's home where he lived with Doris O'Malley (she was pretty and fashionable) when he was not on official business. He would walk in, uninvited, he always seemed to appear if Kelly and Doris were having a row. He would say 'Come on Georgie, I'll take you down to your mother's house'. He appeared besotted with Doris. He would call when Kelly was not in. Kelly one night had soiled his trousers, Balmer put them in a brown paper bag and took Kelly down to his mother's house. They entered the house, Balmer carrying the bag with the soiled pants. Kelly laughingly shouted to his family 'Hey folks look at the great Inspector Balmer, carrying Georgie Kelly's shitty trousers'. Balmer glared at him, 'I'll have you one day for that George,' he said. This was only a month or two before the murder...

...Why did Stutty Northam give false evidence?

He stated that the day following the crime, 'I walked into the public house, The White Star and told Kelly that I would get him away to sea'. I was not in any pub on that Sunday. I didn't then and don't now, know the man Northam. The only man who knew I could go to sea was Balmer. Northam did not know, he would not know where I was. No doubt he had been well-tutored what to say. But why would Northam do that? Well, I can only suppose.

Some months before the Cameo murders, some mystery man climbed into a lorry in Skelhorn Street in the centre of Liverpool. He drove it madly across Lime Street and into the front of a public house known as Connors Bar. A passing woman was killed. No one was ever arrested for this offence. In view of Northam's later newspaper story of how he would drive flashy cars around that area, suppose he was the driver of the lorry that killed the woman and Balmer knew that but there would hardly be much credit for solving that crime. Supposing Balmer told Northam, 'I am going to put you away and Jackie with you, unless you make the statement I will tutor you to make'.

Balmer, thinking of Kelly, now had the perfect set-up for a frame, not to mention all the credit and glory for solving this crime. 'I would repay Kelly for beating up Doris and for insulting me, Inspector Balmer, with his shitty pants..."

APPEAL AND EXECUTION

The murderer should be destroyed

It was several weeks after George Kelly had been sentenced to death, on March 5th 1950, that Rose Heilbron took his case to the Court of Criminal Appeal in London. Kelly was brought from Liverpool to be at the hearing. The appeal judges were Lord Chief Justice Rayner Goddard, Lords Christmas Humphreys and Norman Birkett.

It must have been with terrible apprehension that Rose Heilbron presented her case, in the majesty of the Court of Appeal in London. Lord Chief Justice Goddard was the last of the infamous hanging judges, a man who showed no signs of regret, less still of remorse, when sentencing a man to death, his inhumanity such that, on one occasion, in 1946, when he had sentenced a convicted man to the ultimate penalty and was later challenged with a medical view which blamed the man's distorted personality, his response was, 'If that is the medical view, I am afraid, frankly, that it is one of the reasons why he should have been put out of the way'.

Late in Judge Goddard's career, in 1953, Aneurin Bevan, the Welsh MP and founder of the National Health Service, in an emotional outburst in the Commons, reflected the feelings of most people in the country. 'A three-quarter witted boy of nineteen is to be hung for a murder he did not commit and which was committed fifteen minutes after he was arrested. Can we be made to keep silent, when a thing as horrible and shocking as this is happening?'

The man who sentenced Derek Bentley to death was Rayner Goddard. The death sentence was mandatory, even though the jury recommended mercy. The evidence at the time suggests that Goddard wanted Bentley to hang to discourage others. Yet it was the anguish over this case, despite opposition from Judge Goddard, which led eventually to the abolition of the death penalty.

Rayner Goddard's background was immensely different from that of James Cassells. Born in 1877, he was the son of a successful Kensington solicitor, educated at Marlborough and Oxford. Like James Cassells, he ventured into politics but his bid for election was unsuccessful. He was made a Law Lord in 1944 and a life peer in 1967. A year later, Labour won the General Election and Lord Goddard, against all expectations and almost by default, was offered in January, 1946, the post of Lord Chief Justice. He held the post until 1985, when he reluctantly retired at the age of eighty-one.

By the time of the trial of George Kelly, he was an institution, identified in the public mind with the fight against crime, particularly violent crime, which had become more commonplace in the wake of the war, criminals said to shudder and turn pale at the thought of appearing before him. Their fear was not misplaced.

Within weeks of his appointment, he was using his powers of the Court of Criminal Appeal, to increase rather than decrease sentences, courts throughout the country taking their cue from the Court of Criminal Appeal, longer and harsher sentences beginning to be imposed. His maiden speech in 1948 in the House of Lords was chilling.

"I know, that in uttering this sentiment, I shall not have the sympathies of everyone. But, in my humble opinion I believe that there are many many cases, where the murderer should be destroyed."

It was a phrase that was to be remembered and quoted often, before the death sentence was finally abolished seventeen years later. However, Rayner Goddard's views about the cat, were not as strong as those of Chief Inspector Herbert Balmer. His maiden speech continued,

"I think that the 'cat' is an instrument which ought not to be used. But when people talk about the birch, it is always thought that they are talking about juvenile offenders. I am not. The birch is an instrument that can be used as a strong deterrent."

On June 2nd of that year, Rayner Goddard described the action of the Home Secretary, Mr Chuter Ede, in reprieving existing, convicted murderers as 'illegal and altering the law by administrative action'. The consequence of Lord Goddard's intervention, was the failure of the 'Silverman Amendment', to suspend the death sentence for five years. Goddard's views were attacked strongly by Michael Foot and Labour supporters, such as Sydney Silverman, must have bitterly resented Clement Attlee for recommending a reactionary such as Rayner Goddard to the post of Lord Chief Justice.

Shortly before Rayner Goddard's retirement, in 1958, Bernard Levin, the writer, referred to; 'Goddard's intellectual megalomania and the girlish emotionalism which seems to be his only reaction to such subjects as capital and corporal punishment, his views in general, a wretched blot on the English legal system. Lord Goddard walks hand in hand with ignorance on one side of him and barbarism on the other'.

When Rayner Goddard died, at the age of ninety-four, Levin published a long judgment on him, which initiated a debate which took up columns of correspondence in 'The Times'.

'Goddard as Lord Chief Justice was a calamity. Goddard's influence on the cause of penal reform was almost unrelievedly malign; with a coarse callousness, there was not only a desperate ignorance of the springs of human behaviour but what seemed a positive pride in his ignorance.'

This, then, was the man Rose Heilbron had to appeal to, his reputation enough to discourage even the most fervent defending counsel from relying on his charity. But, despite this, Rose Heilbron was resolute, standing alone before the might of this awesome figure. Her appeal was initially against the fact that Kelly and Connolly had been tried separately.

"The trail at which Kelly was convicted was the second. He had previously been tried with Charles Connolly and the jury had disagreed. This first trial was reported extensively in the local newspapers and intense excitement and interest was caused after the disagreement. I objected to separate trials and applied to Mr Justice Cassells for a postponement because of the great local interest and prejudice and suggested that it would be fairer to Kelly, if the trial could be heard at another place. This application was refused and Mr Justice Cassells ordered that the trials of Kelly and Connolly should be heard separately, Kelly's being first." She then gave a brief outline of the facts of the case. Lord Goddard remained impassive as she was questioned.

"What did the prosecution have to say about your application?"

"They did not say anything. It was left entirely to the judge's discretion."

"Until it had been decided whether or not there had been a murder by Kelly, Connolly could not have been tried or convicted as being an accessory. The rule is that it is for the prosecution to decide which indictment shall be tried first."

"I agree, but the matter seems to have come in such a peculiar way."

"You are not making any point, then, that Kelly's case was taken before Connolly?"

"Yes."

"Then I suggest that is the business for the prosecution."

"The prosecution never said one word in court as to what their request was. The judge did ask them what they wanted and they said they were entirely in the judge's hands."

"The judge had an opportunity of reading the depositions or knew something of what had taken place before and he saw, I should think, that there was a difference between the two accused. He would obviously think that the case against Kelly, who is alleged to be the actual murderer, should be taken first."

"My point is that they could be properly and easily be tried together, because the evidence against the two was substantially the same. One of my points in dealing with the separate trial, was to some extent wrapped up with the question of an adjournment."

Rose Heilbron paused, her initial plea was falling on stony ground. Almost as a gambler's last throw, by now appearing totally convinced of a miscarriage, she introduced the startling information that a member of the jury at Kelly's trial was disqualified. It perhaps says much for the determination of Harry Livermore to do his level best for his client and, also believing in his innocence, that this information was discovered.

"I wish to raise another point. A few days ago, I was informed that one of the jurymen had been convicted of a felony and was therefore disqualified from sitting on a jury. If that was so, it might be grounds for the court to say that the trial was a nullity. I cannot, of course, get his conviction from the police, unless some order is made, because they will refuse to divulge such confidential information."

Lord Goddard frowned at her.

"If you have the information that the man has been convicted, I suppose someone could be brought here to say, 'I know that man has been convicted because I was present at his conviction'. Have you got that evidence?"

"I have not got anyone who can say I know he was convicted. But it could be proved by a certificate of conviction."

"You are applying under Section 10 of the Jurors Act, which disqualifies a person who has been convicted of a felony?"

"Yes."

"When did this knowledge come to you?"

"I think last Tuesday or Wednesday. At first I did not think there was anything in the point. It was only when I went into it with my junior, that I felt I must go into the matter."

Goddard conferred with his fellow Appeal Court Judges before commenting.

"We do not ask you the source of your information but you will recognise, in asking for an adjournment, this is a serious thing. The court is entitled to ask you, on your responsibility as counsel, whether the source of your information is such that you have more than idle talk."

"I have been supplied with the name and address of a man who is said to have served on the jury. I have had a phone call put through to Liverpool. I cannot say I am certain that the information is correct but there may well be something in it. I hope your Lordships will not blame me, if it turns out to have no foundation."

Lord Goddard turned to William Gorman, who was still acting for the Crown.

"It would be a great misfortune if this case had to be adjourned. Is there any reason why a telephone call should not be made to the Liverpool CID?"

Miss Heilbron handed a name and address to Mr Gorman.

"The records will be at Liverpool and the Clerk of Assizes is at Manchester and may have the jury list with him."

Lord Goddard nodded.

"The first thing is to find out whether this man was sworn on the jury and the second is whether he is a convicted felon. This point must be properly inquired into and we cannot do it before tomorrow morning."

The hearing was resumed several days later, on March 10th, George Kelly again present.

William Gorman opened the proceedings.

"Inquiries have been made about the juror who was mentioned before the adjournment. In April 1945, the man was charged with feloniously receiving articles of clothing knowing them to have been stolen. He was convicted and sent to one month's imprisonment which he served. There was no evidence that the man named was in the jury book and he was on the jury panel."

Lord Goddard nodded.

"If you agree the juror had been convicted of a felony, there was no need for formal proof or for the name of the juror to be mentioned."

Miss Heilbron stood to speak.

"I accept the facts, as presented by Mr Gorman and submit that a juryman was disqualified by conviction of a felony. Even a pardon would not remove the objection to his sitting on a jury." She then quoted precedent.

Rayner Goddard questioned her.

"This all comes down to the Jury Act of 1870, doesn't it?"

"Yes, but I have raised the common law position. It has been laid down in early cases that where a juryman has been convicted of felony, conspiracy, perjury or giving a false verdict, such offences are not absolved by a free pardon, so far as jury service is concerned."

Goddard was not to be bettered.

"Miss Heilbron, has your attention been drawn to the Administration of Justice Act of 1883, which contains a formidable point in your favour? Parliament apparently recognised that a man who had been, or shall be convicted, shall not be qualified to serve on any jury."

"Apart from anything else, it amounts to a good sense, otherwise one might have a man convicted of a capital crime, reprieved and having served his sentence then free to sit on a jury."

"You had better not talk about the sense of it, because it means if that a boy of thirteen is convicted of stealing threepenny worth of sweets, he is thereafter for ever prohibited from serving on a jury. It is obviously a matter which ought to engage the attention of Parliament, Miss Heilbron. Is this matter more than one of challenging the jury? I have not been able to find any authority. Can you say, if a juryman is not challenged, whether it renders a trial abortive?"

Rose Heilbron quoted cases where new trials were ordered when jurors were found to not qualify as a juror.

"The courses open to this court, therefore, if it holds the trial to be a nullity, would be to order a retrial. There are unusual circumstances, in that there have already been two trials."

Lord Goddard raised an eyebrow.

"If you establish your case, the court will not quash the conviction and order the discharge of the prisoner. There would have to be a retrial. But let me remind you, the other prisoner pleaded guilty to being an accessory after the fact."

"That is another difficulty. And the appeal also raises other matters."

"These have not yet been considered. If this point is good, the trial was a nullity and will have to take place again."

At this point, William Gorman took up the case for the Crown.

"The juryman had never been attainted of felony or convicted of an infamous crime within the meaning of the Juries Act of 1870. There is a distinction between attainder and conviction and mere conviction of a felony does not disqualify a man from service on the jury."

While these arguments were going on, Kelly had been sitting in the gallery, out of sight of those in the court below, listening attentively. Rose Heilbron's arguments had raised his hopes. Now, as William Gorman spoke, he shook his head slightly, slumping in his seat and closing his eyes in a moment of contemplation. He breathed deeply and then sat upright again as Lord Goddard spoke.

"Your argument is that a distinction is drawn between attainder and conviction and that a mere conviction of a felony does not disqualify a juryman?"

"That is so." William Gorman presented a detailed legal argument which distinguished between felony and infamous crime. "My first submission is that this juror was not in fact attainted of any felony or convicted of an infamous crime. And if that is the position, then it does not affect the case here at all."

He then quoted the Juries Act of 1922. "Every member included in the jurors' book, notwithstanding that he might have been disqualified, or have grounds for exemption, is liable to serve on a jury. This particular man was, in fact, on the jurors' list and, in fact, on the panel and, in my submission, qualified, subject to the right to challenge, notwithstanding the fact that he has this disqualification."

Rose Heilbron stood to respond.

"I contend that once a man is disqualified, he is prohibited from sitting on any jury."

Lord Goddard, rather impatiently, commented,

"The root of the whole question appears to be whether there is a difference between attainted and convicted. If Miss Heilbron's argument is right, every child brought before a juvenile court for stealing some sweets or something of that sort, and many hundreds are a year, is for ever afterwards prevented from serving on a jury. It would reduce the number of jurymen."

Rose Heilbron continued.

"If my argument is wrong, it applies also to serious crime. There is no distinction."

"Where would this stop, if everyone who had discovered a good ground for challenge, which must have prevailed had it been made, acted in this way? We should never finish." The Lord Chief Justice held up a hand to bring the discussion to an end, deciding that the judges should adjourn to consider the argument. He allowed Rose

Heilbron one further statement.

"I have other points to raise on the appeal if this one fails."

The adjournment was brief, the judges resuming their places on the bench before Lord Goddard gave the decision of the court.

"The first point is one of great importance. It has been the subject of doubts expressed in some of the leading text books. The point that has been argued is that there was a mistrial, owing to the disqualification of a juror on the grounds that he had previously been convicted of a felony. The court has come to the conclusion that it is our duty not to give effect to this objection and that we will overrule it."

George Kelly took a slow intake of breath, causing Rose Heilbron to glance towards the gallery with concern. He was again slumped in his chair, his eyes staring unseeingly straight at Lord Goddard. Miss Heilbron turned her attention back to the Lord Chief Justice who was still speaking.

"Owing to the importance of the matter, we will later put our reasons in writing."

She nodded in acquiesence, before starting to deal with her appeal on the grounds of misdirection by Judge Cassells. Lord Goddard intervened.

"We are quite familiar with the facts of the case."

She bowed slightly before starting.

"The first point of misdirection, is that the judge did not remind the jury that the case for the prosecution was that Kelly had thrown the gun in the lake in Botanic Park after the murder and, if that was so, he could not have been in the Leigh Arms at 9.45pm."

Lord Goddard responded, revealing a woeful lack of appreciation of the importance of time in the case.

"It is not part of the prosecution's case to account for the disappearance of the revolver. The prosecution's case was that this man had shot two people and the judge was not bound to go into every point in the case."

Again, Rose Heilbron bowed slightly.

"My second point, my Lord, is that two important witnesses were called for the defence and the way the judge put it was that unless the jury believed these two men, they were to find Kelly guilty. The judge also stressed the point in Dr Grace's evidence, that his impression was that the cinema manager had been shot when he was on his hands and knees. His Lordship did not remind the jury that speculation was involved in this opinion. The judge also directed the jury that if the evidence of the brothers Bampton was correct, Kelly could not be guilty. He did not tell the jury that if the Bampton's evidence raised any doubt, Kelly was entitled to an acquittal."

Lord Goddard responded.

"If the judge gave a general direction to the jury that if they were left in doubt, Kelly was entitled to an acquittal. If he had to give such a direction in regard to each individual witness, I wonder how a judge was going to try a murder case?"

Rose Heilbron stood her ground.

"I submit that the trial judge did not remind the jury of the implication relied on by the defence, arising out of the contradictions in the evidence of Northam and Dickson, relating to the anonymous letter. The defence attached a great deal of weight to this. And let me refer to the evidence. The people at the cinema did not attempt to identify the man. The one thing they swore to, was the coat. And the mask. None of them said it was a brown mask. The judge should have pointed out this contradiction as to colour, for the jury to make up their minds."

Lord Goddard shook his head slowly, gaining approval from his fellow judges before speaking. "I mean no disrespect to your arguments, Miss Heilbron. You have done the best you could, but a more hopeless appeal has seldom been before this court. This man was convicted of a cruel and deliberate murder, for the purpose of gain, as can well be imagined. The case against him is that he went into the cinema with an automatic and shot two men there, as though they were dogs and left them dying on the floor of the cinema and took the money which was what he was after. He is a man who, according to the evidence at the trial, was accustomed to boast about the violence he would offer to people who stood in his way. If the jury in this case believed the evidence which was given, and that is a matter for them, the case is proved against this man beyond the possibility of a peradventure. It is proven as conclusively as any case can be proved, short of actually finding the man with the revolver. Two people of bad character testified that this man had come, earlier in the evening, before he went off and performed this ghastly deed and told them what he was going to do. One of them was undoubtedly a professional thief and, as many professional thieves, was averse to the use of firearms. Despite this man having tried to persuade him not to, Kelly went off and came back to the public house after he had committed the deed. The other evidence that puts the matter beyond doubt, is from a man who was in gaol when Kelly was taken there. According to that convict, Kelly told him exactly what he had done and how he had done it. The question is whether the jury believed this evidence and we are not surprised that they did. The judge then gave as careful and impartial a summing up as was possible in a case of this description. He warned the jury of the advisability of having corroboration, with regard to certain witnesses who might be accomplices, of the danger of convicting without corroboration. That warning was given in full measure by the judge. It was the judge's duty to go through the evidence as witnesses and counsel had gone through it but to represent it fairly to the jury." Lord Goddard paused, staring intently at Rose Heilbron.

"This court has read with care, the long and painstaking charge of the judge to the jury. I have never read a summing up which more fully answers the qualities I have laid down, as to what a summing up should be. The points taken on this man's behalf can only be described as trivial. This court is of the opinion that there is nothing in any of the points made and, consequently, we think the appeal should be dismissed."

The strength of Rose Heilbron's argument was such that the Appeal Court Judges felt it called for a major statement in law. Three days later, the Lord Chief Justice gave the reasons for the court of Criminal Appeal over-ruling the objection submitted on Kelly's behalf. (Appendix 26)

A few day after Lord Goddard had given his decision in writing, the defence made an application to the Attorney General for his fiat to appeal to the House of Lords.

The application was refused, the Attorney General, Sir Hartley Shawcross KC, and Member of Parliament for St Helens, stating that he could find no grounds on which to issue his fiat to enable an appeal to be made to the House of Lords, adding that the Home Secretary had the power to intervene, if he wished.

On March 24th, just over a year after the murder, the Home Office reported that the Secretary of State had failed to find sufficient grounds to enable him to advise His Majesty to respite the death sentence.

It would be carried out on March 28th.

182

Last minute bid

On March 14th, the Governor of Walton Prison received a letter from one of his prison officers, Mr EC Leach.

Re: "CC" Visit Geo. Kelly.

Sir,

I beg to report for your information that several threats were made by the above prisoner's brothers, Jim and Frank Kelly, on a visit on the above date. The following were the threats used: "We will get Connolly and Northam, especially Northam, we will slice his ears off. He's got it coming." (by Frank Kelly)

Jim Kelly added that Connolly will be out in seven years and he will pay if you take the short walk, George, I promise you this."

The above were the actual words used.

I am, sir, Your obedient servant

On March 24th 1949, Mr Philip Allen, an official at the Home Office, telephoned the Chief Superintendent of Liverpool CID at 3.30pm.

"This afternoon, the Home Secretary has been approached by an MP concerning the Kelly case and the Home Secretary would like information on a number of points. The MP was Sydney Silverman.

(1) That the man, Johnson, knows who the murderer is and that he is not Kelly.

(2) That a letter had been received saying that the woman, Dickson, is known to have had a gun in her possession before the murder.

(3) That the police bargained with Connolly to turn King's Evidence.

Can you please let me have this information as soon as possible."

Twenty five minutes later, Chief Superintendent Smith telephoned the Home Office and spoke to Allen with a reply to the questions. He also put his response in writing to the Chief Constable.

(1) Johnson is the man who was arrested last summer in connection with the case against the man, George Kelly. When in custody, he made a statement saying he knew who had committed the Cameo murders. While on bail, he was watched by the police but he spent all his time with his brother's wife, his brother at that time being in custody, also for robbery. Johnson was arrested and tried before Mr Justice Lynskey. After a legal argument, he was acquitted on the accessory charge. I am completely satisfied that Johnson knew nothing at all about the crime at the Cameo Cinema, or the man who committed it.

(2) The woman, Jacqueline Dickson, had been known to us for some years but at no time have we ever had reason to believe that she was in possession of a gun. She is a prostitute and I am sure that if she had ever had a gun, we would have learned something about it.

(3) The police only saw Connolly on one occasion after his arrest and that was when Connolly asked a police officer to visit him regarding something he had heard in prison. The police had nothing to do with Connolly pleading guilty to the conspiracy and robbery charges in the Cameo Cinema murder case and did not know that he was going to plead guilty until the day on which he was sentenced.

Sydney Silverman MP, was Harry Livermore's partner in their law practice and, by now, very concerned about what both he and Harry Livermore saw as a major miscarriage of justice. He attempted to have new evidence brought to the attention of the Home Secretary. He supplied a letter concerning Kelly's alibi, which was of sufficient concern to the Home Office that they asked Philip Allen to again contact the Chief Constable of Liverpool and ask for his comments. He, in turn, asked the Chief Superintendent of the CID to formulate a reply.

The letter was headed: 33 Cecil Street, Wavertree, Liverpool 15. 27.2.50

Sir,

You will excuse me writing direct to you, as I and number of gentlemen whose names you will find appended know and think a grave injustice is being carried out in the instance of the Cameo murders here in Liverpool. We do know that the accused man Geo. Kelly was in the Leigh Arms that night at 9.30 and a number of us was not called to give evidence to the fact. Also the Landlord, who had twenty-three years service with the police, will swear that this man was in the public house on Sunday March 20th. We would like to stress upon you the wrongful evidence of the police ie Insp. Balmer re. the place of the gun. He stated it was in Wavertree Park lake in eight foot of mud. This is a lie because the children of the neighbourhood are walking across it every day, when they would be drowned. Sir, we bring this to your notice as the only means to get satisfaction and we are sure you will give this your valuable attention, as we do not believe in the methods adopted in this case. We crave your indulgence on this issue, as good living citizens of this area.

We remain, Yours obediently

Henry Harrison, Reginald Charles Bampton, Walter Bampton, HE Vickers.

The reply from the Chief Superintendent of the Liverpool CID gave the addresses of the signatories to the letter, acknowledging them to be 'associates of George Kelly'.

'The brothers Bampton gave evidence to the effect that they went to the Leigh Arms public house, Picton Road, at 9.30 on the evening of the 19th March 1949, the date of the murder. In cross-examination, Reginald Bampton said that when he entered the public house he looked at the clock and saw the time was 9.30. They said they stayed in the public house for about twenty minutes and that Kelly was present all the time and was still there when they left.

Doubt was thrown on the accuracy of their evidence because the licensee of this public house, Frederick Thomalla was called as a witness for the defence and gave evidence that it was his custom to keep the clock twenty minutes fast which would have then meant that the Bampton brothers actually saw Kelly at 9.10 whereas, in fact, it was proved by the prosecution and admitted by Kelly, that he was in the Spofforth Hotel, which is some few hundred yards distance from the Leigh Arms Hotel, between 9.20 and 9.25. A colleague of Bampton claimed he had told him that Kelly had come into the pub at about 9.40. Bampton denied this statement, which the judge would not allow as evidence.

Regarding the man Henry Harrison, he was seen by the police and volunteered that he had seen Kelly in the Leigh Arms public house at 9pm and again at 9.35pm. He fixed the latter time, because the licensee then closed play on the dart board. On this point, however, the licensee was seen and he told the police that he is so busy on a Saturday, he closes play at 9pm. Harrison was subpoenaed to give evidence for the defence but he was not called, for what reason we do not know.

It is suggested in the letter, that the landlord of the Leigh Arms, a former police officer, with twenty-three years service, would swear that Kelly was in his public house on Sunday 20th March 1949. This licensee, Frederick Thomalla, now aged fifty, was, in fact, formerly a member of the Liverpool City Police and was pensioned off on medical grounds. He was subpoenaed to give evidence for the defence and, when called, he did say that Kelly frequented his house.'

As a result of this reply, the Home Office decided not to take any action. On March 27th, at 4.30pm, a telegram was received at the Home Office. It was from Kelly's brother, Joseph.

Re. George Kelly. Vital information received, on behalf of George Kelly, please delay execution. Joseph Kelly

At the same time, Sydney Silverman approached the Home Secretary to tell him they had a signed statement concerning evidence given by Robert Graham against Kelly. Philip Allen of the Home Office again telephoned Nichols, the Chief Constable of Liverpool at 4.55pm that day and said that the Secretary of State would like some enquiries made regarding these matters and would like the reply sent to the Home Office by 7pm that evening.

The evidence consisted of a signed statement by a man called Patrick Mahoney who had served a sentence for shop-breaking at Walton Prison. Mahoney called at the Central Police Office, Liverpool, at 6.30 that evening, with Joseph and Frank Kelly, brothers of George Kelly and with Thomas Gill, a brother-in-law. Kelly said they had been in touch with Harry Livermore, who had advised them to tell what they knew. The statement was then given by Mahoney and signed in the presence of the Chief Superintendent, CID. (Appendix 25)

The important parts of the statement are that Mahoney, while an orderly in Walton Hospital, got to know Robert Graham. Mahoney claimed that Graham was in the hospital for forty-eight hours and could not have got the information from Kelly and Connolly, that Graham gave in evidence, in the short time they might have been together.

As the statement was being completed, a phone call was received from Sir Frank Newsham, from the Home office, asking if he could be informed of the result of the enquiries. The statement was then read to Newsham over the phone, a report from the Chief Superintendent, CID, being dispatched immediately it was completed. The report read. 'At the interview with Mahoney, he was asked if he knew Northam or Dickson and he replied no. He was then asked if he had ever referred to Northam, when in conversation with Graham as 'Stutty Northam' and he said, "No, George Kelly called him Stutty Northam".' The police statement then gave the Home Office a damning breakdown of Mahoney's previous convictions, all concerned with shop-breaking.

The Chief Superintendent's comments to the Home Office continued. 'I am, however, convinced that Mahoney's statement was solely inspired by the Kelly brothers and that its substance of truth is so small as to be almost negligible.'

The statement from Mahoney must be considered in the context of the cross-examination by Rose Heilbron, when it was suggested to Graham that he got his information from a prisoner called Marney but Graham denied this, although he admitted that he knew a prisoner called Marney. There is also conflicting evidence as to how long Graham was in the prison hospital, the police claiming he was there for ten days, during the time Kelly and Connolly were there. This point was never resolved. However, the total time Graham was in the prison hospital, including the time spent there in September, was ten days.

As a result of this report, the application for a delay in the execution was rejected by the Home Secretary, Mr Chuter Ede. And one other request for clemency to the Home Office was ignored. The widow of one of the murdered men, Mrs Catterall, wrote to the Home Secretary. She was opposed to the execution and wrote, 'another death will do nothing to bring my husband back'. At this time, Mrs Catterall was pregnant with the child her husband would never see. A religious man, at the time he was murdered, he had given up drinking for lent.

In a skilful, humane and decorous manner

Even in the condemned cell, George Kelly still could not believe that he would face the ultimate sentence. Harry Livermore was one of his many visitors for who, he put on a brave face, asking him, on one occasion,

"When I'm out of here, I hope you'll get me off that other charge to do with the wellingtons. I don't know anything about it."

One of his earliest visitors was Doris O'Malley, her words to him overheard by the warders.

"You know why I couldn't give evidence for you, George. But I've told them I will now tell them everything." But Doris O'Malley never spoke another word about the case.

Kelly never stopped protesting his innocence. In a final, poignant letter to his friend, Harry Harrison, he wrote. '...I'm going tomorrow. I want you to prove my innocence'.

On the morning before the execution, George Kelly's family attended a Mass for him at St Nicholas Church, off Brownlow Hill and, on that night, his family were allowed their last visit. They went, in twos, into a small room, adjacent to the condemned cell, where he said his last goodbyes; the women first, his mother, sister Sally, his sisters-in-law and then Colleen Dutton. Kelly appeared almost happy when he saw Colleen Dutton. She had dressed specially for the occasion, a bright red coat with a light summer dress underneath, bringing with her a nine carat gold engagement ring, with green stones, which Frank Kelly had paid for. Brennan, one of the warders with Kelly, allowed him to take the ring and Kelly kissed it, before Brennan returned it to Colleen Dutton. Kelly watched as she put it on her finger. She smiled tearfully at Kelly who, despite just being told that his last minute appeal had failed, was again putting on a brave face,

"I love you, Georgie. There'll never be anyone else. I will never marry anyone except you, George."When she left, she turned to Kelly's sisters. "George and I are unofficially engaged. That's all we can be, as he is married. If his appeal had been allowed, we would have been married as soon as possible. He is an innocent man. The murder for which he has been sentenced to hang, he never committed. I will never marry. I will always be faithful to George. He said he will march to the scaffold singing his favourite song; 'I lost the sunshine and the roses when I lost you'.

Kelly's sixty-two year old father, Peter, and his older brother, Frank, were the last to see him and were shocked by his physical condition. He had lost weight and had turned to prayer, the green jade rosary beads he had been using, on the small table in the cell. His father had to know.

"Tell us the truth, George, for Christ's sake. If you did it, we can live with it but if you didn't, we have to know."

George looked at him, shaking his head slowly, almost resignedly.

"I didn't do it, Dad."

In his final words to his family, he told them that he had asked one of the warders watching him, Mr Brennan, who had been particularly good to him, if he would be with him at the end. Brennan had told him he would and had particular reason to be sympathetic to Kelly. It was he who had made a note of statements made by Donald Johnson, he also who had said of Johnson, 'We all know he did it, but what can we do?'

Kelly had one last message for his father.

"Tell my nephews and nieces that their Uncle George did not die a murderer. Always remember that. I will be watching over them."

When his family left, George Kelly made his peace with God, Cannon Lane, the Prison Chaplain, taking his last confession. But the priest would tell nobody what it contained.

His own clothes were waiting when Kelly woke on that last morning, laid out for him during his last few hours of fitful sleep. When he had dressed, Brennan gently took the rosary from Kelly's uncomplaining fingers, as the door of the cell opened and Albert Pierrepoint, the public executioner, entered the cell, closely followed by the chaplain. Kelly lifted his arm in response to Pierrepoint's outstretched hand, only for his arm to be swiftly moved behind this back, to be strapped together with his left hand as the concealed door in the cell was swung aside.

"This way, lad, it'll be alright."

Numbed, Kelly, flanked by the two warders, followed his executioner. He had no need of support, his nerve staying to the end.

Already waiting in the execution chamber were the Under Sheriff of Lancaster, the Chaplain, Canon Lane, the Medical Officer, Dr Francis Brisby and Alfred Richards, the Governor, who was unable to meet the condemned man's eyes as he glanced around, almost deliberately ignoring the noose which hung before him.

Within seconds, he was hooded and his ankles strapped. Pierrepoint glanced at the Governor, who nodded almost imperceptibly, his eyes closed, head bowed, those watching, shuddering as the trap opened and George Kelly disappeared from view, the rope trembling for a while, before becoming still. From reaching out his hand to his executioner, to his life being extinguished, had taken less than twenty seconds.

Immediately afterwards, Pierrepoint, followed by the Prison Medical Officer, descended the steps beside the gallows, Brisby quickly examining Kelly's body and pronouncing him dead.

An hour later, Pierrepoint and his assistant, Harry Allen, returned to the chamber and removed the body, lowering it into the metal bath below the scaffold before transferring it into a plain, unvarnished coffin.

When the notice of execution was posted on the prison door, the crowd of hundreds who had been there since the early hours, rushed across the road to read it, filing slowly past. Twenty minutes later, the crowd was still there and had to be dispersed by police officers. Meanwhile, a man walked up and down before the prison gates carrying a placard bearing the text; 'Thus sayeth the Lord, be sure your sin will find you out'.

The inquest was held later that morning, in the small board room near the Governor's office. The jury had viewed the body, which had already been made ready for burial. Their duty was to confirm the identity of the dead man and that the judgment of death had been carried out. The Liverpool coroner, Mr Cecil Mort, presided. He took a deposition from the Prison Governor. It stated:

'The sentence was carried out this morning, at 9 o'clock, in accordance with law. I was present at the execution and there was no hitch in the arrangements. Everything was carried out in a skilful, humane and decorous manner. The body of the prisoner lies at the prison and has been viewed by the coroner's jury and it is the identical body of the said George Kelly.'

The Medical Officer's deposition stated:

'There was no hitch in the arrangements and everything was carried out skilfully and decorously. Death was due to judicial hanging and was instantaneous.'

Among the signatures of the coroner's jury who signed the inquest verdict was that of Herbert Balmer.

AFTERMATH

A disgrace to a civilised country

George Kelly was one of the few men in history to be tried twice for a capital offence. This, together with the way the trials were handled, were looked on with abhorrence in many quarters.

In April 1950, an outspoken criticism of English criminal law and of the procedure at the Cameo murder trial, was expressed in a memorandum from the Muir Society, an organisation of Scottish lawyers, which was submitted to the Royal Commission on Capital Punishment.

'Many Scottish lawyers view with distaste the preliminary procedure in an English murder case and believe that the private nature of the preliminary enquiry, in Scotland, ensures that a person will appear before a jury, less prejudiced, than a similar jury would be in England. Disadvantages of the English rule of unanimity were sharply illustrated in the Cameo murder case in Liverpool. Connolly and Kelly were charged jointly with the murder of a man named Thomas. After a trial lasting thirteen days, the jury disagreed and separate trials were ordered. Kelly, after a second trial, lasting six days, was sentenced to death.

This society wishes to express very bluntly the view that a criminal system which permits such a procedure, is a disgrace to a civilised country. The strain on an accused person in a murder trial is immense. To require an accused person to undergo such an ordeal a second time is unpardonable cruelty. Nor can it be overlooked that it may seriously prejudice the fairness of the second trial because the jurors may have read condensed and misleading accounts of the first trial and, if, in a second trial, the accused is again subjected to the terrible ordeal of the witness box, he might do himself serious injury.

The proposition which arose in the Cameo murder case could not arise in Scotland. In Scotland one of the pleas in bar of trial is that the accused has 'tholed an assize' that is, that the case has already been brought to proof and cannot be tried again.

It is urged that steps be taken, to render an occurrence of the position which arose in the Cameo case, impossible. If an English jury cannot reach a unanimous view, the result should be a verdict of acquittal or, 'not proven' and the accused should thereafter be able to plead he has 'tholed an assize.'

Alternatively, if eight or more jurors found a person guilty of murder, that should result in conviction and, if six or seven found him guilty of murder, that should be treated as a finding of guilty of culpable homicide. Any alteration in the English law of unanimity might well result in increasing the number of jurors from twelve to thirteen or fifteen.

The death penalty should be abolished in Scotland and there is no reason why the law of Scotland should wait upon the more backward law of England. It is only on the assumption that every person accused of murder had an equally fair trial, that capital punishment could be justified.

A jury is too fallible an instrument to be entrusted with a decision on which a man's life depends. The death penalty is irreparable and an irreparable judgment should never be pronounced, save by an infallible judge.'

The conviction and execution of their son split Kelly's family and destroyed his father, who never recovered from the tragedy. He left home and went to live with his son, Frank and daughter-in-law, Agnes. He became devoutly religious, to the point of obsession.

Charles Connolly served his sentence and was released in October 1956, his conduct earning full remission. He started a regular working life and remarried after the death of his wife. He maintained his innocence until his death from a heart attack in April 1997. If not convicted for a part in the crime, he may well have started the new life he had envisaged for so long, in Australia, with his wife and child.

James Northam and Jacqueline Dickson parted, perhaps because they could not live together with the shared guilt of what they had done. Northam married twenty-one year old Mary McCabe, a hospital cook, at Birkenhead Registry Office on April 4th 1951. He was then twenty-five. They lived for a while at his parent's home in Wood Street but the publicity of the case still lived with Northam and, in the 1960s, he changed his name. The motor business he had started became successful and he raised a large family of seven children, in an imposing house on the edge of Birkenhead Park.

Other principals in the case did not change their ways. Jacqueline Dickson sold her story to the News of the World and lived on in Liverpool for several years afterward. In Manchester in 1952 she received a gaol sentence for robbery with violence. When she was released, she settled in Manchester.

Robert Graham, who was sentenced to six months at Bolton Assizes in January 1950, was released on March 18th, after serving only six weeks. In return for his help, Graham asked to be moved to Manchester but, on the 15th March 1950, the Director of Public Prosecutions, Mr G Dowling, wrote to the Chief Constable of Liverpool to inform him that he had been told by the Home Office, that the Secretary of State had decided to recommend remission of the remainder of Robert Graham's sentence and his immediate release. On release, Graham spoke to the waiting press. Again, he lied about the circumstances in which he gave a statement.

"I have done wrong myself but the gravity of the information which I got on the Cameo case, gave me no alternative but to tell the police at the first opportunity. I was then on remand and I told the Preston police when I was taken to Preston for the Magistrates Court. I have been told there may be some danger to me but I have no regrets."

On June 18th 1950, Graham was remanded in custody on a fraud charge. His solicitor, Mr D Taylor, stating to the court that the Governor of Walton Prison had intimated that it would be most undesirable if he went there. Taylor added that there were certain circumstances, to which he would not refer, that led to such a conclusion. Also at the hearing, was a solicitor acting for Graham's wife, who said she was applying for a maintenance order on the grounds of adultery and desertion. Graham pleaded not guilty, the case going to the Quarter Session where, on July 12th, he was sentenced to three years. He pleaded to the court for a chance.

"Since I came out of prison last time, it has been hell. I was kept in solitary confinement in prison and was not allowed to mix with other prisoners. I am afraid of prison."His plea was ignored.

At Liverpool Assizes, on June 5th 1953, Judge Lynskey sentenced Jimmy Skelly to four year's imprisonment. He was convicted on two cases of wounding with intent and two cases of causing grievous bodily harm. Two other cases were taken into account, a supervision order made to be effective after his release from prison. It was Skelly's 14th conviction.

Donald Johnson did serve his full sentence of three years and then quietly disappeared from sight.

After the trial, the Chief Constable sent Chief Inspector Balmer away to the Police College for a three month's course. While he was there, he was awarded the King's Police Medal for Meritorious Service, which was presented to him personally by King George VI. Also at that time, the Watch Committee of the City Council, whose Chairman, Arthur Collins, was later Chairman of the Liverpool/Bootle Joint Police Authority, awarded him, and other members of the murder team, with an inscribed silver cigarette box.

Surprisingly, despite these awards, the investigation of the Cameo murders was used for many years, in police training procedures, as an example of how not to conduct a murder investigation.

Balmer returned to the city from the Police College in June 1950 and took up the reigns again as Inspector, CID, Central Division. He was involved in several other murder enquiries in which a disturbing verdict was obtained, some of these relying on the evidence of an informer inside prison. Among these was the 'Old Curiosity Shop' murder, in which Harry Livermore always claimed that the convicted man, John Todd, was innocent. In another murder, the Cranbourne Road murder of an elderly woman in a street very near the Cameo cinema, two young men, Devlin and Burns were found guilty and executed.

In 1958, Balmer became Acting Chief Constable, serving until 1964, his first act being to create the city's first Vice Squad and Criminal Intelligence Section.

He failed to achieve the rank of Chief Constable, something which always rankled with him, the official reason being that he was ineligible, as he had not served in an outside force in a senior capacity for at least two years. In January 1961, he received the BE, his four awards of merit being the greatest number bestowed on a member of the Liverpool Police since its inception in 1835. In April 1969, he stood as the Tory candidate for Church Ward in the local elections but was defeated by the Liberal candidate. After forty-five years of service, he retired from the force; he was almost sixty-five years old. He then took up a position as Vice Chairman of Securicor.

After the death of his wife, Balmer had been a widower for many years, until he became engaged to be married for a second time. The engagement was short-lived. He collapsed and died from a heart attack on a Saturday in May 1970, in the garden of his fiancee's home, less than a week before they were due to be married. His friend of many years, who was also his successor as Deputy Chief Constable, David Dalzell, paid tribute to him at his funeral,

"He was dedicated to a lifelong task of making our streets safe for the old and helpless and their homes, places where they could sleep in security against the cowardly thug and murderer. He was a great detective, an inspiring leader and a very sincere friend."

Was George Kelly guilty beyond reasonable doubt or did Chief Inspector Herbert Balmer procure his death, after failing to convict Donald Johnson?

There were many who, believing in the innocence of George Kelly, gave their time in trying to prove he did not commit the murders at the Cameo Cinema. Tommy Gill, the husband of Sally, Kelly's sister, who was present at the trials, believed fervently in Kelly's innocence and tried hard for a judicial review of the case. In 1956, after Charles Connolly had been released from gaol, Gill, together with Frankie Kelly, arranged for a Daily Mirror reporter to meet with Connolly in the hope that the truth could be brought out. They met in the Greyhound pub in Huyton, in Liverpool, the reporter offering money for the true story. But there was none, Connolly refusing.

"I'd like to tell but, while my mother is alive, I can't. It would break her heart."

In April 1956, Gill made representations through Bessie Braddock, MP, his letter being passed to the Secretary of State, asking that the case be reopened. His request was based on an interview he claimed to have had with Jacqueline Dickson, in which she admitted that she knew the man who sold the gun and that she had given this man's name to Inspector Balmer.

The Chief Constable of Liverpool was asked to prepare a reply and passed the request to the Chief Superintendent of the CID. The Chief Superintendent's reply was succinct but failed to address the question of Dickson knowing about the gun. (Appendix 26)

In 1960, Gill continued his efforts to clear Kelly's name. On August 29th of that year, he wrote to the Secretary of State and enclosed a statement by Hilda Kelly and her husband. (Appendix 27)

On receipt of this letter, the Under Secretary of State wrote to the Chief Constable of Liverpool. The reply was again prepared by the Chief Superintendent, CID. In it, he commented that Balmer had interviewed Hilda Kelly on October 2nd 1949. She had said Kelly was at her home at 9.30pm and, according to her, Kelly said to her that he had found a note in the sugar basin from Doris O'Malley, saying that she was at the Spofforth Hotel. However, when Kelly was arrested, he made mention of having found the note, but said she was at Bramleys Hotel, which is several hundred yards distance from the Spofforth Hotel. Balmer added that Hilda Kelly said that when Kelly left her house, she saw him go across the street to the Spofforth Hotel.

In May 1965, Gill corresponded with Harry Livermore's partner, Sydney Silverman, also a Member of Parliament. It was Silverman who had tried to obtain a stay of execution, on the basis of fresh evidence. Silverman was sympathetic, but without Connolly's help, could see no further way of reopening the case. (Appendix 28)

In April 1966, Gill approached the Prime Minister. The reply from Marcia Williams, the Prime Minister's personal and political secretary, was brief:

'The case you raise is a matter for the Home Office and I am, therefore, referring all the papers to them, so that they may be in touch with you on the question you raise.'

The Home Office reply was brief.

'The Secretary of State has carefully considered the points you raise but I am sorry to have to tell you, that he can find no grounds for taking any action.'

Gill was not to give up. In January 1967, the correspondence with Sydney Silverman was renewed. Silverman's reply again sympathetic, but emphatic that there was nothing further he could do. He did, however, refer to the allegations made by Northam against Harry Livermore and agreed that these would have some effect on the jury's thinking. (Appendix 29)

In December 1967, after a further exchange of letters, Silverman could not raise Gill's hopes,

'I am afraid that I cannot take the matter any further and, at this time, suggest that you have, in all conscience, done enough. I myself can do nothing more. The Home Secretary, in the absence of new evidence, as the case of Hanratty shows, will not do anything to reopen the matter and I venture to suggest that you have done all you can and need do nothing more.' (Appendix 30)

In fresh correspondence with Downing Street, in August 1968 and August 1971, Gill questioned the right of Judge James Cassells to preside at Kelly's trial, having previously presided over an earlier trial, at which Kelly was the accused.

The reply, on behalf of the Prime Minister, concluded that there was no irregularity in the judge, who had been concerned on the case in 1943, also presiding over his trail in 1950. (Appendix 31)

Still Gill would not be deterred and, in July and October 1968, he again wrote to the Prime Minister, but received no further encouragement. In August 1971, he repeated his requests and, this time, Harold Wilson replied.

'I have now received a considered reply from the Home Secretary about the representations which you have been making, concerning your brother-in-law, Mr George Kelly.'

There followed a detailed, page long review of the case, but Tommy Gill was again to be disappointed. The letter from the Home Secretary finishing.

'None of my predecessors found any grounds for action. I have now considered all that Mr Gill says in his recent letters to you but I find that he has adduced no new evidence and I am afraid that I am unable to reach any different conclusion from that reached previously.'

Civil liberties

Thomas Gill had one more resource to turn to. In 1971 he asked Bessie Braddock MP, to support his approach to the National Council for Civil Liberties, to have the case reviewed. They agreed to this and appointed a barrister to examine all aspects of the case. His report makes interesting reading.

'I have been asked to examine and report on the case of George Kelly who was executed for capital murder on 25th March 1950.

The application has been requested by Mr T Gill, brother-in-law of Kelly, at the instigation of Mrs Bessie Braddock MP. The purpose is to institute an enquiry into the circumstances leading to the conviction and execution.

There are certain disquieting and, in some cases inexplicable, features which merit looking into. Gill says he has known Kelly since early childhood and that, although he was a little 'wild' and inclined to drink too much, he was not the sort of man who would commit such a brutal murder.

The case rests almost entirely on two factors.

(1) Kelly's alibi

(2) Did Kelly and Connolly know each other? Kelly has consistently denied that he knew Connolly at all.

The features which raise doubts in my mind about Kelly's guilt and especially, in some instances, the manner in which his conviction was obtained, are as follows:

(1) The morning after the murders, the first man Balmer called on was Kelly, who he knew not only for his record but for the fact that he was a police informer. Balmer had stated that, asked to account for his movements the previous evening, Kelly's account was so exact that 'his alibi bristled with suspicion'.

The house was thoroughly searched but nothing incriminating, such as money or a revolver, was found.

(2) Balmer received an anonymous letter stating, inter alia, that the murder weapon had been thrown into a pond at Edge Lane Park. Despite an intensive search, the revolver has never, to this day, been discovered. When the writer was subsequently traced, it transpired that she was a prostitute, with a very bad character and record. Since the trial, she has been convicted of robbery with violence.

(3) The writer of the letter said, 'If you want to know all about it, go and see Connolly'. She did not then mention Kelly. At the trial, she identified Kelly as the man who had the gun while the robbery was being planned. She was the principal witness for the prosecution.

(4) Almost every witness for the prosecution either had a police record, which would tend to make them curry favour with the police, or was serving a sentence, in which case, their evidence consisted of conversations with the accused men in prison.

(5) Dickson's statement was that she and Northam, Connolly and Kelly stood in a passage of a public house, discussing various projected robberies and one of them mentioned the Cameo Cinema. It was stated that a gun would be necessary. Kelly produced this and loaded it. Northam opted out and it was eventually agreed that Kelly and Connolly should do the job. All this time they were within sight and hearing of the licensee and a barmaid. This story sounds most unlikely, even having regard for the fact that most criminals of this type are unintelligent.

Kelly said all along, 'I have never had a gun in my life, I don't know how to fire one.'

Balmer says this was untrue and that Kelly would have been familiar with firearms owing to his service in the Royal Navy. Seeing that the Royal Navy use rifles only, and then only on rare occasions and, that Kelly was either on the run, or in prison, during almost the whole of his service, I cannot accept Balmer's version.

(6) Two identification parades were held. Dickson and Northam identified Connolly and Kelly as the men present when the robbery was planned. If this evidence is accepted, it may be proof of conspiracy but not of murder.

(7) At the first trial, when the men were charged jointly, the jury disagreed. The second trial opened five days later. I have never known a case when, after a jury disagreement, a second trial is held five days later.

(8) Gill alleges that a deal had been arranged between Connolly and his counsel that the prosecution would accept his plea of not guilty to the murders, if he would plead guilty to conspiracy and armed robbery. At that time, Kelly had already been convicted and sentenced to death. Connolly knew this and, after thinking the matter over, eventually agreed.

(9) According to Gill there is a woman in Liverpool who will swear that at the time of the murders, Kelly was with her, that she had made a statement to that effect to Kelly's defending counsel, that the husband of the woman would corroborate her statement but that she was not called as a witness for the defence. If any part of this is

true, then it provides new evidence in support of a request for an enquiry, as the woman was not in fact called as evidence for the defence.

(10) Kelly appealed against his conviction. One of these grounds was that a member of the jury was a convicted felon, which made him ineligible to serve.

The appeal was dismissed but the Lord Chief Justice apparently considered the submission important enough to deliver a considered judgment some days later.

(11) The trial judge awarded the two principal witnesses for the prosecution twenty pounds each, not as expenses, but as a reward, which he was entitled to do under an Act passed one hundred and twenty-five years ago but which I have never known to be invoked.

(12) The Lord Chief Justice, in dismissing Kelly's appeal, said, 'It is not without a sense of satisfaction, that the court has been able to come to the conclusion it has in this case'. This gratuitous remark seems to be consistent with the atmosphere which pervaded the whole case, from the time of the crime, to the execution.

(13) Sidney Silverman says, 'It is perfectly obvious, on the facts, that either both men were innocent, or both were guilty'.

(14) The Home Secretary, in deciding whether to recommend a reprieve, must have been aware of the following:

The jury at the first trial had disagreed, leaving some possible room for doubt.

That every witness for the prosecution, with the exception of Balmer, was a person of known bad character and that little reliance could therefore be placed on their testimony.

That the murder gun has never been found.

That a search of Kelly's house, on the morning after the murder, revealed nothing incriminating.

That Balmer continued to employ Kelly as a police informer when, according to him, he had a strong reason to suspect Kelly of capital murder.

It therefore seems to me surprising, that the Home Secretary declined to recommend a reprieve. It is equally surprising that the Attorney General should have refused his fiat to appeal to the House of Lords, on a matter of law, when there was, to say the least, some doubt about the validity of the second trial, at which Kelly was convicted.

All the circumstances surrounding the case are extremely disturbing and I feel that there is an element of doubt whether there may have been a miscarriage of justice. Certain it is that, according to the letter from Sydney Silverman, full justice has not been done.

I want to emphasise that there is no implication in what I have said, of any improper conduct on the part of prosecution, or defending counsel, or the judges.

I have given anxious consideration to this highly complicated case and, having regard to the fact that not only must justice be done but must be seen to be done, I recommend.

(1) That an approach be made to Miss Rose Heilbron QC seeking her co-operation in clarifying some of the points I have raised.

That Frank and Hilda Kelly be asked to give a statement, that at the time of the murder, Kelly was with them, at their home. Although they gave Miss Heilbron statements to this effect, neither of them was called in evidence for the defence. I cannot accept that Miss Heilbron would omit to call evidence which would furnish an alibi for her client. Nevertheless, I consider that this should be established.

In the light of the results of these enquiries, consideration should be given to requesting the Home Secretary to institute an enquiry into;

The conviction of Kelly.

The appeal against his conviction.

The refusal of the then Attorney General to grant his fiat for an appeal to the House of Lords, on a matter of law.

The refusal of the Home Secretary, having regard to the evidence presented, of not recommending a reprieve.'

APPENDICES

Appendix 1

Statement by Donald Johnson to Detective Sergeant Jack Farragher, May 2nd 1949.

I remember reading about the Cameo in the Sunday papers. On the Friday night, or the Monday night before the murder, I was having a drink in the Boundary pub at the top of Smithdown Road and Lodge Lane, when I met Charley Duggan from St Helens. I was in Walton nick with him in 1945. He asked me to go to the Cameo with him and I said alright 'cos I go there occasionally. He told me he was going to do a job there and I went with him on the Monday before the murder. He asked me to look around the place and weigh up the women who worked there, while he was supposed to be looking at the pictures but I was scared and told him I was going out and, anyway, I didn't reckon much on the film, so I told him I was going for a bevvy. He said he wanted to see the end of the picture, so I said I'd see him outside the Boundary at about half-past seven the next night. Anyway, he didn't show up.

Well, the Friday after, I was on a team in Church Street when I saw Duggan again, so I got of the car and shouted to him. He saw me like but then he ran off into Woollies. I was a bit puzzled about that because we hadn't fell out or anything, so I went after him but couldn't find him.

It's no use telling lies. Duggan wasn't the man's name but if I tell you the truth, it would put a rope around his neck. The real truth was that he showed me a gun and asked me to go with him, but I wouldn't. I know he done the murder. It's kept me awake at night worrying about it.

I've even been to confession but the priest won't give me absolution until I tell you about it. But I promised Charley on the Holy Eucharist that I wouldn't tell anyone. What do I do? My mind is a lot easier now that I've told you. Have you seen Duggan? Has he told you about me?

Appendix 2

Statement by Donald Johnson, taken by Chief Inspector Jimmy Morris, May 6th 1949.

One thing is certain and that is that I could tell you who the fellow who did the killing is and where the gun is now but I made a promise and it was a promise on the Holy Eucharist that I would give the chap a chance to give himself up, before I said anything about the murder. I had nothing to do with it myself, although he did want me to go with him but I would not have anything to do with a gun. He told me he was going to do a job at the Cameo and I went with him to the Cameo on the Friday or Monday before the murder. He was asking me to look around at the place and weigh up the women who worked there, whilst we were supposed to be looking around at the pictures but I was scared and told him I was going out. He said,

"Oh well, I'll see you later" and he gave me a few bob. I saw him afterwards and he asked me to go with him on the Saturday and I told him I would not and he then told me he would see me on the Saturday night, at a quarter to eleven, outside the Boundary. I got there at half past ten and whilst I was waiting for him, a policeman came to me and asked who I was and to see my identity card. He did not tell me why he wanted to see my card and, after looking at it, he went away. After the policeman had gone, the chap came over to me and said,

"What was the copper talking to you about?"

I told him that he asked me who I was and to see my identity cards. He said,

"Catch hold of this and get rid of it. It's too hot for me". He then gave me a gun and I said,

"Nitto but what have you done?"

He said,

"Oh, I've just shot a couple of lights out."

I said,

"I think you have done more than that," but he walked away down Parliament Street saying,

"I'll see you tomorrow at the Pier Head." I then walked down Smithdown Road towards the Cameo and, when I got near, I saw a lot of cars outside and a lot of policemen and then I knew that he had done more than shoot a couple of lights. I got scared because I had the gun on me and I did not want to be stopped with it, so I walked further along Smithdown Road and climbed over the cemetery wall near the hospital. When I got into the cemetery I climbed over the wall into the hospital and walked a bit and then climbed back into the cemetery. I don't know why I did that but I was frightened and I then walked across the cemetery, in a line with Smithdown Road and climbed onto another wall, which I found was the backyard wall of some houses. I then walked along a dividing wall and dropped into the road. I walked past some blitzed land and realised I was walking towards Smithdown Road, so I turned back and went the other way and found myself in Croxteth Road.

On the next day I saw him, after I had seen the papers, and I told him that he should go and give himself up but he asked me to give him a week to think it over and I promised him, on the Holy Eucharist, that I would do so. I was pulled up after I had left Croxteth Road the night before by a policeman but I had planted the gun then. I had wrapped it in my handkerchief, as I did not want my fingerprints to be on it but I have been back since and taken my handkerchief away. Nobody will find it and the only things that might go near it are the birds. I have seen the fellow two or three times since and each time I have given him a promise, on the Holy Eucharist, that I would not give him up without giving him another chance to give himself up. I saw him when you were searching the lake and we were watching you and he said,

"You haven't thrown it in there, have you?"

I said,

"No" and he laughed.

I knew something serious had happened on the Saturday night before I saw him and he gave me the gun, because the police were pulling everybody up.

I can't tell you who the fellow is, because of my promise and I had nothing to do with the job. The only way I have helped him, was to get rid of the gun. I can't tell you where the gun is, because you would find his fingerprints on it and that would be as good as telling you who he was. If it wasn't for my promise, I would tell you. He has been no good to me. I saw him yesterday and he asked me for the gun back. He said he would pay me for it but I told him he couldn't get it and I couldn't. If I could see him and give him a chance to give himself up I would be free from my promise and would tell you who he is and where the gun is but I have made my promise and I can't break it. It has worried me for weeks and I haven't been able to sleep. I haven't been able to work properly and nobody ever complained about my work. I fell off the ladder too and that was because I was frightened. He told me that the gun he gave me was the gun he used. He had another gun as well. He lives with one girl and she is no good. He is going about with another girl but she is decent and I would not like to see her get into trouble. Each time I have seen him since the job, he has given me a few bob and a few rums.'

Appendix 3

Statement by George Johnson, Wallasey Police Station, May 6th 1949.

When I was at Wallasey Police Station, my brother Donald went away from his cell and, when I heard him come back, I shouted to him. "Where've you been?"

He said, "Upstairs,"

I said, "What for?"

And he said, "The Jacks have been giving me a grill."

I said, "What about?"

And he said, "The Cameo murder."

I asked him what he knew about it and he said,

"You'd be surprised what I know, I could tell you something about it."

I asked him what he could tell me and he said,

"Never mind."

This talk I had with him, was on Monday night of this week. He went out on bail on Tuesday morning.

One day in the week following the murder I called at my mother's house, 102 Hill Street, where my brother Donald lives. My mother said,

"The police have been here asking where Donald was on the night of the murder."

I said, "What did you tell them?"

And she said "I said he was at home."

I said, "What time did he come in, that night?"

And she said, "I don't know."

I said, "Blimey, I hope he's had nothing to do with that"

And she said, "If he had, I'd turn him over to the police but he couldn't have had."

I don't know where Donald was on the night of the Cameo murder, because he wasn't with me. I was at the Dingle public house in Park Road, from about 7 o'clock to 10 o'clock. My wife might have been with me but I can't remember exactly.

Whilst we have been in prison, he has been looking very worried and I asked him why. He said it was because of the two girls Clara Gallimore of Essex Street or Stable Grove and Sarah Griffin of Leonora Street.

Appendix 4

Statement given by Mrs Ellen Johnson, May 1949.

My son, Donald, was living with me from January up to the end of April when he was arrested. Regarding the night of the murder at the cinema in Webster Road, on the 19th March, he left the house to go to the Pavilion, Lodge Lane. It must have been around seven to half past. He came home shortly after 11 o'clock. I know he wasn't late but I couldn't say to the minute. He always told me about the programme and I'm sure he did on this occasion. I first heard of the murder the following morning in a shop nearby. I don't know how he got to know about it.

Donald had never mentioned the murder to me, except in ordinary conversation, but I remember him telling me one night that they were dragging the park lake at Botanic Park for the gun.

I don't know any of his friends because he is in more than he is out.

He was working with a window cleaning firm in town, up to the time of his arrest.

Appendix 5

Statement by Clara Gallimore, May 1949.

I am a factory worker and I live at 12 Stable Grove, Liverpool. I got to know Donald Johnson about eleven or twelve weeks ago. My cousin is Florrie Johnson, Donald's sister-in-law. We went about together for a time, although my father did not like him. On the 17th March, I was at Florrie's house. She and her husband were both there. I had stopped going with Donald then, for about a fortnight, because my father had stopped me. As I say, on that date I stayed very late at Florrie's house and my father was wild with me when I got home and stopped me going out at all until the Sunday night, so I wasn't out on the Saturday 19th March. I didn't see Donald for another fortnight after that again. So that was a month altogether. When we did start going out again, my father was cross about it.

About this time, but the exact date I'm not sure, Donald told me he had fallen down the ladder at work, but he didn't say what caused him to fall off. He never mentioned the Cameo murder at any time.

I am absolutely definite that I didn't see him at all on the night of the Cameo murder.

Appendix 6

Extract from letter from Donald Johnson to his sister-in-law, Florrie, May 1949.

However, I was foolish and didn't think, I just done it for you and George, plus children and Clara. In a sense, I was loyal to the one I loved and to others that was very dear to me but, as I said, I did not really think and now I am being cruelly punished for not thinking but I will see it through, even if I have to fight it alone. My spirit has nearly been broken and I don't need to go into why it is broken. You should know. I am going to fight this case with all I have got in me and I suppose some people's names will appear in papers and upset them but that can't be helped, I am fighting for the verdict which I hope will mean that I get acquitted. So no matter the cost, or how mean people think I am being by mentioning them, I shall fight what is a name on paper when being there. It was indirectly the cause of me getting acquitted but, on second thoughts, if it is not there and I get a sentence, which you know how large, how would they feel after it, knowing that I helped to gain a true verdict.

Appendix 7

Statement given by Prison Officer Brennan, Walton Prison, May 13th 1949.

D Johnson.
The above named was visited by his brother's wife today. He asked her had she anything and she said no. He said 'Don't forget I was with Clara on the Cameo night'. She said, 'Don't you mean the 19th March? Oh yes, you were at our house and you went with Sarah on the following Saturday'.

He said he could prove that because he was at the Pavilion where a chap cut his finger on a piece of glass and it was dressed there so it could be traced though the accident report.

Appendix 8

Letter to the Governor of Walton Prison, 30th May 1949, by Prison Officer, J Le Poideevin.

McBride told me that one of the murdered men was a relation of his and Johnson told me who had committed the murders, he said that his brother, who is also in the prison, had committed them and had given the gun to Johnson who had hidden it safely away. The gun was in Johnson's house up to a couple of days before his arrest on a charge at Wallasey. He said 'I have carried the can back for my brother' as he is a married man with two children and, apparently, his wife knows all about it. The other Johnson had also shot a man in the Ocean Club and had injured his eye. D Johnson was put up for identification, but nothing could be proved. He had taken the blame for several crimes of his brothers, owing to him being a family man.

Appendix 9

Statement by Bernard Joseph McBride to Chief Inspector Jimmy Morris taken at Walton Prison on June 7th 1949.

I am at present serving a sentence in HM Prison Walton and for the past eight months I have been engaged as a hospital cleaner. About 2.30pm on Sunday 29.5.49, while I was in the hospital, Donald Johnson, who I met some three years ago and who was in hospital as a patient on remand, said,

"Are you the same fellow I met in Wandsworth in 1946?"

I said

"Yes, you seem to have a load of trouble on this charge."

He said,

"Well, it wasn't me who did the job, it was my brother. I was in a woman's house that night, when my brother came in and told me he had shot two men. He showed me a gun and asked me if I would take it. I told him I had taken the can back for him before but he would have to get himself out this time. I went to have a wash and, while I was out, he must have put the gun in my pocket but I didn't find it until I got home to my mother's house. The next day he came round and asked me for the gun but I told him he couldn't have it because I had hidden it. I had hidden it where nobody would find it. I held it with a handkerchief and if the police ever get hold of it, they will only find one set of finger prints and they would be my brother's."

I left Johnson then but, on the Tuesday or Wednesday following, Johnson spoke to me. He had a visit from his solicitor after he had been to court on the Monday. He said to me,

"My solicitor has told me that my girl friend is in the family way and, if I don't tell the police all I know, in three or four days, she will." I asked him the name of his girl friend and he said,

"Clara Gallimore."

He went on to say,

"I didn't know she was in the family way when I came in here and she must have said this to the solicitor, so that I would be frightened and tell the truth."

He didn't tell me that Clara Gallimore knew anything about the gun but, from the trend of his story, I got the impression that she knew something about it.

Appendix 10

Letter to the Governor of Walton Prison, June 13th 1949, from Prison Officer Cork.

On Friday 10th June, I accompanied DTJ Johnson to Chester Assizes. In consequence of my conversation with the prisoner re the Cameo murders, he gave me to understand that the gun concerned in the case had been thrown into the Mersey. I questioned him as to how there were no fingerprints, considering the murderer did not wear gloves and to this he replied,

"I never leave fin…" and then corrected himself and said, "the bloke wouldn't be stupid enough to leave prints."

During the course of the trial at Chester, I was again in conversation with Johnson after he had been sentenced to four year's corrective training. I informed him that his brother, who was also in the Chester case, had been bound over for two years. He replied,

"This is the third time I have allowed myself to take the rap for our kid."

During further conversation he said,

"How do you think I will get on Tuesday, at Liverpool Assizes?"

I reminded him of the grave charge he was accused of committing and he replied,

"They can't top me for it."

I said,

"The sentence, should you be found guilty, will be very heavy."

And to this he answered,

"If they find me guilty, I shall own up to it."

I said,

"Own up to what?"

And he replied,

"The Cameo job."

I asked why he should own up if he had not committed the murder and he replied

"He has more to lose than I have."

He then started to talk about how bad the living conditions were in his brother's home and how often, he had done robbery solely for the purpose of helping his brother's wife and two children. I said to him,

"You must think a lot about your brother's wife and kids."

And he replied,

"I idolise them."

I said,

"To the extent of taking the rap again for him?"

He replied,

"Let's see how things go on Tuesday. If I am found guilty, I will talk."

I respectfully suggest that, should the prisoner be found guilty at Liverpool Assizes, it may be possible to defer sentence until later in the day, during which time, I am convinced he will make a statement and break down his silence.

Appendix 11

Statement by Robert Graham to Chief Inspector Herbert Balmer at Walton Prison, September 15th 1949.

For the past eight months I have been serving a sentence of twelve month's imprisonment in Walton Prison.

About a fortnight prior to Donald Johnson being tried at Chester for the robbery job with his brother, I came into close contact with him in prison. I was a hospital cleaner and he was in the hospital.

One Sunday morning, prior to his trial at Liverpool for the Cameo murder, his mouthpiece came to see him. Her name was Miss Heilbron. She stayed with him about two hours. When she left him he said to me,

"She says that everything depends on legal arguments on the statements." He was very upset and he went on, "I don't know whether to tell her everything or not. She says that if she fails on the legal argument, I'm bound to get life. Well, if she fails I'm going to tell the truth and go into High Wing. I couldn't do twenty years in here." (High Wing is the condemned cell)

From that Sunday, until the following Tuesday, when he was taken out for his trial, he said this many times. Sometimes he said he'd be topped any time but he wasn't going to do life, he'd tell the truth and get it over.

On the Wednesday he was acquitted and came back into hospital from Liverpool about half past two. He was in great spirits and had been ever since.

That apparently opened his mouth and he has said many times how he did the murder. He used to say,

"I can tell you now, because they can't try me again, they've finished. That is, unless they find the gun and they'll never find that in this world."

He said,

"I had the place lined up for some time. I often used to go there. Anyway, on this night, I went up to the manager's office. I thought it was good for four or five hundred pounds. When I went in, they were both sitting there. Both the manager and his assistant. When I asked them for the cash, one of them went for me, so I let him have it right away. The other fellow then went for me, so I put a bullet into him too but it went into his neck and he dropped to his knees and turned over. The first was killed right away and I thought to myself, well, this bugger might recognise me, so I shot him in the back to finish him off. I put three bullets into him before he went out, but the first chap went out when I put the first in him.

I got scared then and got nothing out of the bloody job. I took a powder then right away and, as I was going out, I bumped into the fireman by the top of the stairs. How that fellow didn't recognise me I don't know. He's the fellow I was scared of right through. I ran out and, funny enough, I didn't like to leave the district. I mooched round and then, to finish it off, I was stopped by a copper. He asked me for my identity card and I thought he was going to search me but he didn't. If he had, I was finished because I had the gun on me then. Anyway, I went and got rid of it right away.

I know I was bloody silly sticking round there but I couldn't leave. I think I must have been shocked because I didn't expect to have to do any shooting. I thought as soon as I showed the gun, they would be frightened.

Anyway, they'll not get the gun and they can't get anyone to identify me when the fireman couldn't. In any case, they can't pinch me again for the job."

He also said that when Miss Heilbron came to see him first, she told him that his only chance was the statement being thrown out on legal grounds. If she failed in this defence, she could only promise him life.

Last week he got three day's punishment for insolence and he said to me,

"These buggers know I did the murders and they're going to make sure I do my full three years. I'll get this all the time I'm in."

He also said,

"It's funny, Miss Heilbron never asked me if I'd done it. She only asked me if I was going to plead guilty or not guilty."

I reported it to the warder the first time he told me he had done the murder. The warder was Mr Brennan. Mr Brennan said, '

"We all know he did it but what can we do?"

He also told a prisoner named McBride that he'd done it. I am willing to give evidence any time you want me.

Appendix 12

Statement by Jacqueline Dickson to Chief Inspector Herbert Balmer at Dale Street Police Station, September 29th 1949.

On the 19th March, the night the murder was done at the Cameo Cinema, witness Northam and I came to Liverpool from Birkenhead, arriving about 7.30pm.

Northam and I first walked around the town and we had an argument about where we should go. Eventually, we went to the Beehive Public House in Mount Pleasant.

When we got there the accused, Connolly, was in a passage in the public house. I spoke to the accused, Connolly, and, as the witness Northam did not know him, I introduced them to each other. After about twenty minutes, it would be approximately 8pm, the accused, Kelly, came into the passage and, as he did so, a dark-haired girl came to him and spoke to him. Kelly then started talking to the accused, Connolly, and me. I told the accused, Connolly and Kelly, that the witness, Northam, had only come out of prison that morning and the accused, Kelly and Connolly, started talking about breaking into places. They both said that stealing stuff wasn't any good, as you couldn't get rid of it and they wanted a job where there was hard cash. Connolly asked me if I could get hold of a taxi driver, named Harry, so that they could do him over, as he always had money on him, but I told them I could not do this. There was some talk about a hold-up in New Brighton.

The accused, Connolly, then said,

"I know a smashing picture house called the Cameo up Webster Road. It will have to be a stick-up job and you will have to have a gun."

The accused, Kelly, said, '

"I've got one here." And he pulled out a gun.

I said,

"Put it away, you soft thing."

The accused Connolly said,

"It's a Webley."

Kelly then pulled a case out of the end of the gun and I said,

"Where did you get that from?"

And he said,

"You should know." He then took some bullets from his pocket and put them in the case and shoved it back in the end of the gun. We were all standing facing each other in the passage and I again told Kelly about showing the gun and he put it back in is pocket.

The accused, Kelly, then asked me if witness Northam was going on the job. The witness, Northam, said,

"No, I want a bit of freedom. I have only just come out of jail."

I called the witness Northam names for not agreeing to go but he said he would not do so. The accused, Kelly and Connolly, then talked over the job and the accused, Kelly, said,

"I'll go in and hold him up," and he said to Connolly, "You stand by the door and keep douse." Connolly told Kelly that it was dead easy and that they would manage it alright.

The accused, Connolly and Kelly, and I then left the public house, leaving Northam inside. We walked across Mount Pleasant, and waited at a tramcar stop. A No 8 tramcar then came up Mount Pleasant and either the accused, Connolly, or Kelly, said,

"Here's our car."

As people who had been waiting at the car stop were getting on the tram car, I took

"I'm not going without Jimmy," and I ran back to the public house and rejoined witness Northam. The witness Northam and I then went back to Birkenhead, where we were living. On the following day, Northam and I stayed in Birkenhead.

When I saw Kelly in the Beehive public house on the 19th of March, he was wearing a dark raincoat or overcoat with a belt around it.

Appendix 13

Statement by James Northam to Chief Inspector Herbert Balmer at Dale Street Police Station, September 29th 1949.

I want to tell the whole truth about the Cameo murder because it has been worrying me for a long time.

On the night of the murder, in March, me and Jacky Dickson came over from Birkenhead about half past seven at night. We had a walk around Lime Street and then Jacky said,

"Let's go in the Spanish Bar and the Big House."

I wouldn't, and suggested the Beehive in Mount Pleasant. We went there. When we went in, we saw Charlie Connolly standing by himself in the corridor. Jacky went up to speak to Charlie and left me by myself. A few minutes later, she called me over and introduced me to Charles Connolly. He didn't speak but laughed.

About ten to fifteen minutes later, Kelly walked in. He went up to Jacky and Connolly and they started talking for about five minutes and then called to me again. I had been standing a yard or two away. Jacky told them that I had only come out of from Durham Prison that morning. They then started talking about jobs that were ready for doing, especially one that had a burglar alarm in Islington.

Kelly then said,

"Those kind of jobs aren't any good, you want a job where there's cash. You can't dispose of stuff easily except cigarettes and things."

Connolly turned around and said,

"There's a taxi driver round town whose a 'stooly' for the police, he's got plenty of money."

They asked Jacky to go down and get him up so as we could do him, but Jacky wouldn't. Kelly said he had a job all ready picked out for him at the fun fair, New Brighton. It was a hold-up job and he was definitely going to do it on the Sunday but he had a mate for that. Kelly said they would have to cut the wires there and, when his coat or mac was open, I saw the two prongs of a pair of pliers sticking out. Charlie Connolly said,

"I know where there's a smashing picture house up Webster Road, it's called the Cameo."

I said,

"Where is it?"

He explained the way to get there by walking it. Connolly went on to say,

"There's one thing, it'll have to be a stick-up job and you'll have to have a gun or a dummy."

Kelly said,

"I have a gun here." He pulled it out.

Connolly said,

"That looks like a Webley." Kelly then pulled a thing on the butt and pulled out the case and it was empty. I forgot to say that Kelly had definitely had a few drinks.

Jacky said,

"Where did you get that from?"

And he said,

"You should know, you've had dealings with the same man." He put his hand in his pocket and pulled out about a handful of bullets.

Jacky said,

"You'd better put those things away before anyone sees you."

He said,

"I don't care who sees me." He then counted seven cartridges in the gun and pushed the magazine back in the butt. He shoved the gun back in his pocket. He said,

"You'd better ask him if he's coming."

Jacky spoke to me then and told them definitely I wasn't going on the job. They didn't like that but I didn't care and Kelly, Connolly and Jacky walked out and didn't even say a word to me. About five minutes later she came back and said,

"Let's go home." We went home.

The next day it was all in the papers about the murder. Jacky and me stayed in Birkenhead all day.

On the Monday we both went over to Liverpool.

Appendix 14

Statement taken from Mrs Hilda Kelly on October 2nd 1949, by Chief Inspector Herbert Balmer at the Central Police Station and signed by Mrs Kelly and B Kelly.

I remember the night of the Cameo murder very well. It was the 19th of March. I remember Georgie called at our home at half past nine. The reason I know it was half past nine is that he has a habit of calling at half past nine, to see Doris. I remember he asked where she was and he said he'd found the note in the sugar basin to say she was at the Spofforth, so he said he'd go there for her. As he left the house, I saw him go across the street to the Spofforth. I had seen the note in the sugar basin and I'd told him where she had gone. My husband came in just after and I told him.

Appendix 15

Statement from Charles Connolly taken at Walton Gaol on October 4th 1949, by Chief Inspector Herbert Balmer.

I want you to find who Nobby Clark in Bootle is, and where he is. Also to tell you that a man named Skelly is a mate of Kelly's. Just the same build as me but a little bit heavier. I know Kelly told this to Dennis Barker on the truck and I heard it and heard him say that Skelly and him were together that night. No, no, don't write that, I don't mean all night. Kelly was with Skelly up to 8 o'clock and then Kelly left. I heard Kelly say that. I want you to see Dennis Barker who was in the other cell near me. He will back up what I say.

Dennis also told me that Nobby Clarke knows something about the murder. No, I don't mean the murder, just put it that he knows something. What I mean is this. It may be Skelly who was with Kelly that night and they only said they split up at eight.

It seems funny that they should leave so early. You know what I mean? I am told by my mate, I won't tell you who he is, but he says Skelly is away at sea and he won't be home for six months. No, cross that out, I mean six weeks. It seems funny he should go away immediately after the murder. This is his first trip because he was in the army. I know Skelly but I don't know Kelly at all. Never seen him in my life before. Fitzsimmons of Huyton knows him well. You well know Fitzsimmons. You had him down once. He will tell you that Skelly is very like me. Now, Don't go to Skelly and show him this paper to read. Don't forget this is not a statement, this is something I am telling you I want you to do. Why are you writing it down? Don't forget it is only notes. Can't you see that Kelly had his alibi all fixed up right away but I have got to find one now.

I feel a lot better now. My people have just been to see me and have found my alibi. No, I don't want to sign it, because it is not a statement and I have been told to sign nothing at all.

Appendix 16

Statement taken from James Northam by Chief Inspector Balmer on October 10th 1949.

One thing I should have told you and want to tell you, is that Jackie and I went to the Beehive on the night of the Cameo job and I was carrying my overcoat over my arm. Whilst we were talking to Kelly and Connolly, Kelly asked me to lend him the overcoat, as he was cold and I gave it to him. He said he would give it back later in the

"It fits fine." When he left the public house he was wearing it, with the belt fastened around him.

The overcoat I have given you tonight, is the overcoat I gave him but I cannot now find the belt off it. It has belt loops on it.

Kelly also had a woman's small brown apron and he showed it to Connolly, Jackie and me and said,

"This will do for a mask." He then put it in the overcoat pocket.

When I saw Kelly in Lime Street, on the Monday following the Cameo job and he told me about what happened, he told me to wait and he would get my overcoat. He went away from me and came back about a quarter of an hour later and gave me the overcoat saying,

"I couldn't sling it, in case they traced it to you, but if I was you I would burn it." When he gave me the overcoat he also told me that he had hidden the gun in the soil of Wavertree Park near Edge Lane and that there was one bullet still in it. Before he went away for the overcoat, he had told me that he had thrown the gun in the lake. When I lent Kelly the overcoat, it was before he and Connolly said they were going to do the Cameo.

Appendix 17

Statement taken by Chief Inspector Balmer from Jacqueline Dickson, October 10th 1949.

When Kelly, Connolly, Northam and I were in the Beehive public house, Northam lent Kelly his overcoat, as Kelly said he was cold. Kelly put it on and he was wearing it when he left the public house with Connolly and me and when I left them at the tram stop in Mount Pleasant. The overcoat you have shown me is the one Northam lent Kelly. It had a belt all around and he had the belt fastened.

Before Kelly left the public house, he took a trilby hat from his jacket pocket but I can't remem, which he said would do for a mask.

When Northam lent Kelly the overcoat it was before Kelly and Connolly talked about going to the Cameo.

Appendix 18

Evidence-in-chief by James Northam, January 16th 1950.

I was in the Beehive public house with Jacqueline Dickson. Connolly joined us about 7.40 and Kelly came in fifteen minutes later, at about 7.55. He bought some drinks and we all stood together talking. A short time afterwards, a girl came out of one of the back rooms. She was very dark and had plenty of powder on and lipstick. Kelly went over and spoke to her but I did not hear what was said. I was carrying a brown coat over my arm. In the public house Kelly said he was cold and he asked for the loan of the coat, which I gave to him. Kelly put it on and said it fitted alright. While Kelly, Connolly, Dickson and me were chatting together, the well made-up woman stood in the background.

A particular job was mentioned in Islington but the idea was abandoned because it had burglar alarms. Another job at New Brighton was then mentioned by Kelly and Connolly, and they also mentioned a taxi-driver who was a 'stool pigeon' for the police. Then Connolly mentioned the Cameo Cinema and said it was a smasher. Connolly said that the cinema would have to be a stick-up job and that a gun would be needed. When he said this, Kelly pulled a gun out of his hip pocket. There was no ammunition in the magazine. Dickson said

"Put it away, because you might be seen."

Kelly said

"I don't care who sees me, my name is Kelly," and then he put a shell in the breech. Then he put six more shells in the magazine and others that were left in his hand he put back in his pocket. Kelly then asked me if I was coming. I said no. I said to Kelly,

"You might be seen up there," meaning the cinema and Kelly said

"I will wear a mask." He tried on his own handkerchief over the lower part of his face but it was too small. Then the dark girl, who was standing quite close, produced a small brown apron. I think she brought it from her handbag. She handed it to Kelly and he put it in his pocket. It was much bigger than Kelly's handkerchief.

It was arranged that we would meet next day at one o'clock, in a public house at the corner of Clarence Street and Brownlow Hill. There was talk about the best thing to do, the best way to get into the picture house. I cannot remember just what was said but Connolly, Kelly, and Jacqueline Dickson left the public house about 8.20 to 8.30 and the dark girl remained in the passage along with me. There was no one else there. In about five minutes, Jacqueline Dickson came back alone and soon afterwards we went to Birkenhead.

The following morning, me and Dickson went to the public house at the corner of Clarence Street. Connolly and Skelly were already there. Connolly appeared to be pale and frightened. There was some conversation about Connolly getting out of the country and then Kelly came in with the dark girl who had been at the Beehive the night before. Connolly told Kelly he was getting out of the country and Kelly called him a yellow bastard. Kelly said that he had a good alibi and told Connolly if Balmer comes to you, say you don't know me and I don't know you. Then Kelly told Connolly to find himself an alibi, Connolly said he would fix one up with his wife. When Connolly was talking about leaving the country, Kelly said it will look suspicious.

Kelly told us that if we did not keep our mouths shut they would be shut for us by him or his brothers. I asked Kelly for my overcoat and Kelly told me he could not fetch it that day, but would fetch it the following day.

Dickson and me left about 2 o'clock, and we returned to Liverpool the following day, Monday March 21st. Dickson left me and I walked towards the Adelphi Hotel. I saw Kelly near the Palais de Luxe, in Lime Street, at about 2 o'clock. I asked him for my coat and Kelly told me, if I waited here, he would fetch it. Kelly went away and returned in about fifteen minutes with my coat. He said,

"The best thing you can do is to burn it." He said he would have aimed it, meaning got rid of it, but he thought it might be traced back to me.

I said,

"You made an awful mess of that job. How did it turn out like that?"

Kelly said,

"I stood outside until the lights in the cash desk went out, then went round to the side door. Connolly waited outside the picture house but did not come in. I went up the spiral staircase and saw the door leading to the office and walked in. I saw an old fellow sat at the desk and, on the desk, I saw a bag. I went over to him and said, 'I want that bag'. The man then turned round and said, 'Don't be such a fool, put that thing away. That is not a toy. You can't take that money. It belongs to the company but you can take some of my own money'. The man pushed aside the gun, so I shot him as I could not be bothered with him any more. I picked up the bag, put the gun in my pocket and turned to go out. I got two or three paces from the door, when the door opened and another man came in. The other man stood with his back to the door and hands behind his back. The bag was in my left hand then, and my right hand was free. The man moved towards me, as if to put his hands around me. I then butted the man and, taking the gun out of my pocket, shot him in the chest. The man fell on his knees and started to tear at the shirt on his chest. He tried to tackle me again, so I shot him again and he fell. The money was then scattered all over the floor. I thought the man had locked the door, so I shot off the lock. I had to pull the man away from the door. I went down the spiral staircase and dashed out but I could not see Connolly. I have a cast-iron alibi. The police cannot break it in a thousand years, especially Balmer."

A few days later, Dickson gave me twenty-three shells in a handkerchief, like those I had seen before, but of two different makes. I took six and told Dickson to take the rest back to Connolly. I kept six in my pocket and some time later, Dickson took them away.

Appendix 19

Evidence-in-chief by Jacqueline Dickson, January 18th 1950.

I went to the Beehive public house with James Northam at about 7.30. We went in the lobby and I saw Charles Connolly there. Northam ordered two drinks and, while he was doing this, I walked over to Connolly and started talking him. Northam returned with the drinks and we stood together and I introduced Northam to Connolly. About ten minutes later, George Kelly came in. Kelly walked through to the back but within a couple of seconds he returned and joined us with a dark girl. She wore dark clothes, a suit, and she was heavily made-up. Connolly asked me to go downtown and bring up a taxi driver whose name was Harry and who was a stooge for the police and always had plenty of money. I did not go and Connolly said never mind, I know a smashing job up Webster Road, it's a cinema. He also said, you will need a gun or a dummy gun. Then Kelly brought out a gun, I think from his belt. He said it was the real thing and put some things from his pocket into the gun. I said to him,

"Why don't you put that thing away? Someone might see you."

He replied, '

"I don't care. My name is Kelly," and he put one of the cartridges in the breach of the gun and put the gun back in his pocket.

Kelly tried on Northam's overcoat. He said it was a smashing fit. Later, Charles Connolly, George Kelly and me left the Beehive and went across the road to a No 8 tram stop. It would be about 8.20 at that time. I waited at the tram stop for a bit and, when the car came, I realised it was not the right thing to do and I ran back to the Beehive to join Northam.

When we got back to the Beehive, Northam was still there. We went straight out of the public house and got a train to Birkenhead. The next day we read about the murder in the Sunday newspapers.

On the previous night, we had all arranged to meet in a public house on Brownlow Hill on the Sunday and Northam I went to the public house about 1 o'clock. Charley Connolly was there with a fellow named Skelly. Connolly looked awfully frightened. Connolly said he was going to leave the country and Skelly said he would get him a ship. George Kelly then came in with the dark girl and when Connolly told him he was going to leave the country, Kelly called him a yellow bastard and added that he was sticking here. Kelly then told them,

"That bastard Balmer has been to see me this morning," and he said "I wish I had a gun. He would not have stood there so cocksure of himself."

Kelly told me he had got an alibi for himself but Connolly would have to find one for himself and Connolly said he was trying to get one with his wife.

Northam asked Kelly for his overcoat and Kelly said he didn't want to go and get it then and would give it him tomorrow. Kelly threatened us all and said if you say anything, I will get you or my brother will. The following day, me and Northam came to Liverpool and I left Northam in Lime Street and said I would return in about an hour. When I returned, Northam had his overcoat.

I met Connolly round about Lewis's and he gave me a handkerchief with some hard objects in, telling me to give them to Kelly the next time I saw him. I showed these to Northam and he kept six before handing the remainder back. He said,

"You just go and tell Connolly to go and do his own dirty work." Later I gave the rest to Connolly.

On a Saturday, I think a fortnight afterwards, I met Connolly and we went to a cafe. Connolly asked me to come to the Smoke with him. I said no and he started telling me about the Cameo. He said, '

"I didn't go in, I waited outside the door. Kelly went in and when I heard the first shot, I ran away."

Connolly told me Kelly had told him he had shot the first man but did not want to shoot the second man but he stood with the door closed behind him. He thought he was either locking or jamming the door. The second man came for him for him, so he just had to shoot.

Kelly said he went through the park and had thrown the gun in the lake. On that Saturday evening Northam wrote a letter and I helped. I put the letter in my pocket and posted it at the corner of Crown Street about 4.30 on the Sunday. Northam wrote the letter for himself and for me and I helped him to write it. The same day I wrote the letter, I found six bullets in Northam's pockets, so I took them and threw them away by putting them down different drains by Reece's, up behind the Adelphi.

A few days after we had written the letter to the police, I met George Kelly near the Palais de Luxe Picture House in Lime Street. Kelly came up to me and exclaimed,

"Good God, Jacky, What is the matter with you?"

I told Kelly I was a bit frightened because there was a man named Bobbie Woolerton looking for me. Kelly said,

"Oh, come along with me then," and he took me down a back street and into a public house. I think it was the Caledonian public house, somewhere near the fish market. George Kelly bought two whiskies and said,

"This is the stuff you need to cheer you up," or something like that. He bought another drink and I mentioned to Kelly,

"You must have plenty or money to throw away on this stuff."

Kelly said,

"I would have had more, if I had got what I went for at the Cameo."

I again told Kelly that I was frightened to go outside, on account of Bobby Woolerton. Kelly tapped his pocket and said.

"There is no need to be frightened while I have this." I didn't see what it was in his pocket but I said,

"Why don't you get rid of that thing?"

He said,

"I will. I will take it to pieces and throw it away."

As we were leaving, Kelly said

"Mind, not a word of this, or I will knife you! If I don't, somebody else will."

I cried, because I was afraid and Kelly gave me a handkerchief from his pocket, saying,

"Hey, nark that, people will think I have done something to you."

Appendix 20

Evidence given at the first trial by Robert Graham, 19th January 1950.

On Monday November 14th, I was in the hospital at the gaol. Connolly and Kelly were also in the hospital. I didn't know either of them before. I exercised with them on alternate days, when there were usually about twenty other men exercising at the same time. On the morning of November 14th, after a few moment's general conversation, Connolly told me he was there in connection with the Cameo murder and asked me if I knew prisoner Kelly. Connolly said if I exercised with Kelly tomorrow, would I ask him how he was going on. He said that, apart from being with the chap that day, he had nothing whatever to do with the killing and that, when he heard the gun fired, no one was more surprised than he was and he ran away. He said he did not expect any firing, or any gun to be used at all.

He said that he and Kelly had been with Jacqueline Dickson and Stutty Northam in a public house. He told me that he did not want anything to do with that job but wanted to do a job at Birkenhead but they decided on the Cameo. Connolly told me they met in a public house at 7.30. He did not say anything more about what happened on that night but did tell me about the following day. He told me they all met at dinner time. He told me they met in a public house named The Star. After he had told me that, I told him if he took no part in the affair, why didn't he tell the whole story to the police, instead of running a risk?

Connolly told me he had sent for the police officer in charge of the case and that he was going to tell him everything. He mentioned Detective Inspector Balmer and said he had written to him to come up to the prison but, in between the time of writing and the police officer's arrival, he had changed his mind. He said that he told the inspector something a man named Barker had said to him, instead of telling him what he had intended. Connolly asked me to find out from Kelly how everything was going.

The next day I was on exercise with Kelly and gave him Connolly's message. Kelly told me to ask Connolly how many witnesses Connolly had. Kelly said,

"I have about sixty witnesses and sixteen of them have never been in trouble before. Kelly started to tell me about the circumstances of the murder and said he went into the cinema manager's office, shot the manager and also shot the assistant manager. Kelly said he had shot the lock off the door. He found out that the door opened inwards instead of outwards and said that the police view was that the shooting was done at 9.40 but that he had run down the spiral staircase, got rid of his hat and coat and was having a pint of beer in his own public house at 9.45. He said there were several people to prove he was in the public house at 9.45 and then said that his life hung on those five minutes. He told me that before he actually went to the cinema, he had been with Connolly, Jacky Dickson and Stutty Northam and that they had talked about doing a job. Kelly told me that he wanted to do a taxi-driver but they decided on the Cameo. Kelly told him that he had borrowed a coat from Stutty Northam to do the job.

The next time I was exercising with Connolly, I gave him Kelly's message and Connolly told me to tell Kelly that he had about twenty witnesses but only about six of them were any good. Connolly then went on to tell me about his work and said,

"I don't know whatever made me think about doing a job like that, because I had £15 to draw, including holiday money." He said, "I'm scared of my mother-in-law. She turned my wife out of the house the day after I was picked up and told her to pack her furniture. I don't know what she will do."

Connolly also said that when they were taken to the police station, Kelly did a damn fool thing. He said, straight out,

"You don't know me, do you?" Connolly said that stuck out a mile. Kelly said he told Connolly the day after the murder what he thought about him for running away. He said he wished he had burned the overcoat.

Kelly said it was queer the way they locked me up. I went to see an Inspector on something which had nothing to do with this job and the next thing I knew I was going to be charged with murder. I told Connolly, whatever happens we don't know each other. I met the girl Dickson at a pub in Liverpool. She started to squeal and I put my hand in my pocket, as if I had a gun, and pointed it at her.

Appendix 21

Letter from Mrs Mary Connolly March 18th 1949.

I went to a dance last week with Irene and Doris, I didn't half enjoy myself, with not going for a long time. It was smashing. We are going again on Saturday. We had our photographs taken with a flashlight camera. I don't know what they will be like until Saturday. There was also a crooning competition, which I went in for.

I got the surprise of my life when he shouted my number out when it was over. Charlie was made up because I won. The prize was not much to speak of, but I will keep it always. We are going to Reece's Ballroom three weeks from now, to the staff dance of Bibby's. Charlie is going to wear his black suit and a dickie bow and I am wearing a turquoise blue evening dress. It should be a good show. It would be smashing if you could come too. I have got the baby's photograph taken and would give you one if I had one.

I am starting work on Monday in Maison Lyons Cafe in Church Street, and I am glad. It will be a big help to me, because I need such a lot of things which I could never afford on Charlie's money.

If you do decide to come home for a few days you might arrange for the 2nd of April and then you can come to Reece's dance with us.

Appendix 22

Evidence-in-Chief given by George Kelly at the first trial, 23rd January 1950.

I met James Skelly near Central Station about that time and went to a public house in Hannover Street. We stayed there until 3pm and then went to the bombed site in Lime Street, where I helped my mother, who sold fruit and flowers, for about half an hour. About 3.30pm me and Skelly went to the Ludo Club and remained there until about 5.30pm. We then went to another public house called the Royal William, and left there about 8pm. Then we went on to the Liverpool Arms and later to the Coach and Horses. We left the Coach and Horses around 8.30. I couldn't get a tram car to Wavertree so I cut across by Hall Lane. I went to the Leigh Arms and remained there for about fifteen minutes. I then went to look for Doris O'Malley and went to the house at 67 Cambridge Street for her. I called next door to enquire if she was there and was told she had gone to the Spofforth public house. I got there about 9.15 and had a drink. After four or five minutes, I left the Spofforth and went back to the Leigh Arms, arriving there about 9.25 and I remained there until closing time. After closing time, I went home to 67 Cambridge Street.

On the Sunday, I can't swear to the time, the police came to my house, I can't remember whether it was morning or afternoon. I went to the Leigh Arms at a quarter to one and stayed there until 2pm. When the police came to the house in Cambridge Street on that day, I was in the kitchen with Doris, young Doreen and the son Charles and a Mrs Matthews. There was Inspector Balmer with another officer. The inspector told me he had come in connection with the Cameo. I asked them to come into the backyard. The inspector said,

"Well, Georgie, there was a murder committed last night." He asked me had I any firearms and I told him, no. He also asked if I had a brown overcoat and I told him again, no. I said that I had a mackintosh.

The inspector then asked me to account for my movements the night before.

I told him I was with Jimmy Skelly and that I left Skelly at the Coach and Horses at 8.30. The Inspector asked me if Skelly could corroborate my story and I said yes. Inspector Balmer then asked me which public house I had been in and I told him all of them. I told the inspector that I left Skelly because I wanted to see Doris O'Malley and that Skelly wanted me to stay with him. I told the inspector that, after leaving the Coach and Horses, I went along Hall Lane and got a tram to the Leigh Arms. From there, I went to the Spofforth Arms to see Doris O'Malley. I had a pint of beer and left right away. I walked back to the Leigh Arms.

I said I knew Jimmy Skelly lived in Holborn Street, Low Hill but did not know the number and we went to Prescot Street Police Station to get the number. Before we got to Skelly's house, Inspector Balmer said to me,

"When we go in, I will do the talking, Georgie, and not you."

The Inspector asked Jimmy Skelly where he was the night before and Skelly told him that I had left him at the Coach and Horses. The inspector also asked Skelly about firearms and an overcoat. Skelly said he never had any firearms and he also showed the Inspector his overcoat.

Appendix 23

Statements taken by Chief Inspector HB Balmer, relating to the night of March 19th 1949, in the Beehive public house.

Doris Campbell says:
I know George Kelly, I have known him about eighteen months or two years. I have known Charles Connolly for about four years. I have known Jackie Dickson for about two years.

On the Sunday after the Cameo murder, I was in the Beehive Hotel, Mount Pleasant when I saw George Kelly standing in the passage by the second window from the front door. He was by himself then. I saw old man Skelly and Jimmy Skelly come in then and join him. Georgie Kelly was in a bad temper and was scowling at everybody. I laughed at him and said,

"You sour-faced old thing."

He said,

"I'm a Kelly."

It was either the Saturday, which was the day before that, or the Saturday before that again, that I went into the Beehive about half past six at night and stood in the passage. I saw Jackie Dickson, Charlie Connolly and Georgie Kelly. Jackie was sitting on a stool in the corner of the passage, Kelly was stood up against the wall and Connolly was alongside Kelly and Jackie Dickson. I don't know Northam but another man was standing by the window and Norwegian Margie was in the far passage by the lavatory.

I do not remember any other people in the passage where Kelly, Connolly and Jacqueline were. The time was then about quarter to eight.

I have only seen Kelly and Connolly together about three or four times previously.

Appendix 24

Ruling by Lord Chief Justice Goddard of the Court of Criminal Appeal, 8th March 1950.

The point was taken by Miss Heilbron that there had been a mistrial because one of the jurors was disqualified from sitting on the jury, as he had been a convicted felon. The ground of the disqualification alleged that the juror had been convicted of felony.

It was said that under the Juries Act 1870, a conviction constitutes such a disqualification, that the trial should be considered to have taken place not before twelve but only eleven jurymen, that that constituted a mistrial and that the court would be obliged to award a new trial. That would have been the result, if the court had been obliged to give effect to the objection and a further trial would have had to take place.

It is necessary to state that the name of the juryman in question, which for obvious reasons I do not mention, appeared in the jurors' book as a person qualified and liable to serve as a juror, that he was duly summoned, his name appeared on the panel of jurors, that he was duly called, was unchallenged and sworn. But it also appears that, some three years ago, he had been convicted of the felony of receiving stolen goods and sentenced to one month's imprisonment.

Section 10 of the Juries Act of 1870, provided that 'no man attainted of any treason or felony or convicted of any crime that is infamous, unless he shall have obtained a free pardon, nor any man who is under outlawry, is or shall be qualified to serve on juries or inquests in any court or on any occasion whatsoever'.

The act re-enacted the provisions of Section 3 of the Juries Act 1825. It has been argued for the appellant, that at Common Law, a convicted felon was disqualified from serving on a jury. The court, however, is of the opinion that, since 1825, the qualifications and exemptions of jurors were governed by Statute Law.

We are satisfied that the whole law is now statutory. The importance of this case is manifest, as there are conflicting views disclosed in text books which deal with the matter and the exact point never seems to have been the subject of decision, although, as I will show before the end of this judgment, a point which is, in our opinion, indistinguishable, was the subject of a decision by a court of high authority in 1828, very soon after the first Juries Act had been passed.

Section 10 of the Juries Act of 1870, dealing with three classes of persons, those attainted of treason or felony, those convicted of any infamous crime, unless in either case he obtained a free pardon, and a man under outlawry. But outlawry, which was abolished by the Administration of Justice Act 1938, need no longer be considered.

As the juryman in question had not been convicted, however, of a crime that was infamous, the remaining point to be decided was whether he was a person attainted of felony.

No doubt the distinction between 'convicted' and 'attainted' had often been regarded as distinguishing between the verdict of the jury and the sentence. But the true meaning was the result of a judgment following on conviction or judgment on outlawry, in cases of treason or capital felony.

If a person were convicted but no judgment was passed, attaint would follow. The attaint was the result of the judgment in a capital case because thereby corruption of blood, with all its consequences in the old law, followed.

The Juries Act 1870, received the Royal Assent on August 9th 1870 and a month previously, the act to abolish forfeitures for treason and felony was passed.

It was to be observed that the act made no distinction between verdict, conviction or judgment, as the cause of the attainder. But it seemed clear that, after July 1870, there was no such thing left in the law as attainder, except in regard to persons who were outlawed.

The court cannot read a person attainted of felony as meaning 'a person convicted of felony' capital or non capital and the juryman in this case, although he had been convicted of receiving, was not attainted and therefore the objection cannot be sustained.

It seemed as though the fact that Parliament, by the Administration of Justice Act 1938, had expressly repealed only the words dealing with outlawry, might be used as an argument that they intended to have the rest of the relevant section effective but, as in the view of the court a person convicted after the coming into force of the Forfeiture Act was not attainted, whether the section was expressly repealed or not, it could have no effect.

Two other matters had been raised. One was the effect of the Juries Act 1922, which contained elaborate provisions for the preparation of the jurors' book. It provided that every person whose name is included in the jurors' book as a juror or special juror shall be liable to serve as such, notwithstanding that he may have been entitled, by some reason of some disqualification or exemption, to claim that he ought not to be marked on the electors' list as a juror or special juror. Section 8 provided that, 'a person whose name was not included in the register of electors, should not be qualified or liable to serve'.

Though one would not expect a person disqualified, for instance because he had been convicted of an infamous crime, to disclose that fact by claiming he was disqualified, it seems to the court that whether the person concerned claimed he did not claim exemption did not matter. If his name was included in the jurors' book, he was liable to serve. It was true that his name may have been taken out if he had objected.

It was true his name might not have been included if the registration officer was aware of his convictions, but it seemed to the court, that the act provided in terms of that person whose name appeared in the jurors' book, was liable to serve as a juror and that that again was an answer to the present objection.

There always remained the right of the accused person to challenge. That right remained unaffected, but it was said how could he challenge if he did not know?

It was also contended that the case showed that where information had come to the knowledge of the accused, after conviction, with regard to the qualification of a juror, effect had been given to it by the court and the trial treated as a nullity. Such cases had all been either impersonation of a juror or a mistake as to the identity of a juror.

In a case in which objection was taken because an unqualified alien had sat on a jury, the court saw no difference between a case where the disqualification arose from the juryman being an alien and one in which it arose by reason of his being convicted.

The court could find no case in which, where there had been no doubt as to the identity of the person called, the court had ever set aside the verdict.

It is not without some sense of satisfaction, that the court has been able to come to the conclusion that it has in this case.

While no doubt it is desirable that persons who have real criminal records should not serve on juries, if we had to give effect to this objection, it would mean that any juvenile who had been convicted of a petty theft would, for the rest of his life, be disqualified from serving on a jury and whatever may have been the position in the time of Chief Justice Hale, when all felonies were capital, it would, indeed, be disastrous, if we were obliged to hold that a petty crime, which is technically a felony, conferred disqualification for life on the offender, who might indeed have escaped with no more than a nominal penalty.

It is worth remembering that when the Juries Act 1825, was passed, all but the most petty felonies were capital, so that, with conviction and judgment, attainder automatically followed. Though in that year a statute was passed, empowering the court to abstain from imposing the death penalty on persons convicted of any crime except murder, if the offender seemed to the court a fit subject for the exercise of the Royal Prerogative, it was not until 1826 that at the instance of Sir Robert Peel, Parliament began to pass a series of acts, whereby the capital sentence was abolished for nearly all felonies, so that, by 1870, it was only treason, murder and setting fire to HM ships and dockyards that remained capital and in which attainder followed.

The appeal is accordingly dismissed.

Appendix 25

Statement by Patrick Mahoney, March 27th 1949.

At the beginning of June, I was appointed an orderly in the prison hospital and remained in that post until discharged in November.

At the beginning of October, George Kelly and Charles Connolly were put into the prison hospital. I knew Connolly but did not know Kelly. They told me what they were charged with and what the evidence was against them.

Whilst an orderly in the hospital, I got to know a man named Robert Graham, working in the hospital as an orderly. He was discharged from prison in September and he came back to prison at the beginning of November and was put into the hospital for observation. He was only in the hospital for forty-eight hours and could not have got the information he said he got from Kelly and Connolly and which he gave in evidence. He could have got the information from me, or from newspapers floating round the hospital. Kelly and Connolly told me all the evidence against them and I told it to practically all of the prisoners on remand, including Graham.

The longest period that Graham could possibly have spent, with either Kelly or Connolly, would be about three quarters of an hour a day. They could talk during the exercise period. I am sure that neither Kelly nor Connolly could have told Graham the things that he said they told him, in the short time they were together. Graham told me that he had never met either Kelly or Connolly before he met them in the hospital.

Today, 27th March, I met George Kelly's brother. He told me he had been looking for me, regarding the case against George Kelly. He said to me,

"I wonder if Georgie confessed to that murder?"

And I said,

"No, he always maintained his innocence."

Joseph Kelly then said,

"It's funny he should confess to Graham and not to you, seeing that you knew him much longer."

I told him that so far as Graham's evidence was concerned, he could have got part of it from me, or other cleaners, or from newspapers which were about the hospital, although they were not supposed to be there, officially. I could not have told Graham all the evidence that he gave.

Appendix 26

Reply from the Secretary of State to Thomas Gill, April 26th 1967, prepared by the Chief Superintendent, Liverpool CID.

Following the arrest of George Kelly and Charles Connolly, Mr H Livermore, Solicitor for Kelly at the first appearance at court, said that a tragic mistake had been made and asked that the trial go forward as quickly as possible. Indeed, the case was committed for trial at the Liverpool Winter Assizes but there a different attitude prevailed.

Miss Rose Heilbron QC, leading counsel for Kelly, intimated that she required more time to prepare her defence. The Learned Judge therefore agreed to the case being put back to the next assize, when Kelly and, Connolly, who was represented by Mr Basil Nield QC, were arraigned before Mr Justice Oliver. After a trial which was extended over some thirteen working days, the jury disagreed and it was arranged that the retrial be taken by Mr Justice Cassells. On that occasion, Mr Rowson QC, the Recorder of Blackpool, appeared for Connolly, while the defence of Kelly remained in the hands of Miss Heilbron. Mr Rowson asked that the men be tried separately, a request to which Mr Justice Cassells acceded.

Kelly appealed against his subsequent conviction and sentence to death and one of the points put forward by Miss Heilbron, was that the trial was invalid because one of the jurors himself was a convicted felon. After due argument on this point and other points raised by Miss Heilbron, the appeal before the Lord Chief Justice was dismissed and, indeed, the Lord Chief Justice said that the weight of evidence was such, that even if Miss Heilbron had succeeded on this point, he would have ordered a third trial.

Appendix 27

Reply prepared for the Under Secretary of State by the Chief Superintendent, Liverpool CID.

I beg to report that on 2.10.49, Chief Inspector Balmer interviewed Hilda Kelly and she made a statement. She says that she remembered George Kelly calling at her home at 9.30pm on 19.3.49 and the reason for remembering it was 9.30pm, was that he was in the habit of calling at that time.

It is of interest that, according to her, Kelly then said he had found a note in the sugar basin from Doris O'Malley, with whom he lived at 67 Cambridge Street, saying that she was at the Spofforth Hotel and that he would go there for her. In fact, when Kelly was arrested, he made mention of having found the note from Doris O'Malley, saying she was at Bramleys Hotel, which is several hundred yards distance from the Spofforth Hotel. Mrs Hilda Kelly says that when Kelly left her house, she saw him go across the street to the Spofforth Hotel.

At the trial of Kelly, Edward Ellis, licensee of the Spofforth Hotel, who knew him well, said that Kelly was in his hotel between 9.15pm and 9.25pm on 19.3.49 but Kelly, when giving evidence for himself, denied having been in this hotel on that night.

I would point out, that in the statement forwarded to the Home Office, Hilda Kelly said that she and her husband looked in the Leigh Arms Hotel about 9.40pm on the date in question and there saw George Kelly standing at the bar, but they did not speak to him. It is most peculiar, however, that she made no mention of this when interviewed by Mr Balmer on 2.10.49. Incidentally, her husband, Bernard, was also seen by Mr Balmer at that time and, although he could not assist in any way, he did countersign the statement then made by his wife.

At the trial of Kelly, his movements during the evening of 19.3.49, particularly between 9pm and 10pm, were thoroughly explored, mention was made of the note which had been left in the sugar basin and the time of his visit to the Leigh Arms Hotel received the widest publicity. So far as I can recollect, however, neither Hilda Kelly nor her husband, Bernard, was called to give evidence.

I would mention that AT Gill, writer of the letter dated 29.8.60, to the Home Office, is a brother-in-law of George Kelly. He has long had an obsession that Kelly was innocent of the murder and has approached many people in order to convince them that this is so.

Under the circumstances, I have not made further enquiries, as a result of the communication from the Home Office.

Appendix 28

Letter from Sydney Silverman MP, to Thomas Gill, 24th May 1965.

I did not say that nothing could be done; what I said was that nothing could be done in the absence of further evidence. A statement in full detail by Connolly, would provide further evidence and I asked you in a former letter, whether there is such a statement in existence and, if there is, where could it be obtained?

I see no way of re-opening the case otherwise. I think your letters really are bitter but I do not complain of that. In the circumstances, and believing as you do, you would have no right not to feel bitter.

It is a very sad and tragic story and the saddest and most tragic part of it is just that so little can be done to help. But for the wretched death penalty, which I hope we will now abolish, Kelly would still be alive and if he were still alive, a further enquiry could always be asked for.

Appendix 29

Letter from Sydney Silverman to Thomas Gill, dated 5th January 1967.

I am sure that you are right in saying that you have done all that one man can do, to establish the truth of what you believe and I am sorry that there is nothing more that I can do to help you. If there were any new and positive evidence to show that a miscarriage of justice really occurred, I think something might yet be done with the Home Office but it seems to me, that the key to the whole story now, so long after the event, is the willingness of Connolly to come forward now and tell the whole truth, so far as he knows it.

If he will do that, I think a new opening might be made but if for any reason he is unwilling to do so, then I am afraid there is nothing further that you, or anyone else, can do.

I feel sure that Mr Livermore and Miss Heilbron did all they could at the actual trial and the accusation that Mr Livermore contacted Northam, was denied at the trial. I do not think Mr Livermore was ever much troubled by the accusation but I agree with you, that the making of it, had some effect, probably, on the minds of the jury.

Proving Kelly's innocence of the murder, must depend on the direct and not the indirect evidence and the only person now alive able to give direct evidence about it, would seem to be Connolly.

Appendix 30

Letter from Sydney Silverman to Thomas Gill, 7th December 1967.

I recognise how long and how hard you have worked to secure evidence. I repeat, that if Connolly will sign a statement which could be used in evidence, something further could be done.

In the absence of such a statement, or the refusal of Connolly to make one, I am afraid that I cannot take the matter any further and, at this time, I suggest that you have, in all conscience, done enough. I myself can do nothing more.

The Home Secretary, in the absence of new evidence, as the case of Hanratty shows, will not do anything to re-open the matter and I venture to suggest that you have done all you can and need do nothing more.

Appendix 31

Letter from 10 Downing Street, August 27th 1968.

The records relating to George Kelly's conviction in 1943 of assault, occasioning actual bodily harm, do not contain much detail. I understand, however, that the bill of indictment under which George Kelly was brought to trial at the Manchester Assizes on December 1st 1943, was prefaced with the consent of Mr Justice Cassells, who later presided at his trial for murder.

There was no irregularity in the judge, who had been concerned in his case in 1943, also presiding over his trial in 1950. The Home Secretary has carefully considered the representations which you have made, but I am afraid he can find no grounds on which he would feel justified in taking any action.